Humanizing Environmental Education:
A Guide for Leading Nature and Human Nature Activities

Humanizing Environmental Education:
A Guide for Leading Nature and Human Nature Activities

by
Clifford E. Knapp and Joel Goodman

American Camping Association
Martinsville, Indiana

Library of Congress Cataloging in Publication Data

Knapp, Clifford.
Humanizing Environmental Education.

1. Nature Study.   2. Outdoor Education.   I. Goodman,
Joel B., 1948- . II. Title.
LB1585.K6   796.5   78-51665

Dedication

This book is dedicated to the people of the communities I have been a part of—family, school, camp, religious, therapeutic, and other human communities where I have touched and been touched, especially Barbara, Bev, Big Ernie, Dad, Dawn, Eve, Harold, Howie, Jan, Jenny, L. B. Madeleine, Mary-Louise, Mom, Ryan, Sid, Steve, Sue, Trish, and Vera. (C. E. K.)

To Jeff McKay, who is a living model of someone who has creatively blended caring for people and caring for our environment. His friendship, support, innovative thinking, and pioneering spirit are wonderful gifts. (J. G.)

Contents

Foreword I

Dr. Joel Goodman and Dr. Clifford Knapp give us a warm and sensitive approach to environmental learning. Our personal emotions and attitudes powerfully influence the way we view nature, and this is why the really good environmental educator nurtures a sense of well-being in the child. It's as important to get the child to feel good about (and in) nature, as it is to inform him of issues in conservation and ecology.

The authors have been involved in camp and school programs where respect for self and others, trust and caring, cooperation and a sense of community is explored. Dr. Knapp has described his "secret formula" for these programs like this:

"First I invite the best people I know to join our staff; then campers or students come who want to share outdoor adventure and also to improve their relationships with people. The last step is to give a great deal of energy to helping the group work and play as a community. Fun, learning, and caring just don't appear magically in our lives."

This book shows how Joel Goodman and Cliff Knapp make it work. It will tell you how to teach and encourage interpersonal rapport, open-mindedness and curiosity; a sense of values (personal, social, and environmental); feelings of self-worth and confidence, and a community spirit among children and adults alike.

I met Cliff Knapp recently and was impressed by his gentle and sincere nature. I feel that he is an effective communicator for a loving and caring approach to environmental education. He and Joel Goodman have written a book that truly "covers all the bases" in humanizing environmental education. It is thorough, useful, and always puts the child's highest good—body, mind, and soul—first. I feel that the book will play an important role in helping us to lovingly encourage the child's awareness of and enthusiasm for nature and human nature.

Joseph Cornell
Earth Sky: Sharing Environmental Awareness
Nevada City, California

Foreword II

When I was a kid, I was a boy scout, went to summer camp, and went on family outings with my brothers and sister and parents. I learned to build a fire without matches, to recognize about fifteen bird calls, to swim across a lake, to row a boat, and to paddle a canoe. Along with my mother I helped nurse birds with broken wings back to health. In the summer I would climb the hills behind our houses in Ohio and West Virginia and hunt for snakes and rabbits. In the winter I would climb to the top of a nearby hill to look for deer or to feed the squirrels that were always there. Nature and the outdoors were very much a part of my life. I felt a kinship with all nature and all forms of life.

When I was a junior in high school, my next-door neighbor called me over to his backyard late one night. There were already several other boys gathered there waiting. Tom had caught a bat and he had it in a jar. What happened next has stayed with me ever since. Tom poured gasoline over the bat and lit it with a match as he released it into the air. I was horrified and shocked as the bat flew upward in a circle of flames, hovered momentarily, and then plummeted back to the earth. I was simultaneously disgusted and horrified and yet too afraid of rejection by my peers to say anything. I had just participated in the destruction of part of our natural world. By not speaking up and acting to halt this senseless destruction I had also participated, in some immeasurable way, in my own death and destruction. I had somehow been untrue to myself and to the life force of my environment.

The beauty of this book, which Joel Goodman and Cliff Knapp have created, is that it helps us all to reclaim the boundless life that lies dormant within us and so dangerously threatened around us. The book artfully weaves together activities that expand our consciousness of ourselves and of the natural world around us at the same time. The worlds are not as different as they appear at first glance. Every time I learn to love myself a little bit more, I find that I love all of life a little bit more. Every time I come to a new understanding of the natural processes that abound all around me, I come to more fully understand the natural processes of growth and change that exist within me. The principles are the same—cycles, growth, maturation, decay, rebirth, cooperation, competition, assimilation, integration, and so on. We are of a whole. Whatever affects me affects that which is about me and vice versa.

I have been a classroom teacher, a teacher of teachers, a camp counselor, and a leader of human potential groups. I found that as a professional aid, this book is more than a gold mine of ideas, new perspectives, and practical methods. It is really six or seven books disguised as one. The book contains more activities than you could ever use in two years of teaching or in a lifetime of camp experiences. I am both amazed and impressed at the depth and breadth of what Joel and Cliff know and share with us in this book.

Whether you are a teacher, camp counselor, wilderness trip facilitator, scout leader, environmental educator, concerned parent, or simply a seeker of the wonder and beauty of the universe and the "youniverse," you are lucky to be reading these words, because as soon as you turn a few more pages, you will have embarked upon a great adventure of healing and wholing yourself and the planet. Have a great trip and enjoy sharing it with others.

Jack Canfield
Director of the Institute for Wholistic Education in Muir Beach, CA, and Co-author of 100 Ways to Enhance Self-Concept in the Clasroom

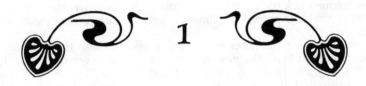

Introducing This Book

It was seven o'clock in the morning and the counselors had just awakened the campers. Everyone except Harold got up quickly and prepared for a typical day at camp. Harold was tired and he pulled the sleeping bag up over his head. After about fifteen minutes more of hiding and groaning, Harold decided to get up. He slowly reached underneath his bunk, found his IALAC[1] sign, and pinned it on his pajamas. He was tired because he stayed up late for astronomy the night before.

"Get up, lazy. Let's get with it or you'll be late for breakfast," shouted his counselor. (Rip: Part of his IALAC sign was torn away with that remark.) Harold quickly threw on his clothes and looked around for his shoes. Apparently someone had hidden every pair he owned. (Rip! More of his sign disappeared.)

He looked around desperately for someone to help him search, but everyone else had gone to the dining hall. He searched everywhere but he could not find his shoes. When he went into the bathroom to look, he spotted what someone had scribbled on the mirror with soap. It said, "Harold has sleeping sickness." (Rip! More of his sign was ripped away.)

He found someone's "flip flops" in the shower and hurriedly slipped them on. When he arrived at breakfast late, one table of boys stood up and pointed to him with big smiles on their faces. (Rip!)

When the camp director noticed Harold's footwear, he said firmly with a scowl, "You know the rules, get back to your cabin and put some shoes on." (Rip!)

Harold went back to his cabin and finally found his shoes in somebody's locker. He returned to the dining hall just in time to see the cook close the serving window. He knew the cook saw him, but the window was closed anyway. (Rip!)

"Oh well," Harold thought, "It's not the first time I've gone without breakfast."

His first activity that morning was softball and he really was looking forward to that. The teams were formed by two captains who picked the best players first. When the teams were even, Harold was the only one left unpicked. The captains had picked both boys and girls who Harold knew couldn't even hit the ball. "You take Harold," scoffed one captain. "No, you take him," said the other. "We want to win today." (Rip!)

At lunch Harold was squeezing between two tables with a loaded tray when someone stuck out a foot. All Harold could hear after the tray of food came to rest with the word, "Clumsy," and laughter and applause in the background. (Rip!)

He couldn't hear the other words being said because the laughter and applause were too loud. (By now you may have figured out the letters in the IALAC sign stand for "I Am Lovable and Capable." Each time Harold was put down and his sign was torn, he felt less confident and good about himself.)

Harold thought the nature class would go better because he liked the counselor. Everything went smoothly until someone found a garter snake on the trail. Harold never did like snakes, and it showed. The girl who found it thrust it into Harold's hands, and as he jumped back in horror he tripped over a log behind him. "Nice slide, you're safe at home," the girl said. (Rip!)

Everyone giggled. (Rip!)

The counselor picked Harold up and said with a smile, "My little sister's not even afraid of garter snakes and she's four years old." (Rip!)

That night, when Harold sat on the edge of the bed to remove his tattered IALAC sign, he hoped that tomorrow would be better for him. He did not feel very lovable and capable today and he hoped that somehow overnight his sign would regain some of the lost pieces. How could Harold's day have been different?

The people around Harold could have behaved very differently. His counselor could have said, "It's hard getting up when you get to bed late. How was astronomy?"

Someone did not *have* to hide Harold's shoes.

The soap scribble on the mirror could have read, "Good morning, Harold. Please hurry to breakfast. We want you to sit with us."

Someone at the table could have said, "I'm glad you made it, I saved you a peach."

The director could have said, "Those 'flip flops' will never get you up a mountain today. I care about your feet, so please put shoes on after break-fast."

The cook could have held the serving window open and said, "There's always room for one more. I think you'll like breakfast today."

One captain could have said, "I'm picking Harold first today because he's my friend."

Instead of laughing and applauding with two hands, someone could have reached down with one hand and helped Harold up when he tripped.

There could have been so many ways that the people around Harold could have added pieces to his IALAC sign and not torn them away.

This book is written for the teachers, camp leaders, parents, and other adults who have opportunities to enrich the life of Harold and other young people like him. What you do with the IALAC idea is up to you.

Since this is a guide to leading nature and human nature activities, we will start by exploring how you can get the most out of your journey through the pages of this book. Every guidebook needs descriptions of some of the places you will want to visit, and a list of what to take.

Guidebooks are useless unless you know where you are going. Here are some ideas to help you determine which routes you would like to follow in this book. Make a note of the questions that you would like answered:

1. What does this book have to offer me? What do the terms "humanizing environmental education" mean? (See Chapter 1—"Introducing this Book."

2. What are some possible goals and organizing principles for humanizing and environmentalizing my program? (See Chapter II—"Designing Your Program or Curriculum."

3. What are some practical activities to help my students/campers/children/staff increase their environmental and human awareness? (See Chapter III—"Coming to Your Senses: Environmental and People Awareness."

4. How can I overcome common roadblocks to effective communication? What are some structured exercises based on these guidelines that I can do with people in my program? (See Chapter IV—"People Messengers: Developing Communication Skills."

5. How can I develop a sense of community among the staff and participants in my program while achieving our goals? What are some ways (e.g., rituals, ceremonies, creativity projects) to build a group? (See Chapter V—"People Harmony: Building a Sense of Community."

6. How can I help people address important values issues? (See Chapter VI—"Trail Markers: Clarifying Personal, Social, and Environmental Values."

7. How can I help myself and others develop more self-esteem? (See Chapter VII—"Making Friends with Yourself: The Nature and Nurture of Self-Esteem."

8. What does the life-skills approach to environmental education look like in practice? How can adventure activities in the outdoors be used as a vehicle to promote personal learning and professional development? (See Chapter VIII—"Adventure Learning: Personal and Group Challenges."

9. What are some of the principles underlying a noncompetitive approach to playing? How can I build cooperation, inclusion, and self-esteem through play and recreation? (See Chapter IX—"Playfair: Everybody's Guide to Noncompetitive Games."

10. What are some guidelines and specific suggestions for humanizing athletics and other traditional forms of outdoor activity? How can I mix the following ingredients: challenge, cooperation, individual excellence, joy, and learning? (See Chapter X—"Creative Leadership: A Humanistic Approach to Coaching."

11. How can I put all the pieces together into an outdoor program? How has a youth camp incorporated awareness, community building, communicating, valuing, self-esteem, adventure learning, noncompetitive play, and humanistic athletics? (See Chapter XI—"Human Relations Youth Adventure Camp: A Model that Really Works."

12. Where do I go from here? What resources can provide me with follow-up help? (See Chapter XII—"Resources: Where Do You Go from Here?"

If you have not found what you are looking for yet, here are some "extra credit" questions for you to consider:

13. As a parent, how can I help my children appreciate both themselves and the environment?
14. As a teacher, how can I enrich my curriculum with hands-on, easy-to-implement, learning activities?
15. As a camp director, what new ideas, approaches, and activities can I use with staff and campers to make our program more exciting, inviting, and effective?
16. As a camp counselor, how can I supplement my activity skills (e.g., archery, crafts, geology, waterfront) with human relations skills?
17. In working with youth groups, how can I help young people practice the skills they will need for the rest of their lives such as communicating, listening, decision-making, and empathizing?
18. As an environmentalist, how can I help people see themselves as *part* of the environment rather than separate from it?
19. In my work in coaching and recreation, what games can be played that will give enjoyment and insights about how to play the larger game of life in a healthier way?

Which questions stimulated your curiosity and have made some sort of connection with your personal or professional life? These are your clues for finding the treasures buried between the two covers of this book. We encourage you to plan your own personalized treasure hunt. In planning your journey, you might want to consider the following things to take:

What to Pack

1. *Curiosity and open-mindedness:* The book contains hundreds of new ideas and activities for you to ponder. For each usable idea you discover, try to think of at least one way to use it.
2. *Creativity:* The power of the activities will increase dramatically if you are willing to modify and adapt them and make your own. We encourage you to create at least one new way to adapt what we have provided as "food for thought."
3. *Risk-taking and enthusiasm:* Your willingness to actually try out these new ideas and activities is what ultimately makes the difference in your program. We support you in your efforts to take the ideas from these pages and put them into practice.
4. *A target:* The activities in this book are best used when they are targeted upon your program goals, principles, and objectives. This implies that activities will only "work" if they are appropriate to the readiness level and needs of the group with whom you are working (or playing). The activities are not "magic" alone—you must provide some magic in fitting them to the right situation and group.
5. *Support:* As in any new venture (or adventure), we often benefit and have more fun with the resources and support of others. We recommend that you consider establishing a formal or informal support group of friends, colleagues, and/or staff members as you think of ways to use the ideas in this book. Discussing the content, adapting it to your situation, and thinking about how to implement the ideas could all be a part of your support group agenda.

6. *Follow-through:* We encourage you to go beyond the covers of this book in pursuing ideas that are of interest to you. Check the references in the last chapter for possible follow-up steps you could take.

Why Are We Taking this Trip?

In the first part of this chapter, you had a chance to examine some questions you may want answered. In addition to the answers to these questions, we would like to paint a broader picture of what we see as the purposes of this book. We are on this trail because:

1. *Increased awareness:* During the past decade there has been a growing awareness of the environment around us. People have become increasingly aware that the survival of civilization depends on the development of an environmental ethic—and of behaviors that support that ethic. The Three Mile Islands and Love Canals of the 70's are reminders of the urgent need to care for the environment.

Over the past ten years, we have also witnessed a booming interest in exploring the world within each of us. The 70's were filled with programs for personal growth, coping with life transition, lifelong learning, and changing life-styles. People are experiencing strong interest in understanding and exploring the universe within each of them.

2. *Personal needs:* Many young people, and adults alike, are experiencing some confusion in their lives. In the face of accelerating change and future shock, almost everyone is dealing with questions in values areas such as: friendship, work, leisure, money, family, love, religion, future, and many others.

Accompanying this confusion may be a sense of devaluation. Anyone who has worked with young people is aware that many of them have a low estimate of their own worth. They seem to lack self-confidence and are often wrestling with issues of competence. Research shows that low self-confidence has a direct bearing on school achievement, task performance, and success. There is a strong need to help young people and adults enhance their self-esteem and to clarify their values in this area in order to create healthier life-styles.

3. *Societal needs:* We are facing and will continue to face oppressive social issues such as racism, sexism, ageism, hunger, poverty, and war/peace. The proper task for camps, schools, and other social institutions is as Mason suggests, "the encouragement of encompassing social visions . . . concern for a more humanized society . . . exploration of renewed social purpose (leading to) full engagement with some of the basic issues of society- racism, environment, health, diversity, work, technology, community participation . . . providing resources for people to participate in change."[2]

4. *Institutional challenge:* Human service agencies and programs are at a turning point. As we enter the 80's, the question of how to respond to increased personal and social needs faces us. Past president of the American Camping Association, John T. Howe also spoke to schools, recreation programs, and families when he said:

Does your camp really build character? Does your camp enable children to develop self-esteem? Does your program really enable campers to be better citizens as a result of their camp experience? We tell the public these things happen in camp, so let's make sure they do . . . [3]

The Synergistic Synthesis

How do we respond to the current needs? How can we tap the energy people have for exploring their internal and external environments? How can we help people to develop the tools to respond to personal and societal needs? How can we support institutions that are facing the challenges of the future?

We believe that part of the answer to these questions lies in the concepts of synergy and synthesis. Synergy is the joint action of separate parts in such a way that the results are greater than the effects of the parts acting alone. Another way to explain this concept is that sometimes, 1 + 1 can equal more than 2. Synthesis is the combining of two or more parts into a whole. The concepts of synergistic synthesis apply to the fields of environmental education and humanistic education.

When we combine the fields, as we have done in this book, we have magnified the possibilities that humanizing environmental education will help meet some personal and social needs. These two fields, which grew tremendously in the 70's, can complement each other well. Goals, principles, and applications from each form a natural bridge. Together, they become powerful allies in meeting institutional challenges for the future.

Environmental Education

Camp leaders, teachers, school administrators, recreation leaders, coaches, naturalists, outdoor educators, and other helping professionals have planted many seeds in developing the field of environmental education. For our purposes in this book, we view the field very broadly. We believe that environmental education embraces the following ideas:

1. Environmental education is a process which uses a wide variety of learning resources, both indoors and outdoors.
2. Environmental education is multidisciplinary in nature. As a means of curriculum enrichment, it applies to many subject matter areas on the elementary, secondary, and college levels.
3. Environmental education, as a means of understanding natural and person-made environments, is a continuous process.
4. Environmental education uses teaching methods and techniques based on a philosophy of experience-based learning through direct contact in the community and nature areas. This involves active exploration and problem solving, along with drawing on the senses of touch, taste, smell, sight, and hearing to the fullest possible extent.
5. Such activities encourage the development of skills, attitudes, and concepts focusing on environmental interrelationships. Human beings are

seen as a part of the natural environment, and not apart from it. Interdependence is an important concept in environmental education.

6. Outdoor learning activities can be coordinated with and complement indoor activities. Knowledge of the out-of-doors can have a significant carry-over value for leisure-time enrichment.

7. Environmental education will become increasingly important as this nation becomes more urbanized and technologized. Planning and decision making, as they regard use of the environment, will rest with all the citizens of the nation. In order to help participants in environmental education programs to develop citizenship skills, we need to create programs that:

a. Facilitate growth in awareness, understanding, and appreciation of the surroundings;
b. Demonstrate concern for improving communication skills, effective group dynamics, and human relations;
c. Encourage the expression of personal values and ideas about the human and natural environment, respect diversity of beliefs, and help participants clarify values;
d. Create an atmosphere which invites environmental awareness and life-styles changes in rational and ecological directions;
e. Respect people for their positive qualities;
f. Encourage trust, caring, empathy, cooperation, and risk-taking through structured experiences and modeling behavior;
g. Structure opportunities for participant involvement in planning, problem solving, and evaluating the learning experience;
h. Provide for differences in participants' needs, interests, abilities, and learning styles by offering a variety of formats and content areas;
i. Build in opportunities for individuals and groups to have successful experiences in the environment;
j. Help people overcome blocks to learning about the natural/human environment, while allowing them to take more responsibility for their own growth.

Humanistic Education

Growing out of the work of Abraham Maslow, Carl Rogers, Louis Raths, Gerald Weinstein, Sidney Simon, and others, the results of humanizing education have touched thousands of schools and other institutions across the country in the past decade. The philosophy underlying this approach seems to have struck a chord in people who want to maintain their humanity in the face of some depersonalizing conditions. Perhaps the major reason for the rapid growth of the field is the fact that the philosophy can be implemented by many practical strategies that helping professionals and parents can employ. This approach is based upon a number of assumptions about people and learning:

1. It is important to address the "whole person" in any educational endeavor. In addition to cognitive learning, it is crucial that we acknow-

ledge the affective areas of human experience. The two areas can not be separated as we learn.

2. People learn best when they feel safe, respected, appreciated, motivated, challenged, when they have opportunities to make choices in their lives, and when they have chances to identify and build on their own strengths and interests.

3. There is a universe within each of us that can be a legitimate and exciting subject matter for exploration. Humanistic education seeks to help people develop self-scientist skills—learning about and from our own thoughts, feelings, and behaviors.

4. We must help people to develop a sense of identity, a sense of connectedness, and a sense of mastery or locus of control. Identity involves one's self-image and feelings of self-worth (e.g., "Who am I? What do I stand for, value, and believe in?"). Connectedness involves one's relationship with other people (e.g., "How do I relate to other people? With whom do I belong?"). Mastery or locus of control involves the extent to which one is in charge of what happens to him/her (e.g., "How can I affect and direct the flow of my life?").

5. We must create learning environments that encourage: pluralism and respect for differences, collaboration and cooperation, nourishment and support among people, and opportunities to generate alternative solutions to problems.

6. Learning will be internalized to a greater extent when: both the experiential (actively participating) and reflective (relating to one's own life experience) modes are employed; different learning styles are incorporated in the program (e.g., listening, observing, reading, touching, discussing, note-taking, playing, working alone, and working cooperatively with a group.

7. Humanistic education is an approach to creating positive learning environments that encourage people to develop *life skills* that they find valuable in addressing personal and societal concerns. Humanistic education helps people develop life skills in four areas: the cognitive (thinking), the affective (feeling), the active (behaving), and the interpersonal (human relations).

—Cognitive skills include: choosing freely (e.g., dealing with peer pressure); developing awareness of available alternatives; choosing with an awareness of the consequences of one's choices; being aware of patterns in one's life; thinking critically (e.g., analyzing, synthesizing, inferring); ideating (being able to generate ideas and alternatives).

—Affective skills include: identifying and acknowledging feelings as one source in making decisions; legitimizing one's intuition as another possible source; focusing on what one prizes and cherishes; empathizing with other people's feelings; enhancing self-esteem.

—Active skills include: acting on one's choices (moving from awareness and insight to behavioral change); goal setting; culling out the inconsistencies between what one would like to do and what one is likely to do.

—Interpersonal skills include: publicly affirming one's choices where appropriate; active listening; resolving conflict situations; asking clarifying questions; cooperating in work and play; validating (focusing on the "positive" in self and others and communicating appreciations).[4]

What Lies Ahead on the Trail?

Based on the guidelines and principles described above, this book takes a humanistic approach to environmental education. We see this as *A Guide for Leading Nature and Human Nature Activities* that will help people learn life skills which will enhance the quality of life, the quality of the human environment, and the quality of the natural environment.

This book is organized in four sections:

I. **Why?:** Chapter one has examined the need for this book, some possible reasons for your picking it up, and our reasons for writing it.

II. **How?:** Chapter two explores the goals, principles, and foci around which you can humanize and environmentalize your program. Chapters three through seven offer many activities that will help you develop and implement your program's goals and principles. Each of these chapters provides dozens of examples that encourage people to learn such important life skills as: awareness, communications, community building, values clarification, and self-esteem. As you will see, many of these activities are interrelated, and can be used together in sequences you create.

III. **Who?/What?:** Who has been implementing these activities, principles, and goals? What do these programs look like? Chapters eight through eleven provide case studies of successful programs. These chapters include insights into what makes a successful program "tick," along with dozens of additional activities.

IV. **Where?:** Where do you turn if you are interested in going beyond this book? Chapter twelve gives references for many resourceful people, organizations, and materials which could provide follow-up support. Our hope is that this book will be a springboard for further exploration.

Coming to Terms with the Trip

There are three terms that we use throughout the book that need explanation. In describing students in a classroom, campers, members of a family, people in an organization, and athletes on a team, we use the word, "participants." In speaking of teachers, camp leaders and counselors, parents, coaches, and other helping professionals who might use or lead the activities in this book, we use the word, "staff." In talking about planned activities for a classroom, outdoor school, camp, family, recreation center, and other arenas in which environmental education could take place, we use the word, "program." As you read through this book, please make your own personal translation when you come across any of these three words.

A Request for Feedback

We hope that your journey through this book will be stimulating, inviting, and impactful. We also hope that we will hear about, and learn from, your journey. Your feedback in the form of questions, activities, suggestions, and leadership tips would be welcomed. Feel free to contact us at Sagamore Institute, 110 Spring Street, Saratoga Springs, New York 12866, and Lorado Taft Field Campus, Box 299, Oregon, Illinois 61061. How about sending the authors a "letter from camp" as you read this book? We extend our best wishes and support to you. See you on the trail!

Footnotes

1 Adapted by Clifford E. Knapp from *I Am Lovable and Capable* by Sidney Simon. Niles, IL: Argus Communications, 1973.
2 James Mason, "Uncertain Outposts: The Future of Camping and the Challenge of Its Past," *Camping Magazine*. (September/October, 1978) pp. 28-29. (An Occasional Paper issued by the Fund for Advancement of Camping.)
3 John T. Howe, "On the Ball," *Camping Magazine*. (February, 1979) P. 7.
4 This list of skills is an extension of what is presented in Donald Read, Sidney Simon, and Joel Goodman's *Health Education: The Search for Values*. Englewood Cliffs, NJ: Prentice-Hall, Inc., 1977, and in Joel Goodman's (editor) *Turning Points: New Developments, New Directions in Values Clarification*, Volumes I and II. Saratoga Springs: Creative Resources Press. 1978-79.

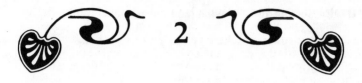

2

Designing Your Program or Curriculum

The intended goals of your organization or school are the foundation upon which the program and curriculum are built. Goals need to be consistent with each other and be attainable with the human and natural resources available. The program or curriculum should reflect these goals in every way. Creative programming is the process of putting together the elements of successful activities in new ways in order to accomplish desired goals.

Broad Goals and Philosophy

The main purpose for providing participants with an environmental experience is to enrich their total education. The learning environment becomes the forests, fields, water courses, a city block, a cemetery, or mountaintop. The use of each of these ecosystems and others should be maximized because this is a prime opportunity for firsthand learning.

Every contact throughout the day is viewed as an educational opportunity (including the tasks of daily living if participants stay overnight in a camp setting). The program or curriculum encompasses all that happens to a participant. We learn from all of our experiences with the environment, whether in a formal class, structured activity, or talking informally with someone. A broad view of what constitutes a learning experience is essential in humanizing environmental education.

A sampling of goals you might consider in designing your program or curriculum follows.

Goal I—Understanding Yourself and Others

Gaining more understanding of one's self and others is a life-long goal. Exposure to new environments often stimulates new insights in both of these areas. Immersion with people and nature, especially in a camp setting, can spark learnings of self and others. Planned activities can be aimed at helping participants cooperate, show empathy, share attitudes and values, and think and act positively toward themselves and others.

Goal II—Respecting and Enjoying the Environment

Our environment is our heritage to preserve, change, or destroy. An important goal of the program should be to encourage participants to respect and enjoy nature and person-made environments whether close to home or far away. One way to do this is to gather staff and other participants who model their values of appreciation and respect for all living things around them.

Examples of wise use and abuse of our environment are all around us. The only rational choice is to live in ways that assure our survival and the preservation of aesthetic surroundings. Planned activities should be woven with the threads of care and concern for preserving the natural world wherever possible.

Informal learning opportunities must also relate the same message in both direct and subtle ways. Care must be taken to conserve food, put out campfires, pick up litter, release captured animals, remove only plants which occur in abundance, plant trees, improve trails, and do other service projects to maintain and improve the surroundings.

Goal III—Living Safely and Healthfully Outdoors

Human health and safety are very important outdoors because of the dangerous accidents that can occur. With the increase in leisure time in our society and the growing popularitiy of outdoor activities, everyone needs to know how to survive without serious illness or accidents. Precautions to be taken in various activities can best be learned while doing them. Safety skills taught in the context of hiking, canoeing, fishing, fire building, sleeping out, shelter building, or eating off of the land are much more meaningful than a film or textbook approach.

Goal IV—Developing Life-Long Outdoor and Environmental Interests

This goal of developing life-long outdoor and environmental interests is possible only if a person has the skills and attitudes necessary for enjoying the natural environment. The exposure to activities such as hiking, birdwatching, natural crafts, creative writing, stream exploration, or whatever outdoor experiences the program provides, could lead to future hobbies and pastimes. The true test of the value of an educational experience is what effect it has on the lifestyle of the person.

These four broad goals can be adapted or expanded to meet the purpose of various organizations and institutions. The important point to remember is that the goals form the springboard from which your program or curriculum is launched.

Take some time now to modify and/or expand on these goals. What visions do you have for your own program or curriculum?

Some Principles of Creative Programming

A principle is a statement of an ideal condition for implementing goals. Principles serve as a checklist for determining if the program's content and process are being directed to your goals. They serve as guideposts along the way to providing a humanistic journey through the environment.

Principle 1—Respect and Support

If the staff does not like and respect the participants it will be difficult to reach any of the goals. An attitude of support is crucial if participants are to take risks, learn, and grow.

Principle 2—Blending

The staff should have an adequate background in both environmental and human relations knowledge and skills. A delicate blend of knowledge and skills in both areas are necessary in order to effectively implement the program or curriculum.

Principle 3—Realistic Goals

The program or curriculum should reflect realistic goals and be attainable within the available time and with the available resources. Not only should the goals be realistic and well-suited to the participants, but the activities should also be clearly directed to accomplishing a desired goal(s).

Principle 4—Understanding Values

The staff should understand their own values and those of the participants before (and while) the program or curriculum is implemented. It is important that the staff be willing to clarify their own values before attempting to work with other people and their values.

Principles 5—Holistic View

The program should be viewed as a totality and include such components as introductory community building, ongoing maintenance of the sense of community, activities for closure and evaluation. This principle stresses the importance of being aware of the developmental phases of any community-building effort.

Principle 6—Adequate Time

The staff should have time to plan together as well as to build personal relationships together. A smoothly operating community just doesn't happen. Adequate planning time must be allotted to coordinating activities. The staff must devote time on a regular basis to getting to know and care for each other, to resolving conflicts, and to solving problems and concerns that emerge during the program.

Principle 7—Evaluation

On-going evaluation may be the most-spoken-about and the least-applied of all the programming advice given. Evaluation is the best means of knowing how to change activities to better accomplish goals.

Program or Curriculum Focus

Once the goals and principles have been thought through and written down for clarity, the program or curriculum focus must be considered. The focus is the organizational mode or way of implementing the program or curriculum. Environmental and outdoor education foci have varied widely.

Focus 1—Subject Matter or Curriculum Approach

The most common focus used by schools conducting outdoor programs has been the subject matter or curriculum-centered approach. This focus organizes activities around subject matter disciplines such as science, mathematics, language arts, social studies, music, art, and physical education. The process of planning starts with the subject such as science and then examines some objectives of the science curriculum at a particular grade level. The next step is usually to select certain objectives that can be best learned outside of the school classroom.

A classic example of this approach is the pond ecology lesson. Most all science curricula contain objectives dealing with food chains and food webs in aquatic environments. Usually, educators conclude that the most efficient and meaningful way to learn about food chains and webs in aquatic environments is to visit a pond or stream and examine the organisms firsthand. Predator and prey relationships among the organisms often can be viewed while the organisms are still being collected.

Focus 2—Problem-Solving Approach

This focus centers around a problem to be investigated. The activities and methods spring from the problem as it is solved. For example, one problem could be phrased, "What can be learned about the lives of people who lived in this area and about ourselves from the evidence found in the cemetery?" With this approach, activities are designed to reveal answers to the problem and are not confined to any particular subject matter area. Rubbings with paper and crayons can be taken of the epitaphs and designs on the tombstones. Some of the old tombstones can provide examples of mechanical weathering and opportunities for rock identification. Participants can write their own epitaphs, and stories of what they would imagine life to be like one hundred years ago.

Focus 3—Pollution Detection and Monitoring

This focus centers around particular pollution problems in the area. Air pollution sources and effects can be isolated and action projects planned to reduce the problem. Litter surveys and pickups can be planned and methods to prevent future littering explored.

Focus 4—Adventure Programs and Outdoor Skills

Adventure programs provide participants with practical experiences in survival skills such as camping, mountain climbing and rappelling, fire building, pitching a tent, outdoor cooking, and other camping skills, as well as lifetime sports such as archery, fishing and casting, skiing, and riflery. Skill development along with self and group understanding are the primary purposes of this approach.

Focus 5—Environmental and Ecological Awareness

This focus concentrates upon a wide variety of structured activities aimed at increasing environmental awareness. The five senses are used extensively as well as the introduction of ecological concepts to explore various types of ecosystems. The popular *Acclimatizing* approach is one example of this "awareness" orientation.

Focus 6—Natural History and Identification

This focus concentrates heavily upon people learning the names and important characteristics of flora and fauna. Knowing the scientific and common names of a plant as well as where it grows, its bark, fruit, bud, leaf, and flower characteristics, and the uses to people are important in this structure.

Focus 7—The Location as the Key to Learning About the Environment

This focus depends upon a particular location or setting to teach environmental concepts, skills, and values. Sometimes these programs use parks, school sites, vacant lots, sanctuaries, or even city streets to present activities. Sometimes participants travel to specific locations for extensive periods of time and learn about these places firsthand.

Focus 8—Personal Growth Through Outdoor Experiences

This focus uses the outdoors and environmental values issues to help participants grow in interpersonal and self-understanding. The outdoor setting and natural and person-made objects are used as vehicles to personal growth and improved human relations.

It may have become clear as you were examining the eight program or curriculum emphases that in practice very few appear in pure form. Various combinations of foci are usually blended to best meet the goals and philosophy of a particular person or organization. No one structure will meet all goals equally well. No one focus is best for all outdoor and environmental staffs to implement. The important point is to be aware of the various foci and to combine them in creative ways to reach desired goals.

Take some time now to focus on these foci in your own program or curriculum. You might rank-order the foci in order of their importance in your own program. Or, you might think of practical applications for how you could integrate and combine these foci in your own program.

Program Activities: Whetting Your Appetite

Once you have identified your goals, principles, and foci, it is time to generate and select specific, appropriate activities. If your staff conducts brainstorming sessions in planning the program, many more activities will be available to choose from. Pooling ideas serves to expand the number of program options and serves as a means of sharing among the staff. Piggybacking on the ideas of others results in many more program activities than any individual staff member could generate alone.

One hundred program ideas resulting from brainstorming sessions of the staff of the Human Relations Youth Adventure Camp (See chapter XI) are offered here as an example of the wide variety of outdoor activities available. We hope this will whet your appetite for the life-skill-building activities described in the following chapters.

(1) Design a banner or symbol representing our group using native materials.

(2) Burn names and symbols of everyone into a driftwood log.

(3) Write a guide booklet for a self-made nature trail.

(4) Choose quiet spots for individuals to use for reflection.

(5) Make nature crafts for a bartering day.

(6) Carve walking sticks with symbols of new experiences gained.

(7) Provide notebooks for everyone to keep journals.

(8) Form back rub chains when people are tired.

(9) Do community service projects such as building a bridge, campfire log circle, trail clearing, sauna, etc.

(10) Build sand castles on the beach.

(11) Build a raft and float down the stream or across the lake.

(12) Spend 24 hours in the woods alone without food.

(13) Make bread, pie, or jam for everyone.

(14) Make new obstacles for the group initiative ropes course.

(15) Eat a meal blindfolded while being fed by a partner.

(16) Set up a board for everyone to share favorite quotes or sayings.

(17) Set up a schedule for an all-night fire vigil.

(18) Invent a new ceremony to increase environmental awareness.

(19) Lead a session in body movement related to movements of nature.

(20) Tell a round-robin story around the campfire.

(21) Read the group a story about a topic related to the environment.

(22) Do values clarification activities on concerns of participants.

(23) Invent new games of cooperation.

(24) Find out what skills participants have that they would lead for others.

(25) Make a tree house or an underground fort.

(26) Lead a guided fantasy pretending to travel inside the vessels of a tree.

(27) Go on a night walk without flashlights.

(28) Walk down the center of a stream in sneakers as a group.

(29) Conduct a '50s night.

(30) Make nature collages showing how you feel about this environment.

(31) Take an early morning "polar bear" dip in the lake.

(32) Prepare and serve everyone a special meal.

(33) Paint each others' faces and bodies with water colors.

(34) Write a community newspaper about a shared experience.

(35) Conduct an interview with different people each day.

(36) Invite someone from the surrounding community to dinner.

(37) Have a good will day in which everyone exchanges good deeds.

Brown

(38) Eat a meal similar to that served in another culture.
(39) Change your personality for 1 hour to understand how it feels.
(40) Put on a circus.
(41) Don't talk for a day.
(42) Don't eat for a day.
(43) Blindfold yourself for a day.
(44) Take a beeline compass hike to a specific place.
(45) Conduct a creativity sharing night.
(46) Make boats from found materials and race them in a stream.
(47) Build shelters from natural materials.
(48) Watch the sunrise and sunset.
(49) Dig for artifacts at an abandoned farm.
(50) Go mountain climbing and rappelling.
(51) Spend time writing creatively and sharing what is written.
(52) Use corn husks to make crafts.
(53) Make nature mobiles.
(54) Paint rocks with designs that have personal meanings.
(55) Dye wool with natural plant dyes.
(56) Make candles and soap.
(57) Make macrame jewelry.
(58) Make and fire clay beads.
(59) Have a non-thumb day (tape everyone's thumb down).
(60) Go jogging in the morning together.
(61) Explore a local cemetery to learn history.
(62) Dress up in a crazy costume.

BROWN

(63) Go on a scavenger hunt with a partner.
(64) Make a group weaving or paint a group picture.
(65) Have a strength bombardment session to tell people what their strengths are.
(66) Sketch nature pictures.
(67) Do ozalid sun prints.
(68) Write a letter to yourself.
(69) Exchange handmade gifts.
(70) Conduct camping skills sessions on knife sharpening, ax use, fire building, whittling, wood splitting, etc.
(71) Find shapes and characters in the constellations at night.
(72) Invent and make wooden toys.
(73) Sleep out on top of a mountain.
(74) Collect and polish driftwood.
(75) Do nature awareness activities.
(76) Invite someone to share what they know well.
(77) Hold a service auction where everyone offers a service.
(78) Talk to trees, rocks, and other objects, and imagine what they would say back to you.
(79) Hug and dance with trees.
(80) Move your body like trees in the wind, clouds moving across the sky, and raindrops falling in a puddle.
(81) Invent games using found items such as branches, stones, grasses, leaves, acorns, etc.

(82) Find objects in nature containing successively higher numbers (e.g., plant with one leaf, two leaves, etc.).

(83) Create a giant sculpture using rocks or logs.

(84) Create a sculpture using people—form different animals, plants, buildings, etc.

(85) Go on a litter hunt to see how large a pile of litter can be built (and then thrown away).

(86) Pretend people are raindrops falling to earth.

(87) Role play earthworms, birds, snakes, insects, and other animals as well as inanimate objects such as rocks, fences, tires, houses, telephone poles, etc.

(88) Find familiar shapes in the clouds and between tree branches.

(89) Make a nest like a bird.

(90) Make paint brushes from pine needles, weeds, and other natural objects and paint a picture.

(91) Search the area for "Guinness world records" for the fattest tree, prettiest insect, biggest acorn, etc.

(92) Find lines (zig-zag, vertical, wavy, horizontal, slanted) in the environment.

(93) Invent solutions to practical problems by getting ideas from nature.

(94) Pick up natural objects and see how many questions can be asked about each one.

(95) On a sunny day play tag with each other's shadows.

(96) Go out in the rain and get wet (not during a thunderstorm).

(97) Role in a pile of leaves and "wash" in a leaf bath.

(98) See how many people can fit on a section of sidewalk.

(99) Dig the deepest hole you can in the ground.

(100) Do something to improve the environment.

Selecting Criteria for a Humanizing Activity

The preceding list of 100 activities can provide hundreds of hours of fun and learning. You can add to this list (and to the activities described in the following chapters) and create your own humanizing activities by considering these criteria as guidelines. These criteria can also double as evaluation principles. Of course, any one activity may not meet all of the criteria—hopefully, you could put together a "recipe" for your program that would be well balanced in terms of the following:

(1) Does the activity speak to one or more of your broad program goals?

(2) Does the activity seem to be consistent with your organizing principles?

(3) Given the particular focus of your program, does the activity fit?

(4) Does the activity provide opportunities for learning new skills (e.g., such life skills as communicating, community-building, decision-making, etc.)?

(5) Does the activity encourage cooperation and group cohesiveness?

(6) Does the activity primarily use the natural setting and local areas and people?

(7) Does the activity enhance self-esteem and feelings of success?

(8) Does the activity introduce a sense of fun and adventure?

(9) Does the activity encourage creative outlets for energy?

(10) Does the activity invite participation and involvement?

(11) Does the activity consider the environment (i.e., does not harm the environment)?

(12) Does the activity accommodate for individual differences in ability and preferences?

(13) Does the activity consider the health and safety of the participants?

(14) Does the activity provide opportunities for the participants to make choices—does the activity offer "structured freedom"?

(15) Does the activity speak to the needs, interests, and readiness level of the participants?

(16) Does the activity flow in a way that is logically and psychologically sound (e.g., moving from lower risk to higher risk; moving from introduction of a new skill to planned reinforcement of that skill; etc.)?

(17) Does the activity include variety (e.g., of groupings; of learning/teaching modes; a balance between seriousness and lightness; energizers and changes of pace)?

(18) Does the activity include opportunities for self-evaluation, for reflection, for "processing" or making sense/meaning of the activity?

(19) Does the activity have follow-up (i.e., do participants know how to springboard off the activity)?

(20) Does the activity include the following steps: (A) attending (have I built in an initial attention-grabber?); (B) experiencing (have I included opportunities for participants to be actively involved?); (C) conceptualizing (have I provided time for the participants to "make sense" of their experience?); (D) relating (have I given the participants a chance to relate these learnings to their own lives and values?); (E) practicing (have I invited participants to "try out" and apply their learnings to their own lives?).

Can you think of other criteria that would be important for you to consider in generating and sequencing your program's activities? Take some time to create your own list (or to add to the list above). This step is crucial if we are to go beyond merely following "recipes" for activities. Ultimately, we need to have more cooks, not more cookbooks.[1]

---

(1) For additional ideas on how to create and evaluate a program on curriculum, see an excellent article by Joel Goodman and Kenneth Huggins, "Confluent Curriculum Development: Achieving Tenure in the Lives of Students," in Joel Goodman's (editor) *Turning Points: New Developments, New Directions in Values Clarification, Volume I* (available from Creative Resources Press, 179 Spring Street, Saratoga Springs, NY 12866). Also, see "A Humanistic Approach to Evaluation and Ways of Evaluating Humanistic Education: Counting the Apples in a Seed" (Chapter 8) in Donald Read, Sidney Simon, and Joel Goodman's *Health Education: The Search for Values* (Englewood Cliffs: Prentice-Hall, 1977).

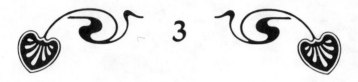

Coming to Your Senses:
Environmental and People Awareness

Buckminster Fuller once defined the word "environment" as "everything except me." Using this definition, you can then consider the environment to include things such as trees, rocks, water, soil, sunlight, *and* the surrounding people. Environmental activities that combine awareness of both nature and people are excellent vehicles for humanizing environmental education. The following activities are designed with this two-fold purpose in mind.

The word "awareness" is used freely and often broadly in writings today. Awareness occurs when you combine the sensory input from the outer environment with thoughts and feelings from the inner environment (yourself) to produce meaning. You must make a personal connection with the environment, and certain conditions must be present before awareness can result. These are: (1) physical comfort (awareness is stifled when a person is too cold, wet, or tired); (2) open or receptive attitude (unless a person wants awareness, no awareness will occur); (3) sensory intake (one or more of the senses must be functioning in order for a person to reach a level of awareness); and (4) environmental stimuli (the environment must provide the stimuli in order for awareness to result). There are several "hooks" that help create the conditions that invite a person to develop awareness.

Hook #1—*Limiting Senses*

At first, the technique of limiting senses appears to be counter to one of the prerequisites for awareness. However, by limiting one or more senses, the others are often heightened. The blindfold which is often used in awareness activities, enables the senses of hearing, touch, or smell to be heightened. Other methods of limiting senses can involve taping the thumbs to the palm, putting gloves on before trying to identify textures, or not talking for a period of time. The limiting senses technique also serves to provide a person with greater appreciation for the limited sense once it is freed for use again.

LESSER

Hook#2—*Expanding Senses*

This technique does exactly what is described—it extends the senses through the use of a sensory aid or gimmick. These techniques can involve gadgets such as toilet tissue rolls used as "cameras," "task cards" to focus attention on something, cupping hands behind the ears to gather in more sound, or merely repeating words such as "Now I am aware that . . ." or "I wonder . . ."

Hook #3—*Questions*

The time-honored question can serve as an awareness hook. Open-ended questions often serve as effective ways of opening a person to awareness. Sometimes, the more ambiguous and unspecific the question is, the more the participant can supply the missing parts and arrive at more creative answers. So often, the answers to questions far exceed the expectations of the leader and provide more environmental awareness for the whole group.

Hook #4—*Role Playing and Using Metaphors*

One method of producing creative thinking is to "make the strange familiar and the familiar strange." This means that by examining the environment in new and different ways, awareness results. By playing the role of an earthworm, for example, we are forced to see new things. The simile, a way of comparing two apparently unrelated things using the words "like" or "as," is another way to encourage awareness. For example, to see a snake like a "painted rope" may help you see the beautiful patterns of the scales. Allegories and analogies will accomplish similar purposes.

Hook #5—*Guide Sheets and Factual Information*

Not to be discounted are the guided discovery techniques similar to those used in nature trail booklets. If a person is motivated to learn about the environment, guided directives can invite new awareness. For example, the direction to "Lift the fallen log to see what you can find underneath" can help expand a person's world. Also, facts such as "The sassafras has three distinctly different shaped leaves," can stimulate investigation. Invitations to count, measure, or estimate can also open up new awarenesses.

Perhaps you can discover other awareness hooks, but most of the awareness activities listed in this chapter can be categorized under one or more of these five "hooks."

#1—*Question Trail*

Prior to introducing the question trail activity, go outside and put numbered stakes or pieces of cardboard at designated locations. These numbered locations will become "stations" or stops along a question trail.

The reason this activity is called "Question Trail" is because instead of factual information being provided at each station, one or more questions are asked. Each question must invite some type of activity and result in a new awareness at that location. Initially, small groups of three or four persons are assigned to each station and told to compile a list of questions about that spot. After each group has compiled their questions, the whole group is led to each successive number and invited to answer the questions. This activity provides for a success experience for most people while asking and answering the questions. This activity also gets people away from the erroneous idea that they must be able to identify a plant, rock, or animal by name in order to learn about it.

For example, when a group is examining a decaying stump, questions could include: (1) Can you find any living things that use the stump for an apartment? (2) Does the rotten wood hold water like a sponge? (3) How is this stump like a person you know? (4) How many words can you find to describe this stump to a friend who is blind? (5) How many colors can you find on the stump? (6) Of what kind of animal does the stump remind you?

#2—*Naming Trail*

Select a location outside where two types of environments join (for example, where a field joins a forest, a vacant lot joins a sidewalk, water joins a bank, or a road joins a field). Usually, the area where two ecosystems meet will provide a great variety of plant and animal life. Ask the participants to each take ten toothpicks or small sticks and ten small slips of paper and use them to mark numbered stations along a section of the edge trail.

The object of this activity is to name the plants or animal evidence by making up names that are based on a characteristic of that plant or animal. No real common names can be used even if the person knows them. For example, a toothpick and paper numbered with a "1" can be placed next to a dandelion plant and called "fuzzy head" after the cottony seed head. The same plant could be named, "garden hose plant" after the flexible, hollow stem supporting the seed head. Next, a toothpick with a piece of paper numbered "2" could be placed next to a clover leaf. This plant could be named "triple leaf" after the three-part leaf. After each participant has named ten plants or animal evidence, they pair up to share their trails. This activity stresses awareness of characteristics and creativity in assigning a name based on these characteristics. This technique also illustrates how many plants and animals are named for obvious physical characteristics.

#3—Awareness Theme Cards

A deck of 3 x 5 cards is prepared beforehand on which a theme word or words are written, one to a card. Words which can help direct awareness in the environment are as follows: decay, life cycles, bark, moisture, coolness, weeds, seeds, roots, animal food, insect evidence, protective covering, arts and crafts plants, fences, water, manhole covers, gutters, telephone wires, motion, patterns, cooperation, textures, waste, cruelty, variety, symmetry, harmony, repetition, etc. Many more awareness themes can be added to explore a particular area. The human interaction is increased if teams of two or three participants are assigned to find evidence in the environment of the theme written on each card.

Another way to use theme cards is to prepare different roles people can play as you walk along the trail. Each role is placed on a card and given to the participants. The fun can be increased by having the others try to guess what role each person is playing as they walk along. Some examples of roles are: toucher, lifter, looker up, looker down, questioner, exclaimer, listener, smeller, and searcher.

#4—Environmental Task Cards[1]

Environmental task cards direct participants to explore the environment. The tasks are usually worded briefly and allow a variety of interpretations and responses. Usually, boundaries of time and location are established and participants choose a partner to explore each card. The tasks may be completed by bringing objects back, sketching them, or verbally describing them. The sharing session following the completion of the tasks is just as important as the discovery part. Participants should be encouraged to select task cards even if the solutions are not clear before beginning. Some of the tasks are purposely ambiguous to force participants to make decisions and be creative. Participants are to answer the task in any way they feel is best. Guidelines should be provided about not picking plants that are threatened, poisonous, or on the property of others. It is important to maintain a nonjudgmental and accepting atmosphere throughout the sharing of the results after completing the tasks. Participants may wish to "pass" if the sharing is considered too personal. Examples of task cards:

(1) Go outside and stand in a spot which is as near to sea level as possible. Prove to someone else that you are at the lowest elevation around. How long would it take you to reach sea level?

(2) Go outside and find pebbles to create a rock rainbow. How many colors are in your rock rainbow? Crush some soft rocks and mix them with water to make "face paint."

(3) Find a collage that was not made by people. Duplicate a natural collage. Rearrange the elements of a natural collage. Add to a natural collage.

(4) Make a list of changes that occur while you watch some things outside. How many can you list in five minutes? Which changes are not reversible?

(5) Look under two things, inside of three things, around four things, and through five things. What other ways can you look at things in your environment? Look in those ways. What in the environment is *not* a thing? How can you examine a non-thing?

(6) Go outside and find plants or plant parts that resemble or remind you of different things. Make sketches of the parts and next to each write what it resembles or reminds you of. Find parts of plants that remind you of body parts (both inside and outside of you). Using plant parts, make something beautiful, useful, ugly, or scary. Try to become a particular plant or plant part. What happened to you when you did?

(7) Go outside and ask a question, make a hypothesis about the answer, and design an experiment to test that hypothesis.

(8) Go outside and crush parts of abundant plants to smell the aroma of each. Which smell would make a good deodorant or perfume?

(9) Go outside and find the home of some living thing that you would most enjoy living in. Describe a house you know that has one feature of this animal home. How would you like to change your house so it is more like this animal's home? How is your present home not like this animal's home?

(10) Go outside and find small objects that resemble squares, ellipses, circles, triangles, diamonds, and rectangles. Group these objects into different categories according to color, texture, living and dead, light and heavy, etc. Make up other categories and group them in those ways. Name three ways that all the objects are similar. Which ones were there because of people? If you were to make animals out of these objects, what animals would you make? Pick one object and use your senses in as many ways as possible to learn more about it.

(11) Go outside and find an insect. Mark the spot where you find it. Follow it for five minutes. How far did you travel? Try to retrace your steps. What do you admire about that insect? Give your insect a name and talk to it for a while. What would the insect say to you if it could talk? If you could choose one kind of insect to be your friend, which would it be? How is a particular insect like you?

(12) Go outside and make a list of rules that people have made that have affected the environment. Which rules are not necessary? What evidence can you find of natural rules? Can you find examples of natural rules and people-made rules in conflict with each other?

(13) Go outside and look up. What do you see that you haven't noticed before? What is the color of the sky? How does this color change? Find some clouds in the sky. Are they moving? Pick a tiny wisp of cloud and follow it for a few minutes. Does it disappear or build in size? Find familiar shapes in the clouds. What can you learn from looking down?

(14) Go outside and select an object that can be found in abundance (e.g., acorns, fallen leaves, pebbles, or sticks). What is the most of any one object that you can carry in one hand? Can you hold twice as many objects in two hands? What tool could you invent to hold more objects in one hand? Invent the tool and see how many objects you can hold.

(15) Go outside and pick an area where you would like to spend some time alone. How much time would you like to spend there? What characteristics of that spot influenced your decision? Find an area that is completely different from the one you picked first. Would you like to spend some time there too? How much? What are some of your thoughts and feelings while spending time in that spot?

(16) Go outside and find a color that represents the following feelings: sad, glad, mad, and scared. How many mood colors did you find? Does the color of something in the environment affect your feelings toward that object?

(17) Go outside and find something that is dead. Write or give a eulogy for it (a speech giving praise for its accomplishments). Try to figure out the following: cause and time of death, names and numbers of survivors, how the object will be missed on earth, and other important information about the departed one. How is death valuable to the environment?

(18) Go outside and listen to some moving water in a brook, gutter, drain pipe, lake or reservoir. Can you hear sounds that resemble words in the English language? Don't give up too soon; you may hear the moving water "speak." Does a brook really babble?

#5—Nature's Band

Give the participants instructions to go into the environment and find objects that can be used to create some music. Objects such as sticks, stones, leaves, husks, and seeds, metal pipes, car brake drums, garbage can lids, bottles, and many other objects can produce tone and rhythm. Conduct a musical "happening" in which instruments join together one by one and blend into an unrehearsed composition. A musical piece can be written be assigning each instrument a line on a grid written on a piece of newsprint. Each time the instrument is to be played, an "x" is placed along the grid horizontally. The conductor moves a baton along the grid horizontally to signal the instruments to be played. Nature's band creates a group effort which tends to expand awareness of nature and the people-made environment as well as results in feelings of teamwork and cooperation among the band members.

#6—Tree Fantasy

Ask the participants to select a tree from the surrounding area. They then assume a comfortable position and close their eyes. The leader conducts a slow-moving fantasy in which the participants pretend that they are small enough to travel inside of that tree. The guided journey can begin by entering the tree through a small hole in the leaf. The inside of the leaf is explored and then the branches, trunk, and roots. With the imagination of the leader and participants, an exciting journey can be conducted. After the journey, the participants can share their feelings about exploring the inside of a tree throughout the seasons. The sharing phase of this activity is just as important as the fantasy journey.

#7—Recalling Highpoints Outdoors

The participants assume a comfortable position and close their eyes. The leader conducts a guided tour of past experiences and memories in the outdoor environment. The purpose of this activity is to relax and recall positive, past associations with the environment. It is important to dwell upon positive experiences in order to accomplish the purpose of relaxation and refreshment. The participants are advised to only think of happy or pleasant experiences that are triggered by the leader's words. You may select words from the following list or make up new ones. Mention them slowly to provide time to savor each one:

The smell of a beautiful flower, the sight of a stream in the mountains, sawdust in a woodshop, freshly cut grass, the sound of crickets chirping, the smell of a campfire, wet sand between the toes, sunshine warmth on a cool day, taste of a freshly picked apple, walking through leaves in the fall, the smell and feel of pine needles on the ground, the sound of a bird in the early morning, a sunset over a lake, and on and on.

It is important to provide opportunities for the participants to share their thoughts and feelings after the experience if they wish.

The activities that follow use a utility pole as an example. Any other object found in the environment may be substituted.

#8—Pretending

Examine your environment from different points of view by role playing various types of people or pretending you are a plant, animal, or object. Allow your imagination to run wild. Here are some examples: Look at a utility pole as if you were: (1) a creature from another planet; (2) a telephone repairman; (3) a child flying a kite nearby. Pretend to be a plant, animal, or object looking at a utility pole such as (1) some grass growing at the base; (2) a hungry termite; (3) or be a telephone cable.

#9—Body Twisting

Examine the environment by adjusting your body position, moving, or doing something different with your body. Examples: (1) How would a utility pole look while lying flat on your back beneath it?; (2) How would it look from on top of a step ladder?; (3) How would it look while standing on your head or lying on your side?; (4) How would it look while hopping up and down on one foot?; (5) How would it look while squinting your eyes?

#10—Analysis of Characteristics

Examine the environment to determine how each characteristic of an object is related to the function. Examples: (1) Characteristic—height of a utility pole and its relation to function: the height of the pole enables the cable to be suspended above the street for safety; (2) Characteristic—straightness and its relation to function: the straightness makes the pole easier to pile, transport, and to erect; (3) Characteristic—Dark colored wood and its relation to function: the dark wood preservative slows decay and insect damage so the pole will last longer.

Some other characteristics you may want to examine: color, size (height and width), composition, location (surrounding objects), shape, decorations or symbols, hardness, sound (or sound when tapped), smell, taste (use caution in tasting some substances), texture, pattern or movement.

#11—Changing Characteristics

Examine the characteristics of an object to see how each one could be changed so the object would serve its function better. Examples: Utility poles can be: (1) made of clear plastic so they will be less visible to those who think they are an eyesore; (2) made of metal so they won't decay as fast as wood; (3) be erected farther apart so that fewer poles are needed along scenic highways.

#12—Compare and Contrast

Compare and contrast characteristics of an object to those of other objects of the same type. Examples: (1) How does the height of this pole compare with other poles I've seen? (2) How does the color of the wood compare with other poles I've seen? (3) How do the symbols (abbreviations, words, and numbers) compare with those on other poles?

#13—New Uses

Examine the object to see how it could be used in new ways. Examples: A utility pole can be used as (1) a unit of length to measure heights of surrounding buildings, trees and other objects; (2) a place to post signs and erect billboards; (3) a place to erect bird houses and feeders to increase bird populations.

#14—Autobiography

Write an autobiography about the object including where it came from, how it got to its present location, how long it has been there, how long it will be there, why it was put there (or is there), who visits it, how it changes, where to go to get more information about it, and how it is important to people and the environment. Here is an example:

"Before I was cut I was a tree growing in the south. I was a southern pine and chosen because I was straight and tall and at least eight inches in diameter. I was transported first by train and then by truck to where I was treated with a preservative called penta. I was purchased by the local telephone company which erected me last year because the previous pole has decayed and was weak. Occasionally, a bird sits on top of me and the sun and rain have caused me to be a lighter color in places . . .''

#15—Sense Probe

Use your senses to learn new things about an object. When you discover some new things about it try using this information to describe the object to someone who has never seen it before. Some examples follow:

(1) *Sight*—With a magnifying lens, examine the wood of the utility pole. Step back from the pole and stare at it carefully. Then look behind the object without moving behind it.
(2) *Hearing*—Does the utility pole make sounds as the wind passes by the wires? Cup your hands behind your ears and face the pole. Does this help you hear better? Tap the area around your ear gently to sensitize your ear to hearing small sounds. Then tap the pole in different places to determine if it makes different sounds. Describe the sounds you hear from the pole using words (whirrr, buzz, etc.) or visual sketches of the sound.
(3) *Touch*—Use your cheek, nose, arm or foot to touch the pole as well as your fingers. Which part of your body has helped you become aware of something new? Make rubbings of the symbols or wood texture by placing a piece of paper over it and rubbing with a crayon or soft lead pencil.
(4) *Taste*—(Taste is a more difficult sense to use with the pole because of dangers of poisonous materials in the environment. Exercise extreme caution in taste experiments and warn the participants against indiscriminate tasting of plants, animals, and chemicals. There are, however, many substances which can be tasted in order to learn more about the environment.)
(5) *Smell*—Smell the utility pole. What is the strongest odor that you smell? Does it smell the same all over? Compare the smells to familiar materials.

#16—Figures of Speech

Use analogies, metaphors, similes, personification, and allegories to enable participants to gain new perspectives of objects. Some examples are: (1) Telephone lines are the veins and arteries of the telephone's body; (2) Telephone poles hike over mountains and through valleys carrying important messages on their backs; (3) Telephone poles are trees stripped of their arms and clothing and replanted again; (4) Telephone poles are like city fence posts.

#17—Assigning Numbers

Examine an object and think of as many ways as possible to assign numbers to it. Examples: (1) How much did the pole cost the telephone company? (2) How tall is it? (3) What is its diameter? (4) How much does it weigh?

#18—If I Had . . .

Imagine that you have superhuman powers such as X-ray eyes, long-distance vision, magnifying eyes, super-powered hearing, very sensitive touch and smell, an immunity to any poisonous chemicals and other materials. Using these imaginary powers, ask the question, "If I had _____, how would I perceive the object differently?" Examples: (1) If I had x-ray eyes, I could see inside the pole to count the growth rings to find out how old the tree was when it was cut; (2) If I had long-distance vision, I could see all the poles in my state to find out how many there are.

#19—Jigsaw Puzzle

Using your imagination, take an object apart and put the pieces back together again. Example:

When I start to detach the wires on the utility pole, I notice that there are wires of different thicknesses. The thin ones are the electric wires and the thicker ones are the telephone wires. The thinner ones lead to a large container (transformer). Some wires are attached directly to the pole and others are connected to shiny, odd-shaped things (insulators). I need to tear off a wire that is attached along the full length of the pole and runs into the ground (ground wire). The crosspieces are bolted and braced with other pieces of wood. They will be difficult to take off. (During the process of taking the utility pole apart, many new discoveries raise many questions which lead to greater awareness of the pole and its function.)

LESSER

#20—*Environmental Factors*

Determine how different environmental factors affect an object. These factors can include: sunlight, precipitation, humidity, wind, heat, cold, animals (including man), plants, and other forces which change and affect objects in the environment. Examples: (1) Rain causes some of the wood preservative to wash away; (2) Sunlight causes some of the preservative to become sticky and some other areas to fade in color; (3) The repairman puts spike holes in the pole when he climbs it with special boots.

#21—*Opposite Lines*

Using the following lines, inventory the environment by placing the names of objects and events in position on each line. Examples:

a. Hot _____Cold
b. Fast _____Slow
c. Light _____Dark
d. High _____Low
e. Loud _____Soft
f. Straight _____Curved
g. Old _____New
h. Quiet _____Noisy
i. Good _____Bad
j. Cooperative _____Competitive
k. Moving _____Still

#22—*Shopping Center Search*

Investigate a shopping center to solve the following problems: (1) How many cars will the parking lot hold? (2) Is there any evidence of traffic congestion? (3) How much water is used each week and how is it used? (4) How is the center lighted at night? How much does it cost? (5) How is the merchandise received and distributed throughout the shopping center? (6) What types of refuse accumulate and how is it disposed? (7) What types of changes could be made in the shopping center environment to attract more shoppers? (8) What are some reasons that customers give for shopping there instead of downtown? (9) Is there any cooperation between individual merchants in the shopping center in regard to refuse disposal, litter cleanup, window washing, or theft protection? (10) What type of communications system is established within the shopping center? (11) How has the building and parking lot affected the water drainage patterns in the area? (12) What types of safety hazards can be located? (13) What kinds of conveniences and services are available to the customers (restrooms, drinking fountains, benches, telephones, etc.)?

"Believe one who knows, you will find something greater in woods than in books. Trees and stones will teach you that which you can never learn from masters."   (ST. BERNARD DE CLAIRVOUX)

#23—The Art of Seeing a City Block

This activity invites you to be creative in how you perceive a familiar environment (e.g., your own block or neighborhood). Generate a series of questions that encourage new perspectives, and then act as a "tour guide" for others. Here is a sample tour arranged for a block in Saratoga Springs, New York:

> Exit this building at Spring Street—Go West, young person. Look very carefully at this old building. Is the brick work uniform throughout? What might account for this.

> Go to the utility pole marked as follows:

> Koppers
> Ch—70
> SP—P
> 5—40

What do you think these codes mean? What other characteristics reveal the story of this pole?

Continue across the street and observe the other church building. What do the two dates mean on the cornerstone?

Look up toward the roof. What animal evidence can you find?

What kind of plant is growing near the roof?

Now look down to see how many different kinds of plants are growing along the base of the building and between the sidewalk cracks. Sketch one plant that you recognize.

How is this building now being used?

Look for a four-leaved clover next to the sidewalk. What good luck has entered your life recently?

If a raindrop fell in the center of the street, where would it roll? Pretend that you are a raindrop and see.

Notice the evergreen in front of the Skidmore Shop. Look at the underside of a needle. Can you find the "railroad track" markings?

Along the way, smile and greet any people you meet. What are their reactions?

Stop for a moment at the corner of Spring and Circular Streets. What would you do if you discovered a fire in one of the buildings nearby? In what direction would you go to find a hospital for the injured?

Examine the old lamp post on the corner. Can you find others within sight?

Head south on Circular Street. How might have this street received its name?

Notice the Christmas tree lights on the tree in front of Skidmore Hall. Are they early for Christmas or late in taking the lights down?

Notice the patterns and textures in the sidewalks. Take rubbings with paper and pencil. Are the cracked sidewalks beautiful or ugly? Explore the vine-covered fence. What animal evidence can you find?

What animal foods can you find? Where was the fence made? When was it patented?

Crush and smell the feathery leaves growing on the grass in front of Route 9P state highway sign. This plant is Yarrow and was sold in old apothecary shops as a tonic. Find other aromatic leaves along the way.

Go East on Union Avenue. What University was once across the street?

Where was the bus stop sign made?

Turn north at the corner on Regent Street. What might have caused the depression in the grass along the sidewalk?

Examine the vines on the fence carefully. Find a leaf scar where last year's leaf was attached. Find a new bud.

Notice the frieze on the brick building ahead of you. From this clue, how might this building be used? What other clues can you find to support your theory?

The next building constructed in 1904 with the Ionic columns has a raised pattern on the side of the steps. Can you take a rubbing of this pattern?

What kind of grey rock could this be?

"A child's world is fresh and new and beautiful, full of wonder and excitement. It is our misfortune that for the most of us, that clear-eyed vision, that true instinct for what is beautiful and awe-inspiring, is dimmed and even lost before we reach adulthood." (RACHEL CARSON)

Which was here first, the twin oaks or the buildings on either side? How could you find out for sure?

Return to our starting point and share some highlights of your walk with someone. Are you more aware of the potential of a city block for learning?

Some Questions and Answers
about Environmental and People Awareness

(1) How important is it to know the names of the plants and animals before going outdoors to explore?

A leader can conduct sessions in environmental education without knowing the given names of anything outdoors. Identification by name is only one characteristic of that object and perhaps the least important of all. Of course, it is helpful to know some broad classes of living things such as trees, shrubs, ferns, mosses, and lichens, but even this isn't necessary. The characteristics of the plant or animal that may be observed through the use of the senses are more important than the name. Virtually hundreds of awareness activities can be led without knowing how to identify natural objects. On the other hand, knowing the specific name of a living or non-living thing may open up more possibilities for program or curriculum planning.

(2) What is the role of asking questions in leading groups outdoors?

Many years ago, the late L. B. Sharp said that it is much more difficult to ask a good question to guide discovery than to give the answers to many questions already posed. The question, "How many living things can you find under this fallen log?" produces more meaningful learning than the question, "What is the name of the animal with a pair of legs on each segment?"

Open-ended questions that invite investigation allow the participant to supply more information to the decision-making process and take more responsibility for learning. Questions can also be asked for which the leader expects no answer. These rhetorical questions can serve to focus awareness on important objects or events in nature. The question, "I wonder how many colors there are on the leaves in the fall?" can draw attention to variety in leaf coloration and tone.

(3) How can the natural environment be used for increasing awareness and still be preserved for the future?

The natural environment must be preserved if future generations are to enjoy and use it. The natural environment is also there to be used for people's pleasure and convenience. How can this dilemma be resolved? Any plant that is in short supply in the immediate area or on the state or national protected species lists should be considered off limits to picking or disturbing.

One general rule is that if you can see more than one hundred of the same plant, it's all right to take a few for a good use. The question also arises as to what is a good use? Perhaps if the nature object can be made into a useful or aesthetic product, it is all right to pick. Also, if people can learn more about the object and in the process appreciate it more, perhaps it's all right to pick. There are few hard and fast rules to apply to the pick or not to pick dilemma.

A survey of the flora and fauna in an area is a necessity if rare species are to be protected. The location of trails, activity fields, campsites, or future buildings should be determined with an eye to environmental impact on the plants and animals. Few animals should be kept in captivity. Perhaps a few hardy species, such as the turtle and snake, can be kept for a short period of time for study if the proper conditions are provided. Animals are often more appreciated in the wild rather than behind the bars of a cage. One reason to learn to identify some plants and animals is to know which are threatened with extinction because of indiscriminate picking and killing.

(4) In summary, what are some tips and suggestions for leading participants in awareness activities?[2]

    a.   Guide people in using as many senses as possible to explore outdoors.

    b.   Try to see nature through the eyes of young people. Encourage role playing, pretending, and creating new ways of experiencing nature.

    c.   Respond to and encourage young people's enthusiasm and curiosity for nature. Show your own enthusiasm and curiosity whenever possible. Try not to convey your own irrational dislikes and fears of nature.

    d.   Develop simple guidelines and encourage collecting of natural objects. Where laws and common sense prohibit collecting, enjoy nature and leave it for those who come after you. Provide places for young people to keep what they find. (Cigar, egg, or shoe boxes are good storage places for, rocks, weeds, cones, and seeds.) Collect things that have fallen to the ground or are not living so that no living thing is harmed or destroyed. Ask permission before collecting objects from someone's property. Avoid picking up sharp objects such as broken glass or thorns. Avoid putting anything found outside in the mouth unless a knowledgeable person gives permission.

    e.   If you don't know the names of something in nature, have the participants make up a name based on some characteristic of that object. Don't let the lack of a name stop you.

"Each part of nature teaches that the passing away of one life is the making room for another."   (THOREAU)

f.   Demonstrate a concern for all living things and be conscious of what young people are learning about death.

g.   Read and provide books about nature and then try to find the objects outside. Help young people see how objects found indoors are connected to the larger world of nature outside.

h.   Go outside in all kinds of weather. If people are dressed properly, nature can be enjoyed throughout the whole year.

i.   Set aside a bulletin board, blackboard, or nature corner where objects and pictures of nature can be displayed.

j.   Provide many opportunities for people to make choices and decisions while learning from the outdoors.

k.   Encourage cooperation, sharing, and teamwork among people as they interact with the outdoors.

l.   Stress the positive aspects of nature such as beauty, balance, variety, complexity, strength, and rebirth.

---

(1) Modeled after *Essence I* and *Essence II*, published by Addison Wesley (see Chapter XII).

(2) Originally appearing in an article by C. E. Knapp in *Science and Children* titled, "Exploring Outdoors with Young People" October, 1979.

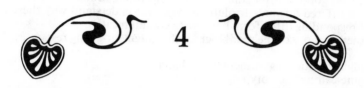

People Messengers: Developing Communication Skills

"I know you believe you understand what you think I said, but I am not sure you realize that what you heard is not what I meant." (ANONYMOUS)

Increasing communication skills is a goal that is difficult to achieve, but well worth the effort. Communicating is important in any type of human contact, and it is especially important when people live closely together over a period of time as in a family, a classroom, a camp, or an outdoor school.

Communication is a process of translating ideas into symbols and then sending them to a receiver who interprets the idea. In this process there are a number of things that can go wrong. How many times have you given what you thought were very clear directions to someone, only to find that she/he did not understand? Perhaps the symbols you chose to represent an idea did not mean the same thing to the other person. Perhaps you assumed that the other person knew some information you did not provide. Perhaps the receiver of your directions had something else bothering him, and he did not listen to all or part of what you said or perhaps the symbols you chose to use in giving directions—the words—were not the best. Maybe drawing a map would have been better. Perhaps the receiver knew how to get to the destination, but was really trying to strike up a conversation to get to know you.

Roadblocks

There are many barriers to effective communication and seldom do we have opportunities to improve our skills in this area. Thomas Gordon lists twelve "roadblocks to communication" in his book, *Teacher Effectiveness Training*.[1] One category of communication roadblocks is the solution-giving responses:

(1) Ordering, commanding, directing
(2) Warning and threatening

(3) Moralizing, preaching, and giving 'shoulds' and 'oughts'
(4) Advising, offering solutions or suggestions
(5) Teaching, lecturing, giving logical arguments

It often feels good to offer someone solutions to life problems. If you have ever been offered unwanted solutions, you will understand why these five ways of responding often form barriers to communication.

Another category of the roadblocks is the judgment-giving responses:

(6) Judging, criticizing, disagreeing, blaming
(7) Name-calling, stereotyping, labeling
(8) Interpreting, analyzing, diagnosing

No one likes to be negatively judged, not even if it is "for their own good." One way to practice being non-judgmental is to "fire" or "suspend" the little judge that sits on the bench in your head. Try looking at people and events without judging them. You may find this difficult to do, but being temporarily non-judgmental is important if effective communication is to take place.

Another category of the roadblocks is the support-giving responses:

(9)   Praising, agreeing, giving positive evaluations
(10) Reassuring, sympathizing, consoling, supporting

It might appear contradictory to present these support-giving responses as roadblocks to communication. In certain contexts, however, they may interfere with really hearing the full expression of another's feelings. Your support-giving responses may be misinterpreted as being insincere and may also take the focus away from the other person and on to yourself. There are many times when support giving is exactly what is needed, but it can sometimes interfere with effective communications.

The remaining two roadblocks are difficult to categorize:

(11) Questioning, probing, interrogating, cross-examining
(12) Withdrawing, distracting, being sarcastic, humoring, diverting

When these responses interfere with the process of conveying and interpreting the meaning of ideas among people, they are inappropriate.

Now What?

According to Virginia Satir, "Once a human being has arrived on this earth, communication is the largest single factor determining what kinds of relationships he makes with others and what happens to him in the world about him."[2] When viewed from this perspective, you might wonder why you have not been required to take courses in communication since you started kindergarten. It is also difficult to understand why everyone seems to have to learn so much about communication through trial and error.

Everyone experiences their environment in their own unique way. We cannot assume that any two people have an identical experience even though they are exposed to the same outside stimuli. When you assume that another person sees the world in exactly the same way as you do, both of you can experience communication difficulties.

Each of us wears a pair of invisible colored glasses that filter what we see in the environment. Our filters include our past experiences as well as our feelings at the moment. Just being aware of your own feelings and needs at the moment is not enough if you need to cooperate with one or more people. You must accurately communicate these feelings and needs to others in order for them to respond to you.

You communicate with much more than words. You can also use physical touch, body movement, gestures of all kinds, and tone of voice. It is important to remember that people have meanings within them, not in the words they choose to use. You may want to ask yourself, "What body language and symbols would best convey the meaning inside of me to another person?"

The brief overview of the communication process in this chapter will be illustrated through the following communication activities involving nature and human nature. These activities can help to overcome communication roadblocks by focusing upon one or more of these guidelines:

(1) Do not assume that any two people have identical experiences from the same stimuli. Do not assume that: (a) others know what you want from them; (b) they understand you when you tell them; or (c) you know exactly how they feel at the moment.

(2) We communicate with different types of symbols including physical touch, body movement and gestures, tone of voice, and words.

(3) Get in touch with feelings in yourself and others in the "here and now"

BROWN

of present time. Look for the sometimes hidden feelings behind the words used.

(4) Temporarily "suspend" the judge within you in order to really hear what another person is saying. Being judgmental often interferes with good communication.

(5) Check out with others how they are perceiving the world around them. Be aware of the filters through which everyone views their environment.

The following activities provide opportunities to learn and practice good communication skills. These skills include: effective listening, empathizing, accurate observing, role-playing and pretending, communicating and perceiving congruence between verbal and nonverbal messages, interpreting the feelings behind the words of others, and becoming aware of your own feelings.

Activities

#1—Word Painting

Find a partner and decide which one of you will start this activity. That person is to go outside alone and find something in the environment to describe to the other. The object or natural phenomenon is to be observed carefully and described in such a way that the other could go outside and find the real thing. The descriptive words should not reveal the identity too quickly, but be designed to create a detailed word painting of the object.

You can modify this activity by having the first person seated facing away from the object. As the second person describes the object in detail, the first sketches it. The sketching is to be done nonverbally, and the word painter is not allowed to see the sketch as it is being done. When the description and sketch are completed, the pair goes to the object to compare it to the sketch on paper. A sharing of feelings of each person can follow the activity. The partners could then switch roles and repeat.

Questions to consider in the sharing include the following:

(1) How did it feel to try to verbally describe an object or natural event?
(2) How did it feel to try to visualize that object or event?
(3) What kinds of description were easiest? most difficult?
(4) How would this activity be different if the sketcher could give feedback to the word painter?
(5) How would this be different if the word painter could see what the sketcher was doing and make corrections along the way?

#2—Nature Charades

Go to a particular place in the environment where a particular event is happening. It could be a tree blowing in the wind, a bird building a nest, an insect crawling on a flower, or any similar event. When an event is selected, return to the group and nonverbally act out the event in charade-type fashion. Different nonverbal symbols can be prearranged to help in figuring out the event (e.g., people event, wildlife event, inanimate object event, etc.). Some familiar charade-like gestures can also be used such as "sounds like," number of syllables, or correct answer. This activity can also be done while walking along a trail or a sidewalk.

#3—Nature Life Symbols

Form trios or quartets. Give everyone approximately fifteen minutes to find objects in the environment to symbolize different aspects of their life. It is best to select objects (e.g., fallen leaves, soil, acorns and other seeds, grass blades, rocks, sticks, litter, animal evidence) that can be transported easily back to a central meeting place and those which will not cause too great an impact on the ecology of the area. When the objects are gathered, they are arranged into a collage on the ground to represent each person's life. The objects may also be arranged along a "life line" to depict various events and life stages. After each collage or life line is created, volunteers can share all or part of their stories with the others.

#4—Variation: Finding Yourself Outdoors

Go outside and find things that symbolize yourself. We often become aware of our surroundings because we see parts of ourselves in objects and events. When you locate what you are asked to find, you can bring it back to share with others in one of the following ways:

(1) The object itself,
(2) A sketch of the object or event,
(3) A verbal description of the object or event.

If you choose to bring back the object itself, you must follow these two rules:

(1) The object can not be part of a living and growing plant.
(2) The object can be easily replaced where you found it without harming it or the surroundings.

The purposes of this activity are: (1) to become more aware of your surroundings; (2) to consider what you think is important about yourself; and (3) to allow the members of this group to get to know you better.

Please return promptly when you hear the signal and stay within the boundaries. Be sure to respect the environment as you discover more about it and yourself. Please return any objects to the places you found them after the activity.

What to Find

Something that symbolizes:

(1) something you are good at doing,
(2) a wish for the future,
(3) something you would like to give to someone special,

(4)   a pleasant memory from the past,
(5)   a quality you have that helps make you a good friend.

#5—Nature Ventriloquist

Select something that can be seen or heard from a particular spot outside. Then give that object or thing a voice and carry on a conversation between each person and that object. For example, if you choose a cloud in the sky, the conversation might proceed as follows:

Cloud: "Hello down there. Don't you wish you were up here with me?"
You: "Well, you know, it might be fun."
Cloud: "Right now I feel warm and comfortable, but it gets pretty cold at night."
You: "Yes, but what a beautiful view of the stars you have."
Cloud: "I don't feel like I have a very solid foundation in life. I wish I felt more together."

Try this exercise by pretending to be the cloud for a while. Take turns in a conversation between yourself and the cloud. Think about how it feels to talk to a natural object. How does it feel when you are pretending to be that object? Did you learn anything about yourself? How was your object like you? Or not like you?

#6—Sensory Sharing

Find a partner and decide who will be blindfolded first. The sighted person then guides the blindfolded person nonverbally to explore the environment. The object is to provide the blindfolded person with the most joyous and sensory experience possible. Care must be taken to make the exploration as safe as possible for the blindfolded person.

Some things to try: sharing many textures, smells, and sounds; walking at different speeds and even running or skipping; sprinkling the blindfolded person with cool water from a lake or stream; touching others in the group as they are met along the way; and just sitting unattended for a minute to experience aloneness. This nonverbal sharing of the environment can be a very satisfying experience for both partners. After fifteen minutes, the partners should switch roles.

After both have had an opportunity to be blindfolded, they can share their feelings on such questions as: (1) Which role was more comfortable?; (2) What experiences created feelings such as fear, joy, curiosity, or surprise?; (3) Did the nonverbal rule heighten or detract from the experience?; (4) If this activity were repeated, what new experience would you each provide the other?; (5) What experiences would you eliminate?; (6) What experiences helped to build trust in each other?

"Learning to suspend judgment is far from easy, because most of us have spent a lifetime being judged ourselves.   (Dorothy Corkille Briggs)

KNAPP

#7—Sharing Branch

Find a large, dead branch to bring inside or suspend from a support outside. Ask everyone to go outside and bring back something that they would like to share with the whole group. When each person returns, provide string and tape to attach the object to the sharing branch. After the branch is decorated with everyone's contribution, each person in turn explains what was hung on the branch and why it was selected.

#8—Group Pictures

Give a small group of about eight persons a large sketching pad and some crayons or magic markers. They are to go outside and create a scene visible from where they are standing. Each person is given a chance to add one part of the scene, then the crayon or marker is passed to the next person. The group picture is continued until everyone agrees that it is complete. This activity can be tried either verbally or nonverbally. This illustrates how each person in the group sees the same scene in their own way and how each selects what is important to them.

#9—Nature Towers

Form small groups of six to eight people. Each group goes outside and finds objects to use in building a tower. The towers can be judged for the highest, best looking, most sturdy, and most ecologically sound. One person is selected from each group to form a panel of judges. One observer is selected from each group to observe and report on how their group completed the task. The only materials provided each group are a ball of string, a roll of masking tape, and some airplane glue. The task is to be completed in twenty minutes and each group is given an additional five minutes to plan. After the planning session, the rest of the task is to be completed without talking. After the twenty minutes of tower building is completed and judged, each group, builders, observers, and judges can talk about their feelings and thoughts stemming from the activity.

#10—Environmental Trio Sharing

Divide into small groups of three. Complete the following sequence of events to explore various aspects of communication: One person volunteers to start and be the focus person. The focus person talks for two minutes on a topic of interest. The other two persons in the trio are to purposely *not* listen. They may ignore the focus person, ask diverting questions, or converse with each other. After two minutes, a second person in the trio becomes the focus person and the activity is repeated. After another two minutes the third person becomes the focus person. After all three people have had an opportunity to be ignored, they can share their feelings.

The first focus person then chooses another topic to talk on for two minutes. This time the other two persons try their best to practice good listening skills. They should make eye contact with the focus person, show attentive body posture, not interrupt to share their own experiences, and concentrate on both the content and the feelings behind the words of the focus person. The other two persons take their turn as the focus person. After all three people have done this, again take time to share feelings and thoughts.

Suggested questions for the focus person:

(1) What does wilderness mean to me?
(2) What does it feel like to be alone in the woods?
(3) How can I have lots of fun outdoors?
(4) What is my biggest fear outdoors?
(5) How does it feel to climb a tree?
(6) What would it be like to not ever see a tree again?
(7) How could I use a park if I lived in the city?
(8) What part of the environment would I most like to save for future generations to see?

#11—Nature Nonsense

You can often get a lot of clues about the meaning of a word when it is used in context with other words. Each person is to go outside and find an object and give it a nonsense name. For example, the name could be "ibble-dibble" for a maple tree. Then a nonsense adjective describing that object should be invented, such as "brigetle" in place of curving. You can then write a story about that object using both nonsense words as many times as possible. The object of the activity is for someone to guess the meaning of the nonsense noun and adjective. Here is one such story:

The brigetle ibbedibble stood silhouetted against the bright blue sky. The brigetle was gradual but distinct. Perhaps it was caused when the ibbledibble was young and bent by some playful farm boy. The brigetle made it easier to climb to the top of the ibbledibble. I thought only birches were brigetle like that, but now I know that ibbledibbles are brigetle too.

#12—Sound Symbols

Sounds can be translated into symbols using words or line segments and curves. Listen to sounds in the environment and put words and line segment symbols to them. For example, a tufted titmouse might appear to call, "peter, peter, peter." Bluejays sometime call "jay, jay." A woodpecker tapping on a tree sounds like "ratatat tat." Translate as many sounds that you hear in the environment using words. Line segments can be used in the following ways to represent various sounds:

Call of a bobwhite quail $\quad - \; \int \; - \; \int$
Call of a crow
Sound of a siren

Have people guess what makes each sound from seeing each type of symbol.

#13—Word and Picture Symbols

Make a list of ten of the most noticeable parts of your surrounding environment. After making this list, compare it with the lists of others who have done the same thing, at the same time, and in the same place. How many of the things on the list were the same? How many were different?

Even if you have the same word listed as someone else, you cannot assume that you share the same concept which the word represents. To illustrate this, ask everyone in the group to draw a tree. The trees that they draw will be as varied as real trees are in nature, maybe even more varied. Try writing down descriptive words about any single natural object, such as a rock, stream, stump, cloud, and bird. Because our experiences with each of these concepts differ, so will our symbols to represent them.

#14—Reading Feelings

Try to tune in to someone else's feelings for a while. The words another person uses may not always be a clue to their true feelings. Try to empathize with someone by walking with them from place to place in your immediate environment. At each place, try to guess how the other person feels toward that spot. After each guess, your partner should tell you how the spot makes him/her feel.

As you go from spot to spot and you learn more about how the environment affects your partner, can you empathize more accurately? Introduce natural objects to your partner and continue this empathizing exercise. Always check out how your partner is seeing and sensing the environment.

LESSER

Ask questions to get a better idea of how stimuli affect another. Concentrate on how the environment affects each of you in the "here and now."

#15—Environmental Pictures

Mount several hundred pictures cut from old magazines on 5" x 8" cards. These scenes can be of rural, suburban, and urban views, environmental use and abuse, and from a wide variety of ecosystems (deserts, forests, beaches, etc.).

Each participant is directed to select about twelve cards on the basis of which ones create a strong feeling inside the person. This feeling could be either positive or negative. The person does not need to fully understand the reason behind the choices at the time of selection.

After the cards are selected, they are arranged on the floor or table in front of each participant. First, the cards can be analyzed according to color; type of scenery; whether the card depicts a person's past, present, or future; the feelings each picture evokes; those places a person would like to live or vacation; and good and bad environmental impact.

Later, a story can be made up about the pictures selected. The pictures can also be lined up according to the one liked most to the one liked least. The results of these ways of looking at the pictures can then be shared with others.

For further discussion with a partner or in small groups, consider the following questions:

(1) Which picture or pictures would you have picked from someone else's selections?
(2) Which pictures represent high and low points in your life?
(3) Why did another person select a picture? Try to guess the reasons for each selection.
(4) Can a poem be written by combining feeling words from each of the pictures?
(5) What would you title each picture if you were the artist or photographer?
(6) How do others feel when you give them one of your pictures?

Here are some comments from people who had just completed this environmental picture card activity. This will give you a taste for what can result from participating in communications skill-building activities:

"I got in touch with some goals I am seeking and also gained confidence that I can recognize what I want. I also liked the way this activity revealed parts of my partner's life in an easy, nonthreatening manner. This was a pleasant memory journey."

"Happy for the opportunity to share part of myself with another, and vice versa. Content with pleasant memories. I would like more opportunities for sharing."

"I felt it put me more in touch with some of the things I value. Wildlife, the outdoors, skiing, and people. I would like to have been able to see more pictures."

"I did learn something of my partner and of myself. I experienced a great deal of beauty and inspiration. I think it's a great way to teach art or science."

"I found this to be a very relaxing exercise. It allowed my mind to wander to . . . places that I have gone to and other areas where someday I hope to be. It made me feel that my life has been full and good so far, and that there is much promise and adventure in the future. There was a lovely magical fusion betwen picture and imagination."

Summary

This chapter has outlined some of the reasons for the importance of including communication skills in your camp or school program. Some communication concepts are briefly discussed along with some barriers to effective communication. The activities provide opportunities for participants to learn about communication by practicing communication skills.

The outdoor environment provides a unique medium for learning about communication. Often a new setting can facilitate skill building and enable the transfer of these skills to occur in other areas of life. Because some of these activities may be new to participants and involve a level of risk, people may be reluctant to try some of them. As a leader, you must demonstrate that the goals of the activities are important and that the means for reaching these goals can be both fun as well as beneficial. We encourage you to modify some of the activities if they do not feel quite right for your leadership style or the participants. We believe that an effective leader must be convinced of the value of structured activities before they can be successful in reaching objectives.

---

(1) Thomas Gordon with Noel Burch, T.E.T.: *Teacher Effectiveness Training*. New York: Peter H. Wyden. 1974, pages 48-49.

(2) Virginia Satir, *Peoplemaking*. Palo Alto, California: Science and Behavior Books, Inc. 1972, page 30.

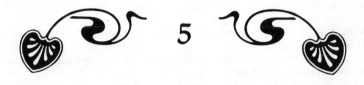

5

People Harmony: Building a Sense of Community

A community is much more than a collection of individuals in one place. People become a community when they cooperate in living, playing, and working together. They agree on certain human values and goals, however few or general in nature. Building a collection of people into interdependent and cooperative community members does not just happen. Community building is both an art and a skill and must be planned in order to achieve the expected ends.

Leaders generally agree that one important aim of outdoor programs is to help people reach more of their potential as human beings. Camps and outdoor schools have been established to facilitate change in the direction of more effective and happier group members. Often it is assumed that personal and social growth occur automatically in outdoor settings and few plans are made to achieve a sense of unity and cohesiveness. Much of the focus in outdoor programming is on knowledge and skill areas such as ecology, campcraft, astronomy, map reading, swimming, or hiking. However, if the goal is better human relations, more thought must be given to community-building techniques. This should be reflected in the scheduled activities and planned time periods of the environmental program.

Whenever individuals come together for the first time in a new setting, they experience many questions about themselves in relation to the group. Some of these questions include:

How do others see me?
Who will become my close friends?
Who can I really trust here?
Will I be accepted by others?
How long will it take to feel a part of the group?
What are the others in the group really like?
Who has the most power in this group?
What will happen while we are here?
How will we work together?
What will I be like when I leave?

These questions are shared by many individuals and can be answered as a community evolves. A fully functioning community is characterized by several elements:

(1) Community members understand their purpose for being together—their goals are clear;
(2) They know the rules under which they will be operating and in turn know their areas of freedom;
(3) They also understand that they have a degree of power in decision-making and a feeling that their opinions count;
(4) They know that although leadership responsibilities will be shared, the staff has the "ultimate responsibility" for the health and safety of the group. The staff must be respected and trusted;
(5) Trust must extend throughout the entire community for growth to occur. A degree of safety and comfort must exist for a community to function effectively;
(6) Mutual caring is the key to success in moving from a collection of individuals to a growing community.

Community-building activities must be carefully thought out in order to achieve the desired results. One way of developing a sense of community is to increase the feeling of cooperation among all group members—competition must be down played in the program. The spirit of a cooperative activity is reflected in the question: How can we all gain by having fun while we learn more about ourselves and others?

In a cooperative program, activities are structured so that everyone wins. Even in the case of an activity that results in one winner, everyone could experience a degree of success in the process leading to the one winner. No prizes or awards are given to a select few. Rewards of personal satisfaction and fun are the prizes for all. Individual differences are recognized and applauded. Everyone is not expected to contribute to an activity in the same way. Each contribution can be viewed as building to the success of the whole activity.

There are those opposed to this program philosophy. Sometimes these critics voice objection to an emphasis on cooperation because they feel that young people need to be trained for the competitive, dog-eat-dog world around them. We contend that our society reflects cooperation to a far greater degree than it does competition. Consider how families, churches, industries, schools, community service organizations, and other elements of society function together to meet their goals. Other critics of cooperation programming contend that young people want competition in games and activities. We believe that most human beings do request the familiar pastimes and games rather than the unknown. Competitive activities are what they know best because their culture has encouraged and supported them most. If people experience more cooperative activities, we believe that then they will request them over the competitive ones. Perhaps the few people who are the winners in competitive games are the only ones requesting their perpetuation.

In this chapter we would like to explore some community-building activities in which cooperation is the glue. As you read and try them out with groups, try to discover some other common elements of community-building activities.

There are many activities which encourage creative expression while also fostering a sense of community in people. These activities pool the creative talents of the group so that each can contribute in a special way.

Activities

#1—Mobile Happening

Go outside and find objects in nature which can be suspended on string or thread to make mobiles. You may wish to bring back items such as evergreen cones, lichen, fungi, bark, husks, rocks, acorns, pods, dry grasses, and many other pieces of nature. (Be aware of destroying and uglifying living things in the environment.) Be sure to collect some dead twigs and branches for the cross-pieces of the mobile. After everyone has collected an assortment of objects, start the mobile happening by hanging a piece of strong thread, fishing string, or monofilament from the ceiling or an overhead branch outside. In turn, each person adds their contribution to the ever-growing mobile. As each crosspiece or object is tied on, the rest of the group shows appreciation in any way they wish. To make the mobile happening more interesting, you and the others could choose an object which represents a quality you admire about yourself. You could also select objects on the basis of beauty, past associations, favorite color, or any other criteria. When the mobile is completed, it will hang as a reminder of the lives of the people in the community. If there are more than twenty people in the group, more than one mobile happening can take place at the same time.

#2—Native American Totem

Group cooperation can occur at various points while erecting a totem pole to depict the life of the community. First, select a tree which not only meets the requirements of a totem but can be cut down without significantly affecting the ecology of the area. Then select a site for the totem and drag the tree there. With chisels or pocket knives, take turns carving the bark to make the totem symbols. Cutting away more than the bark and actually sculpting the wood is much more time-consuming and requires more skill, but makes for a longer lasting piece of art. After each community member has had a chance to carve a symbol into the totem, a hole must be dug and the pole lifted into place. If a large enough tree is selected, it will take a large group to do the job. After the totem is erected, plan a campfire in which everyone takes a part.

#3—Flag or Banner Design

You can design and make a flag or banner which depicts important goals for your program or curriculum. The process starts with a group meeting to brainstorm ideas for color, layout, and symbols. For the flag or banner to truly represent the community, a consensus should be reached on the final design. Reaching consensus takes time, but the point is to decide on a flag or banner that everyone can accept with pride.

The designs and colors can be applied to a piece of material in various ways. Native dyes can be applied directly or can be used to tint wool which can be embroidered. Simple block prints can be made by carving potato halves with designs. The community members can make the many decisions necessary to complete the flag or banner.

If this project seems too large for the time allotted, substitute a large, flat piece of driftwood or split log for the fabric. The participants select their own symbols and initials to burn into the wooden plaque. If a wood burner is unavailable, a large nail fitted with a wooden handle can be heated in the fire until cherry red and used to burn designs. You can hang the finished product on the wall or over the fireplace mantle as a reminder of another group effort resulting in a successful project.

#4—Group Weaving

Group weavings can be fun and can produce surprisingly aesthetic results. Different types of looms may be used. Everyone participating should see the loom to judge the proper size of the materials, and then go outside to gather them. They can be added in whatever sequence the group decides will make an appealing pattern and texture. We have used a simple grass mat loom using twenty-four inch sticks driven upright into the ground.[1] Nine sticks are needed. Two rows of four sticks each, about three inches apart, are driven about four to six inches into the ground. The two rows are as far apart as the grass mat will be long. Warp cords are attached, connecting the four sticks to the ones across from them. An additional set of four warp cords are attached to the rear four sticks and the other ends attached to a cross-bar (the ninth stick). This forms a movable set of cords to hold bunches of dry grass, sticks, roots, or other material. With an up-and-down and back-and-forth motion of the cross-bar, the material is woven into a mat or wall hanging representing the group's creative effort.

In another type of simple loom, warp cords are attached to low-hanging branches. Grasses and other "found" materials can be woven between alternate warp cords to form an outdoor nature weaving. The key to community-building weaving projects is to make them a cooperative event using native materials.

#5—Group Sketching

Community members can work together on a sketch, each person adding something unique. This activity can be done with a group of as many as twenty if the paper is large enough. Smaller groups of about six or eight can work on a piece of paper at the same time if it is large enough. We use thirty-five inch by forty-four inch newsprint because it is relatively inexpensive and large enough. Crayons are especially useful, but any medium may be used for the group sketch. Each person in turn can add a sketch that builds on the ideas of the previous people.

We have found it fun to make a sketch map of our campsite and fill in drawings of the community members engaged in their favorite activities. Directions can be given to do the sketch nonverbally. This type of activity can produce some very interesting results from those people who depend heavily on speech to communicate. After the sketch is completed, the group members can profit from sharing their thoughts and feelings from before, during, and after the exercise. The sketches can be hung on the walls for all to enjoy and learn about others.

#6—Community Newsletter

We have found that a newsletter is a positive force in building a sense of community. This project can involve all of the group members, who each contribute in their own way. Writers can do straight reporting of events, interviews, crossword puzzles, creative writing of poems and stories, gossip and advice columns, editorials, or selections from personal journals. Artists can provide sketches, diagrams, maps, and other visuals. Layout and production people can plan the layout, organize the sequence, type, reproduce, and collate the final product. Special sections might be included such as names and addresses of everyone, birthdays, graffiti (the kind that focuses on the positive aspects of the community), and appreciations of individuals. From start to finish, the newsletter helps build the community and provides a special memory after the experience is over.

#7—Movement and Creative Expression

Wherever possible, outdoor areas should be used for movement activities. The space and fresh air are only two reasons why. It is very important to experience the real objects and processes that inspire creative movement. Movement becomes easier and more connected to the environment among the grasses, trees, wind, clouds, streams, and animals.

The body can express beauty through movement and provide a constructive outlet for physical energy. Gather a group together and interpret the surroundings through body movement. Move like different kinds of trees in the wind, like some of the local animals, like seeds falling from plants, or like water flowing in a stream. Pretend that you are walking through a swamp as the water and mud become gradually deeper. Also walk on ice, between puddles, and through briars. Pretend you are climbing a cactus plant. Imitate a hiker climbing a mountain, rappelling down a steep cliff, or walking at night without a flashlight in the woods.

You can practice free expression to music. We have used a kalimba to provide background music for creative movement. The possibilities for movement exercises related to the outdoors are almost unlimited.[2]

#8—Cooperative Nature Trail

A nature trail is a path which leads people to greater understanding and awareness of the outdoors. Various stops along the way (stations) are usually labeled with words or numbers to guide people. Instead of having the nature expert design and label the nature trail, we have found that everyone has some insight or observation to share.

Approach this project from the viewpoint of helping others to look at the environment through your eyes. You *do* have a unique way of looking at the world because of your use of the senses and your past experiences. You can reveal nature to others by stating facts and concepts about objects or events, or by asking questions about the environment around the station. Both techniques are effective and we have used them successfully.

Giving facts and concepts requires that the senses of observation, touch, smell, hearing, and sometimes taste be brought into play. Sometimes information can be obtained from books or by asking people who know. The goal of all information about nature should be to relate these facts and concepts to the life of the trail walker.

Try your hand at asking questions that will lead people to new discoveries along the trail. We call this a "Question Trail." Questions such as, "What lives under this log?" or "What does the smell of this plant remind you of?" often open new doors. It is sometimes more difficult to ask good discovery questions than to give facts and concepts about natural objects and events. If each community member prepared information or questions about only one station, there would be much to share with everyone.

This group project starts with the selection of the site and trail route and ends with sharing what people create at each station. Again, there are different ways for everyone to contribute to the project. Group members could write poems, draw sketches, ask questions, or give facts and concepts at each assigned or chosen station.

#9—All-Night Vigil

The all-night vigil is a community project that provides for new experiences while contributing to the total group. Start by explaining a new way to cook using hot coals buried underground. To do this, first dig a hole, about three feet deep and large enough to hold cast iron Dutch ovens with food for the entire community.

Then ask everyone who wishes to participate in watching a fire for one hour shifts to sign up for a time slot during the night. People can pair or trio together during each shift. The fire is watched all night and fuel is added as needed. In the morning, the food is placed in the Dutch ovens and covered over with hot coals and soil about two feet deep. By evening the food is done and it is uncovered and eaten for dinner.

Everyone who watches the fire can feel a special sense of having helped to prepare the meal. The anticipation combined with big appetites help make the occasion a memorable event. For some, the fire vigil provides the first opportunity to be outdoors during the early morning hours. The camaraderie and the natural environment are special features of this activity.

#10—Stream Walk

If you are fortunate enough to have a stream in the area, take a group stream walk. All you need is some old clothes and footwear that you do not mind getting wet. The whole group enters a stream and walks right down the middle. Depending on the type of stream, adventures abound and many opportunities arise for helping each other. One rule is that the group must stay together, periodically waiting for the slowest movers to catch up.

The purpose of the walk is not to get it over with quickly, but to enjoy the journey and learn something about the group members. If the stream becomes deep enough to be over the heads of the shorter people, water safety procedures must be taken. It is always a good idea for staff with life-saving skills to be in the lead and to have some follow behind the group. We have found this activity to be one of the best group-building adventures we

---

"If I accept the sunshine and warmth, then I must also accept the thunder and lightning."
                                                    (KAHLIL GIBRAN)

have ever done. If a stream is not available, the same sense of cooperation and adventure can be achieved by taking a bee-line walk through a park or wilderness area.

#11—Compass Bee-Line Hike

A topographic map of the area and magnetic compasses are necessary for this activity. Sight a destination on the map and take a compass bearing. It is best to choose a target which is not more than a mile or two away because there is always a certain amount of error along the travel route. It is also best to choose a relatively large target like a mountain or lake. Buildings and old foundations are good destinations but they take a greater degree of accuracy to locate. As in the stream hike, the group must stay together as they move overland through the woods.

#12 —Gift Giving

Selecting and giving a gift that suits a person is a skill as well as an enjoyable activity. You might set aside a block of time for the exchange of gifts that are handmade. Alert community members a few days in advance and have everyone draw the name of someone else. In the following days everyone prepares their gifts secretly so that the recipients do not see the gifts. Most of the items can be made partly or entirely from natural materials found around the area. Items such as weavings, macrame necklaces and bracelets, wood carvings, homemade blueberry jelly, bread, polished driftwood, nature mobiles, pottery, original poetry and artwork, terraria, and games with native materials can be made with pride and given with pleasure. The gifts can be exchanged one at a time in the center of the group. Each person as they are giving and receiving can be the focus for a minute or two.

#13—Creativity Night

One evening can be devoted to sharing the creativity within each person. Everyone has something that they can do that requires creative talent. Each person in turn can present whatever they wish to share. Sometimes groups of people put on skits or pantomimes. Songs, poems, skill demonstrations, musical compositions, or any other personal contribution result in a pleasant evening for all.

Performing in front of a group is usually a scary thing for most people. We suggest talking about these feelings before the performance and discussing the idea of taking risks in a supportive atmosphere. We encourage you to try, despite the fear of making mistakes. Of course, no one should be forced if they do not wish to participate. After every performance, encourage active appreciation of each person, realizing that each has done the very best possible.

#14—Sensory Feast

Eating together can be a special event. A sensory feast, when carefully planned, can make eating a community-building event also. A sensory feast consists of foods that are carefully chosen for color, taste, texture, sound when chewed, and significance. Foods such as nuts, raisins, cheese, apples, brown sugar, limes, melon, pudding, fruit juices, tomatoes, green peppers, and many more provide sensory delights. You can highlight the sense of taste by closing your eyes as a partner feeds you contrasting tastes—bitter and sweet or salty and sour. If the pace of the meal is slow, readings and songs are interspersed, and if the table and room are approximately decorated, the meal can become a ceremonial dinner.

#15—Earth Day

On a selected day, stress ecology and the environment. Gather the group together and exercise the senses by guiding awareness. Touch your skin with different plant textures, smell the soil, listen for a minute to the sounds of nature, and taste edible plants. Smaller groups can pantomime an environmental story or do a dance. Music can be played and sung. Readings can stress a closeness and dependence upon nature and lifestyles which cause a minimal impact on the land and other resources. Once the theme is chosen, creative minds will take over to produce a many-faceted performance.

#16—Group Living Tasks

Although group living chores such as cooking, doing dishes, cleaning latrines, cleaning tents and cabins, getting water, and other basic essentials are not usually considered part of a scheduled camping program, they can contribute greatly to a sense of community. These tasks are essential for comfort and health and are therefore important. If the chores are shared and rotated, everyone will get a feeling of contributing to the functioning of the whole community. We suggest that staff and participants alike share in the work and that a fair system of assigning or choosing the tasks be decided upon by the entire community. If individuals do not do the jobs or do them poorly, this is a community problem which must be dealt with by everyone.

BROWN

#17—Rituals and Ceremonies

Rituals and ceremonies that become a part of the daily or weekly activities are very important in building an identification with the community. Many camps or schools inherit traditions that bind everyone together. Each program must encourage traditional rituals and ceremonies that are still valued and develop new ones when needed.

Two rituals which have been important to us have been friendship circles and validation circles. In the friendship circle, everyone joins hands while someone reads an appropriate quote or speaks on an issue that is current. A validation circle consists of focusing upon each individual in turn and telling how he/she is appreciated and what special strengths the community members see in that person. You might consider how to build these kinds of rituals and ceremonies around daily events (e.g., waking up, eating meals, going to bed) and special occasions (e.g., birthdays, trips, last day of the program, orientation).

Group Problems

Most of the following group problems are challenges for developing self and group awareness, teamwork, and other human relations aims.[3] Stories and role playing situations may be used to motivate the group and the activities can be adjusted according to the group size, age, time available, and the situation. Many of the activities can be used inside or outside. An important ingredient of these group problems is the discussion process which follows the attempted solution(s). This gives the participants a chance to interpret and internalize their experience.

#18—The Clock

Begin by having your group stand in a circle and hold hands. The object is for the group to rotate clockwise 360 degrees in one direction and go 360 degrees back to the start. The goal is to see how quickly the group can complete the problem. Time each attempt and stop the activity if anyone breaks their grip with another. Group cooperation is obviously essential. Sweatshirts or other markers are placed at both "six o'clock" and "twelve o'clock" inside the circle so the group has reference points for starting and finishing.

#19—Line-Ups

Number Line—Members of the group are blindfolded and quietly given a number. The members are to line themselves up numerically without talking. Time may be given for planning before numbers are given, if desired.

Birthday Line—The members of the group must arrange themselves according to the month and day of birth, without talking.

Height Line—The blindfolded members of the group will arrange themselves according to height, without talking.

Animal Line—The members of the group are blindfolded and quietly given the name of an animal. The group members must then arrange themselves in a line according to animal size from small to large using only the noises of the animals, and no normal verbal communication.

#20—Artist-Clay Model

Break into groups of three. Person #1 is blindfolded and is the artist. Person #2 assumes some distinct position and is the model. Person #3 is the clay. The artist must move the clay into the same position as the model.

#21—Snail

The group forms a long line with hands joined. The line begins to coil at one end until the entire line is in a tight spiral similar to the shape of a snail. The group may move as a unit and then uncoil and coil the opposite way.

#22—People Tree

If an appropriate climbing tree can be found, the group is required to get everyone in it. More challenging variations can be presented by having one person labeled "injured" and unable to move or by having a cup of water (representing TNT) passed from the bottom person to the top person without it being spilled.

LESSER

LESSER

#23—Blind Square

Place pegs, mallet, and rope on the ground and have one-half of the participants put on blindfolds. In this activity the non-blindfolded participants should try to direct the blindfolded participants so that they are able to construct a square with the rope using the four pegs as corner posts. Members without blindfolds may not touch the equipment.

#24—Bomb

Two people connected by locked elbows are the bomb. They will explode if they move their feet, if they are pulled apart, or if anyone talks. The remaining group members must move "the bomb" twenty feet to deactivate it.

#25—Trust Circle

One blindfolded person is placed in the center of a circle. Holding his feet stationary, he relaxes, falls backwards, and is moved around the circle by group members. Group members take turns in the center. The purpose is to develop group cohesiveness and individual trust in the group.

#26—Trust Fall

You can do an effective trust exercise by asking someone to stand on something such as a stump, platform, or ladder rung approximately four or five feet off the ground and fall backward into the arms of the group. There should be at least ten to twelve individuals standing on level ground to act as catchers. To increase the commitment of the person who is falling, ask

LESSER

her to close her eyes before and during the fall. The faller should keep her arms close to the side of the body and fall with the body held rigidly, i.e. not bending at the waist. If the falling person bends at the waist, it concentrates all the force of the fall in one small area and makes catching more difficult. The two lines of catchers stand shoulder to shoulder facing one another. Hands are extended palms up so they are alternated and juxtaposed to form a safe landing area. Catchers should *not* hold hands.

#27—The Four Pointer

The object is to attempt to get a group of seven people across a thirty-foot area, using only four points of contact with the ground. Rules: (1) All seven people must start at the marked starting line and end at the finish line; (2) No props (logs, wagons) may be used; (3) All seven people must be in contact with each other as they progress across the ground.

A large group can be divided into many groups of seven. Have all the groups make the attempt, simultaneously, so they will discover solutions independently. This problem can also be done other ways, such as with five people on three points. You can create a variation of this problem by constructing "a monster" with only a certain number of legs and arms touching the ground, (number depends on number in group) and move it a certain distance.

#28—Ten Member Pyramid

This activity challenges you to build a symmetrical pyramid with a group of ten people as quickly and efficiently as possible. Rules: (1) Timing begins when the problem has been given and ends with the final person tops off the apex; (2) Only a 4-3-2-1 person pyramid is considered symmetrical.

#29—All Aboard

The object is to get all members of the group on a platform (stump, board, tee shirt, etc.) at one time. Rules: (1) In order to be on the platform a person must have both feet off the ground; (2) The group must hold in position for five seconds.

You can motivate the group by challenging them to quickly escape a wave of hot peanut butter leaking from a broken storage tank on the hill.

#30—Reach for the Sky

Challenge your group to make a mark as high as possible on a wall or smooth tree trunk with a piece of chalk or tape. The group is not allowed to use the tree or wall as an aid to climbing but simply as a support. The group members must be connected by touching in some way throughout the activity. Proper spotting techniques are extremely important. As a variation you can have participants mark their territory in the same manner as a male bear would scratch a tree trunk.

#31—People Pass

You can use this activity during the early part of community building. The group forms two lines facing each other. One person stands in front of the line and goes first by lying backward and being picked up by the rest of the people in front of the line. The first person is then passed gently along the line to the end. When the person is lowered to the ground, he/she takes a position there ready to receive the next person who is being passed down toward the end. Everyone who wishes to participate is passed down the line until each has had a turn. Reluctant people should not be forced to take a turn, but they should be told convincingly that they will be cared for safely if they try.

#32—Human Knot

The group stands in a tight circle. People then grasp one hand from a person across from them. When this is done, ask them to grasp another hand without letting go of the first one. The only rules are that no one should grasp both hands of the same individual or the hands of the person on their immediate right or left. A human knot has been formed by everyone clasping hands.

The object of this puzzle is to unwind without unclasping hands until either a circle is formed again or a figure eight is formed. On rare occasions we have seen two interlocking circles formed when everyone unwinds. This activity usually evokes much laughter and provides a great sense of accomplishment when the group succeeds. This exercise becomes more difficult as the group size increases beyond fifteen people.

#33—The Diminishing Load

The goal is to move a group or series of teams across an open field as quickly as possible. The distance can vary with the estimated strength of the groups. Rules: (1) To cross the open area a person must be carried; (2) The carrier must return and be carried himself; (3) The only person allowed to walk across the open area is the last person; (4) If the carried person touches the ground while being transported, both members must return to the start; (5) The number of people being carried and carrying can vary with the strength and/or imagination of the group, i.e., one-to-one is not the only way. You can change the objective by having the entire group move across the distance in as few trips as possible (this changes the emphasis from speed to efficiency).

#34—Happy Landings

Explain that this is a group activity designed to test concentration and the ability to give and take directions. You will need two volunteers—one a rower and the other a dock worker. The rower will be trying to maneuver a "boat" through a rock-strewn channel and land at the dock. Explain that the rower is the lone survivor from a ship that exploded. He/she was blinded in the explosion but escaped in a small rowboat.

"There is only one thing that all people possess equally, and that is their loneliness. No two people on the face of the earth are alike in any one thing except for their loneliness. This is the cause of our growing, but it is also the cause of our wars." (Cheyenne)

The dock worker who saw the explosion is now trying to guide the blind rower to safety. The other participants are to be the rocks and channel sides. Some of them should stand in two lines along the channel (boundaries), while the others (rocks) may stand, kneel, or sit at random in the channel area.

When the rower docks successfully, or bumps into a rock or channel boundary, both he/she and the dock worker lose their turn and must choose replacements. While the new rower is being blindfolded, the "rocks" should change positions in the channel.

The game continues until everyone has a turn at being rower or dock worker. When everyone has had a chance to participate as rower or dock worker, have the group sit in a circle and talk about the experience. These are some questions that might be useful for starting the discussion:

—Did the dock workers find it easier to give directions after they had seen several people try?
—How did it feel to be the rower blindfolded and walking backwards?
—Which commands were easiest to understand?
—Which were hardest?
—Did the rowers trust the dock workers?
—Did the "rocks" want the rowers to make it?
—Which rowers went farthest?
—What accounts for this?

Follow-Through on Activities

Thinking about and discussing each part of a group problem is essential if the aims of the community-building activities are to be met. The exercises can easily become just fun and physical experiences without the additional educational benefit. Evaluation and discussion can take many forms. Questions such as the ones presented in Activity #34 (Happy Landings) might be considered. Other examples include:

Problem-solving:

(1) What problems did we encounter in solving the task?
(2) Did we use the best method for solving the problem?
(3) How could the problem have been solved more rapidly?

Group Functions:

(1) Did everyone in the group participate? Why or why not?
(2) Who provided leadership in the group? Did everyone who wanted to lead have an opportunity?
(3) How many people in the group provided suggestions to solve the problem? Were everyone's suggestions heard?
(4) Did the group help each other? How could people be more helpful?
(5) What different kinds of contributions were made in the group to solve the problems (physical, emotional, mental, etc.)?

Individual Functions:

(1) Did you enjoy the experience? Why or why not?
(2) Did you feel the group accepted your ideas and involved you in the task?
(3) What contributions did you make to the group?
(4) How would you like to change your contributions next time?

Wrap Up:

(1) What did you learn from the group problem? About solving problems? About yourself? About working with others?
(2) Share your completion of these sentences:
     I relearned . . .
     The people in this group . . .
     I was especially proud of . . .
     After solving each group problem, I felt . . .

Since a community is a group of organisms gathered together in close association under common rules and beliefs, achieving a sense of community is a process that is dynamic and ongoing. Groups of people never fully achieve the goal of an ideal community, however, they can approach it.

People generally behave on the basis of what they believe. If people agree that a sense of community is a desirable goal, they are often willing to work toward that end. The development of a sense of community depends upon the extent to which people believe in some of the following ideas:

(1) That they are relatively safe from emotional and physical harm. They feel relatively secure and trusting of others.
(2) That *they* are worthwhile, likable, and competent people who deserve the best out of life.
(3) That *other people* are worthwhile, likable, and competent people who deserve the best out of life.
(4) That they have a great amount of control over their lives within the structure of the community rules.
(5) That they are clear on much of what is important to them and have a realistic plan to achieve what is important.
(6) That the skill of empathizing with others is important (the ability to step inside others' shoes and view the world in a similar way).
(7) That the skill of separating their own thoughts and feelings is important.
(8) That honest and direct communication helps most relationships more than dishonest and indirect communication.
(9) That conflict with others can improve human relationships if dealt with in the proper ways.
(10) That supporting people and telling them what is appreciated about them is more important than criticizing them.
(11) That human diversity in values can stimulate growth rather than stifle it.
(12) That there should be a "give and take" in human interaction and that sometimes you win, sometimes you lose, and many times everybody can win.
(13) That cooperation is more important in community building than competition.

If you would like to evaluate your curriculum or program to determine the extent to which it reflects some elements of a sense of community, use the following checklist:

Does my curriculum or program:

—Emphasize cooperation more than competition?
—Provide time for people to develop new and common interests as well as communicate their present common interests?
—Provide a variety of small group and large group activities?
—Help create a safe environment with rules that protect people from emotional and physical harm?
—Provide opportunities for personal successes in different areas of skill?
—Provide opportunities for people to practice communication skills such as listening, empathizing, and expressing opinions?
—Clarify common values and at the same time recognize the diversity of certain values?
—Provide opportunities for people to take charge of their own lives?
—Structure opportunities for role playing and empathizing to gain greater understanding of others?
—Provide opportunities for staff members to model the behaviors that promote a sense of community?
—Provide opportunities for people to choose and interact within the limitations of the community structure?
—Facilitate the resolution of conflicts rather than pretending that they don't exist?
—Provide opportunities for people to help each other and be helped?

After determining how your curriculum or program can be improved, the contents of this chapter and others in this book may be helpful.

Summary

This completes our chapter on community-building activities. What is the thread that ties them all together? What are the common elements of activities that build a sense of community in people? These commonalities may be considered criteria for judging and developing community-building activities. These activities:

(1) Encourage total group interaction over a period of time;
(2) Promote attitudes of self- and group-worth and capability;
(3) Have as a goal a worthwhile product, or sense of accomplishment;
(4) Are appropriate to the age and interest level of the participants;
(5) Allow individuals to contribute to the task or solution in their own unique way;
(6) Have a high probability for the participants to experience a feeling of success;
(7) Incorporate an inherent sense of excitement, adventure, or importance;
(8) Have a built-in vehicle of cooperation and interdependence.

All community-building activities could be analyzed, discussed, and processed after completion. The dynamics of each activity can be examined from the points of view of the individual and the group. The ultimate test for a community-building activity is the question, "Do you feel better about yourself and more accepted by the group? If the answer is "Yes," the activity is important in developing a sense of community.

---

(1) Ellsworth Jaeger, *Nature Crafts*. New York: The MacMillan Company, 1966, pp. 5-7.

(2) For more ideas on movement outdoors, see *Using Movement Creatively in Religious Education* by Pat Sonen, available from Unitarian Universalist Association, Department of Education, 25 Beacon Street, Boston, Massachusetts, 1963.

(3) Some of these activities were taken from the book, *Cowstails & Cobras*, by Karl Rohnke, published in 1977 by Project Adventure, 775 Bay Road, Hamilton, Massachusetts 01936. These activities include Trust Fall, All Aboard, Reach for the Sky, Happy Landings, Diminishing Load, Four Pointer, Pyramid, and The Clock. Artist-Clay-Model came from a mimeographed paper from the Minnesota Outward Bound School. Blind Square was borrowed from a paper by Jim Merritt of the New Jersey School of Conservation, Branchville, New Jersey.

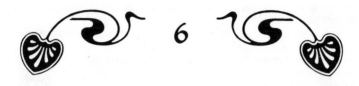

6

Trail Markers:
Clarifying Personal, Social, and Environmental Values

Values are human preferences for specific things that ultimately lead to certain related behaviors. Values serve as guideposts as we experience our life. Our priorities and chosen lifestyle mirror our values. We see a need to insure a connection between the environmental education experience and the rest of the "real world." Values can be the bridge.

Camps and outdoor education programs are in an excellent position to make a difference with regard to helping students and campers develop value systems that are rewarding, both to the individual and to the society. Camps and outdoor programs offer natural environments for people to see, hear, and interact with each other as humans. In an atmosphere of mutual trust, openness, respect for diversity, a sense of wonder, and an excitement about learning, it may be possible to make great strides in examining issues that are often difficult in other settings. These are the very issues which are vital to our nation in the 1980s, and are of interest and concern to young people and adults:

racism	consumerism	lifestyles	citizenship
honesty	pollution	nuclear power	vandalism
sex roles	authority	energy alternatives	justice
war/peace	poverty	death	friendship
aging	drug abuse	hunger	marriage
work	leisure	money	celebration

If we intend to humanize camping and outdoor education programs, it is crucial that we legitimize and build in opportunities to focus on human concerns—and that we create opportunities for people to develop the valuing skills they will need to sort through these complex issues. These skills include the following:

Helping people

(1) to choose freely in appropriate areas of life
(2) to choose with an awareness of the available alternatives
(3) to carefully examine the possible consequences of these alternatives
(4) to prize their choices
(5) to affirm their choices either verbally or in writing when appropriate
(6) to act upon their choices in day-to-day activities
(7) to act repeatedly over time in recognizable patterns.

The key to realize here is that the emphasis is on teaching valuing skills, and not on teaching values per se. Again, we refer to the quotation, "If you give me a fish, I'll eat tonight. If you teach me how to fish, I'll eat for a life-time." We're interested in promoting an effective, lifelong approach to working with values, rather than the hit-and-run moralizing approach or the hit-and-miss laissez faire approach to working with values.

In this chapter, a wide variety of suggested activities to explore values issues and to develop valuing skills will be provided. These are not the only activities that could serve this purpose—again, you are encouraged to create your own, to springboard off the ones offered, to invite the participants in your program to generate ideas as well (we have found the participants in our programs to have a wealth of ideas and creativity).

Leadership Tips: Guidelines for Working with Values

We recommend that you first actually *do* the activities yourself, for as the old Chinese proverb says: "I hear and I forget; I see and I remember; I do and I understand." Afterwards, in applying, adapting, or stretching these activities to fit the groups with whom you work, you might want to consider the following guidelines:

(1) Participants have a right to pass—this is crucial if we are to build a safe atmosphere and if we are to respect the privacy of the individual. If at any point a person chooses not to share his/her thoughts, all that needs to be said is "I pass." We hope this guideline would be respected.
(2) Try to avoid the "right answer" syndrome—this is important if we are to encourage individual creative thinking and to minimize peer pressure. The complexity of many values issues also suggests that there may not be any one "right answer" in the back of the book.
(3) Keep the focus on the positive and on supporting one another—this is especially helpful in addressing issues which may carry strong emotions. We always call for a moratorium on put-downs during values discussions.
(4) It is essential that the activities be understood as a means, not an end, in the process of developing valuing skills.[1] After opening up an area for values exploration, the leader can aid participants in honing their skills by asking clarifying questions. Here is a taste for the kinds of questions which can move people beyond the fun and excitement of the activities themselves:

a. Where do you suppose you first got that idea?
b. How long have you felt that way?
c. What else did you consider before you picked this?
d. Was it a hard decision? What went into the final decision?
e. Is this what I understand you to say . . . ?
f. What will you have to do? What are your first steps?
g. In what way would life be different without it?
h. Is it something you really prize?
i. Would you be willing to sign a petition supporting that idea?
j. What are the consequences of your choice?
k. Who has influenced your decision?
l. Where will this lead you? How far are you willing to go?
m. How has it already affected you life? How will it affect you in the future?
n. Have you done anything about it? Do you do this often?
o. Are you the only one in your crowd who feels this way?[2]

There are three kinds of arenas in which these activities and clarifying questions can be employed:

(1) Time set aside specifically for values exploration and skill development (e.g., at a daily sharing session, as part of the evening campfire, at a staff training workshop, or during a one-day retreat);
(2) Integrated in the study of some other subject area (e.g., biology, social studies, or crafts);
(3) Spontaneously when the opportunity arises. Camping and outdoor education programs, with a multitude of opportunities for people to live, work, and play together, offer numerous on-the-spot invitations to tackle values issues and to practice valuing skills. We just need to be on our toes, and seize the opportunities.

Now, a chance for you to dig in . . .

Indoor Activities

#1—Hand-Wave Voting

Changes in personal behavior sometimes occur after someone simply points out an inconsistency in your life. Just hearing another point of view is often enough to spur people to reflect on the way they think and act.
Hand-wave voting is a good method to create awareness of issues which invite further thought. Read the following list of prepared questions slowly enough so that you and the members of your group have a chance to indicate your position on each. If your response is positive or you agree strongly, then wave your hand wildly in the air. If you are against the idea or your response is negative, then wave your thumb rapidly in a lowered position. If you wish to pass on the question, or are undecided, then fold your arms. The movement of the hand up or down and back and forth gives some indication of the intensity of feeling about each issue.

Here are some sample questions for you to try:

(1) How many of you would like to add new activities to your camp program?
(2) How many of you think the economic recession has had an effect on camp enrollments?
(3) How many of you think camping will decrease in popularity as this country becomes more urbanized?
(4) How many of you have slept in a tent for more than a week this year?
(5) How many of you are against parents tipping counselors at the end of the season?
(6) How many of you enjoy walking in the woods at night?
(7) How many of you believe in setting mouse traps to catch mice?
(8) How many of you believe poisonous snakes in the area should be killed?
(9) How many of you think it's okay for counselors to say "hell" or "damn" regularly while talking with campers?
(10) How many of you admire the teenagers of this generation for their good qualities?
(11) How many of you think that most camps are exciting places for people to be?
(12) How many of you think that camps should help people become clearer about their values in life?
(13) How many of you have changed your lifestyle in the past year to improve the environment?
(14) How many of you have publicly taken a stand on an environmental issue?
(15) How many of you can think of something you could do tomorrow to improve the environment?
(16) How many of you have read something dealing with the environment lately?
(17) How many of you have wondered about how long people will inhabit the earth?
(18) How many of you save scrap paper for writing notes?
(19) How many of you recycle glass? aluminum? paper?
(20) How many of you don't flush the toilet after every use to save water?
(21) How many of you try to enforce no smoking regulations?
(22) How many of you turn out lights when leaving the room to save energy?
(23) How many of you believe that each couple should not have more than two children?
(24) How many of you use a pesticide around the house?
(25) How many of you try to choose the pesticide that is least harmful to the environment?
(26) How many of you pick up litter sometimes?
(27) How many of you join car pools to save gasoline?
(28) How many of you improve the insulation in your home to save energy?
(29) How many of you boycott products of countries that still hunt certain whales?
(30) How many of you are bothered when you walk down a street with many overhead power and telephone liens?
(31) How many of you think the flow of people into crowded parks should be controlled to preserve them?

(32) How many of you think more governmental controls are needed to achieve environmental quality?

(33) How many of you feel that the profit motive of free enterprise is the major barrier to a cleaner environment?

(34) How many of you think that your individual lifestyles reflect an adequate degree of concern for recycling and reusing resources?

(35) How many of you feel that the schools can influence student behaviors leading to an improved environment?

(36) How many of you would sign a petition today banning nuclear plants?

(37) How many of you read newspaper articles concerning environmental issues regularly?

(38) How many of you feel that writing a letter to someone about an environmental problem in your community can help to correct it?

(39) How many of you think that as a group, elementary pupils are more interested in cleaning up pollution than adults?

(40) How many of you believe in zero population growth?

(41) How many of you believe that this planet is already overpopulated?

(42) How many of you would rank environmental quality as this country's greatest concern?

(43) How many of you believe that the "energy crisis" or fuel shortages are man-made and not due to shortages of natural resources?

(44) How many of you choose a car by considering its impact on air pollution?

(45) How many of you think that federally owned wilderness lands should be kept forever wild?

(46) How many of you eat organically grown foods along with the rest of your regular diet?

(47) How many of you think that science and technology will produce enough food to feed the world's hungry population?

(48) How many of you believe that the earth holds vast quantities of untapped natural resources?

(49) How many of you think that urbanization causes alienation and psychological damage to people?

(50) How many of you think that human intelligence will overcome the dangers of pollution?

(51) How many of you would like to ban all strip mining of coal in this country?

(52) How many of you think that atomic energy is one answer to our future energy requirements?

(53) How many of you feel that all hard pesticides should be banned despite their effectiveness for killing pests?

The list of voting questions that can be asked is unlimited. Participants are often interested in looking around at how others vote. The diversity of values often prompts spontaneous discussions which, in turn, may motivate self-examination.

#2—Ten Things I Love to Do in Camp or School

Here is a more private way for you to examine personal values. Start by listing ten things you love to do in camp or school down the left side of a piece of paper. On the right side of the paper, draw six columns to help you examine your loves.

In the first column, put a check by those items that are regularly scheduled activities during the day. In the second column, place an "A" if you like to do the activity *a*lone, a " +1" if you like to do the activity with *o*ne other person, and a "P" if you prefer doing it with lots of *p*eople. In the third column, mark a "B" next to each item that you would like to become *b*etter at. The fourth column is where you can rank your top choices from 1-5. In the fifth column, put an "O" next to those items you would like to do *o*ften. Finally, place a "T" in the last column next to those items you would like to *t*each others to do. After doing the codings, you may find it helpful to analyze the data by completing "I learned . . ." statements. You may also want to do this activity periodically to see if any changes occur over time. Of course, new codings can be used later to examine the same items in different ways.

Experience has shown that few people like to code more than six columns. In addition to the codings listed above, you and your participants might consider these: the initial of the day of the week to indicate when the activity was done in the past week; "SA" for those activities enjoyed with people of the same *a*ge, "SE" for those activities that require *s*pecial equipment; "W" for those done best in the *w*ilderness; " +E" for those having a *p*ositive *e*ffect on the environment; and " −E" for those having a *n*egative *e*ffect on the environment. Feel free to use your creativity in inventing more codings—and encourage your staff and participants to do the same.

#3—Environmental Continua

Continua are excellent means for you to publicly state your positions on issues. Usually, continua are created which have unrealistic extremes at either end as a way of forcing you to stand somewhere in between. Also, the exact middle of the continuum is said to be off-limits in order to encourage you not to fence-sit.

There are a number of ways in which you can use the continuum. It may be done individually on paper. Another option would be for you to draw a continuum on newsprint or on a blackboard, and then have people in the group place their initials on the continuum to represent where they stand. Another way is to create the extremes on either side of a room or outside . . . people could then physically place themselves in a position which represents their view—they would be literally taking a stand.

Here are some continua to consider:

(1) *Use of Electricity:*
Peter Power (lights flood lamps 24 . . . . Carrie Candle (only uses
hours a day)   candles for lighting)

(2) *Greenery:*
Asphalt Arnie (covers the yard with . . . . Flora Flora (grows plants
asphalt)   on every square inch of
                                                                          property)

(3) *Littering:*
Pam Pickup (picks up all litter at all . . . . Tommy Toss (tosses litter
times)   on the ground for a liv-
                                                                          ing)

(4) *Transportation:*
Audrey Auto (uses her car for every-......... Freddy Foot (walks ev-
thing—including "walking" the   erywhere, shoots out
dog)   tires of others' cars)

(5) *Recycling:*
Reusable Roger (repairs paper cups......... Throw-away Thea (after
with tape in order to reuse)   one use, throws away
                                             fine china)

(6) *Environmental Freedom of Choice:*
complete individual freedom   .... total environmental con-
                                           trol

(7) *Gypsy Moth Invasion:*
Spraying Steve (uses any poison at......... Let 'em Be Bert (even if
all)   it costs you your prize
                                            tree)

(8) *Home Water Use:*
capture raindrops to save for drink-......... let water run for one hour
ing   before using

(9) *Hunting:*
kill animals for fun only   .... kill hunters for fun only

(10) *Watercraft on a lake:*
Motoring Melvin (unlimited size of......... No-Motor Mike (canoes
motors)   and sailboats only)

(11) *Energy Sources:*
complete energy self-sufficiency   .... complete dependence on
                                             foreign energy sources

(12) *Participant Choice in Activities:*
Total free choice of activities   .... total scheduling of activi-
                                             ties by staff

(13) *Types of Activities Offered:*
any skill that staff want to teach   .... only those skills that can-
                                               not be learned at home

One other way you may want to use the continuum is in focusing on the
difference between where you would *like* to be on an issue and how you are
likely to act. You could make one mark above the line and one mark below
the line to distinguish between the two. You may choose to set a goal for
yourself—to close the gap between "likely" and "like." The continuum is
also a good stimulus for you to consider consequences and alternatives on a
particular issue—it might be intriguing for you to share your reasoning with
someone who is near you on the line, as well as with someone who is on the
other end.

You might also want to use a series of continua to help people explore a particular values issue. For example, if you were focusing on "wildlife," here are seven continua you could use:

(1) Predators like hawks should be des-. . . . . Predators like hawks troyed when they interfere with should be protected man. completely even when they intefere with man.

(2) There should be no restrictions on. . . . . No new foreign wildlife importing foreign wildlife to this should ever be imported country. to this country for any reason.

(3) Wildlife refuges should be open to. . . . . Hunting should never be hunting. permitted on wildlife refuges.

(4) It doesn't matter at all to me if an. . . . . It matters a great deal to animal species becomes extinct. me if an animal species becomes extinct.

(5) Wildlife is very important in my life. . . . . Wildlife is not important at all in my life.

(6) The great bison herds should have. . . . . It is not necessary to pre- been preserved as they were. serve any bison.

(7) I don't want to spend any time help-. . . . . I want to spend all of my ing wildlife. free time helping wild- life.

Here is another set of continua you could use to help people clarify their values about "open space" issues:

(8) Wetlands are worthless and should. . . . . Wetlands are more valu- be eliminated completely. able than any other type of open land and all of them must be preserved.

(9) Having open space is not important. . . . . Having open space is very at all in my life. important in my life.

(10) National parks and forests should. . . . . National park and forests be open to all people at all times. should be closed to protect them from too many people.

(11) I would never allow national parks. . . . . I would be very willing to to be developed for other purposes have the national in the future. parks developed for other purposes in the future.

(12) Strip mining should not be subject. . . . . Strip mining should be to any governmental controls. banned completely ev- erywhere in the country.

#4—Button, Button, Who's Got the Button?

Pin-on buttons with slogans or messages about the environment or other issues are popular. Take some time to design and make a button which expresses a values position about the environment. Pick an issue about which you feel strongly—here is your chance to use a visual technique to create awareness about an environmental cause. For example, some causes which participants have supported include: protecting whales and porpoises; pro or anti-abortion; "zero" population growth; banning of strip mining; no nuclear plants; reducing air pollution; stopping clear-cutting of trees.

For this activity, provide crayons, magic markers, pieces of oak tag or cardboard, scissors, and different sized objects for tracing circles. Note the variety of shapes and sizes of the buttons being made. When the buttons are completed, tape them to your clothing and share them with others.

To modify this activity, make picket signs or sandwich boards to state your concern. An environmental parade on the order of the original Earth Day can be organized. Floats and decorations may follow if you and the participants want to create a bigger production using this idea.

#5—Environmental Petition

As a follow-up to "Button," you, staff, and participants in your program can write a petition and then pass it around to gather signatures. The act of signing your name to a piece of paper is not only a clarifying experience, but also an opportunity for you to make a commitment to changing behavior and doing more about an issue. Consider some of these questions: How freely do you sign your name to different petitions? Do you ever refuse to sign until you study the issue more thoroughly? When are enough facts present for you to take a stand on an issue? Is it okay to change your mind on an issue when new information is received?

Petition writing and signing can be fun, as well as a means to institute change.

#6—Environmental Geography

Here is an activity which encourages both physical and mental movement. Describe an imaginary map using the walls in a room or other objects outside. The map can be of the United States, a particular state, or a continent. Direct people to move to the area of the imaginary map which fits the appropriate question. For example, go to the location on the map where you . . .

(1) were born.
(2) would like to take a vacation.
(3) would like to live when you retire.
(4) think you would find the most breathtaking scenery.
(5) would least like to live.
(6) have experienced wilderness.
(7) would find the city you most want to visit.
(8) would like to swim or wade in the water.
(9) think you would find the most excitement.
(10) think you would find the most pollution.

Periodically, you can encourage people to discuss their opinions with those around them. This activity is a good one to break the ice with a new group, as well as to learn more about people who have been together for awhile.

#7—Partner Sharing

People like to share their values about many environmental issues, especially when they feel safe. One crucial ingredient of safety is to feel "listened to." It is important to reinforce good listening habits when staff and participants are sharing with one another. It is vital for us to listen with our whole body, because body language usually speaks louder than words. There is nothing more satisfying than to be listened to and to be heard when you have something to say about which you feel strongly.

This activity provides an arena for practicing listening skills while talking about topics of interest and concern. In a group, have people form pairs for a five-minute period (this time can be extended as listening skills increase). Each partner then takes two and one-half minutes of uninterrupted air time to talk about such topics as:

—When you say that you are for clean air or clean water, what do you really mean? How clean is clean?
—Find out what your partner would be willing to pay to reduce smog by fifty percent. Find out how much your partner is willing to pay to reduce other forms of pollution.
—Tell your partner as many things as you can about what you do to maintain a quality environment. In what areas could you do better?
—Do you think that the billions of dollars spent in the space program have been worth it? Has the space program made life on earth any better? How? Do you think there is a danger of polluting outer space? What could be done about this?
—You have just received a federal grant for a million dollars. How would you spend it to improve the quality of the environment?
—What appliances do you use in your home that consume large amounts of electricity? Which ones could you eliminate or reduce the use of?
—Daniel Boone felt crowded when he could smell smoke from a neighbor's fire. When do you feel crowded? What makes a crowd for you?

#8—Environmental Auction

Auctions are fun, and they also reveal a great deal about what you value. Conduct an auction using the following rules: (1) You are to pretend that no one has the items to be auctioned; (2) You have a total of $50,000 to spend; (3) You cannot spend more than $10,000 on any one item; and (4) Bids must open at no less than $100 and no more than $500 for each item.

The audience should keep a record of the amount of money they have before each item comes up for sale, the highest amount bid on each item, and their own bids. This information can be used to draw conclusions about values after the auction. Here are examples of items which could be auctioned:

For Your Personal Use:
(1) a solar-powered vehicle
(2) your home heated for a year with heat from the center of the earth
(3) a wind-driven generator to supply electricity for a year
(4) food containers that are biodegradable
(5) twenty acres of forest land
(6) a garbage-burning furnace run on cheap and abundant fuel
(7) a private well for your house

For Others to Share:
(8) The power to save endangered animals
(9) Elimination of world hunger
(10) Reduction of air pollution
(11) Clean water for swimming
(12) A steady world population
(13) A cheap way to get fresh water from the oceans
(14) A wilderness to stay wild forever

Getting Acquainted with the Human Environment

At first glance, the purpose of this activity seems to enable people to meet each other. However, there is also a strong emphasis on values, as individuals consider some of the items on the list. Some people who have tried this activity seem to enjoy guessing which item may belong to another person.

Here is a list which we have used. Feel free to change the directions or any of the items in order to fit your particular group.

Directions: After each item, fill in the name or names of people here who fit each description. Try to talk with as many people in the group as possible. If you would like to talk with someone later, tell that person you have some "unfinished business." Use each person's name only once.

Find someone who:
—signed a petition expressing a viewpoint on an environmental issue.
—feeds birds during winter.
—has changed his/her lifestyle in the last year to improve the environment.
—maintains a compost pile.
—gets more than twenty-five miles to the gallon of gas in their vehicle.
—has slept out under the stars recently.
—has seen the sunrise within the past year.
—was raised on a farm.
—has been a city dweller all his/her life.
—rides a bicycle to work or school.
—finds peace and relaxation in the wilderness.
—has flown a kite within the last three years.
—has never been to a nature center before.
—likes to walk barefooted through the grass.
—has caught a fish over twelve inches long.
—enjoys the smell of soil.
—likes to grow plants.
—has cared for a wild animal.

#10—Environmental Impact

All humans and other living things make an impact on the environment as they live and carry out life processes. It is impossible to live without making an environmental impact, but it is very possible to control the amount and kind of impact one may have.

This activity asks you to look carefully at your daily lifestyle and to decide how it affects a quality world. Draw a line down the middle of a sheet of paper, making two columns. Head the first column with "Life Support Needs" and the second with "Luxury Desires." Fill in as many items as possible under each heading. After examining the lists, do you see any areas for change in your lifestyle? Check with others on this, too.

Another way to visualize environmental impact is to represent a typical day in your life with a circle. Divide the circle into slices proportionate in size to the specific ways in which you make an impact on the environment. For example, if you ride in a car for one hour a day, make a thin slice about 1/24 of the circle and label it "car rides." If you watch television for two hours each day, make a slice about 1/12 of the circle and label it "TV." It might be interesting for you to color the "negative" influences red and the "positive" influences green. How do you draw the line between "positive" and "negative" influences? Compare a typical day at home with a typical day at camp or school. Which location shows a greater impact on the environment?

Still another way to examine impact is to list all items you use that consume electricity. After doing this, code the items in the following ways: put a "P" after those items which provide pleasure; place a "C" next to those items which are conveniences; mark a "W" after items which are used while doing necessary work; put "BN" after those that you consider to be basic needs; place a "D" after items that you use daily, an "O" for those used occasionally, and an "R" for those used rarely. It may be very revealing to compare your lifestyles in your program setting with those at home. How could the lifestyles in your program be simplified even more (e.g., suggest fasting for one day as an experiment and as a way of reducing environmental impact; suggest eating simple meals of rice and other vegetables to experience the diets of people from other countries).

Spin-offs of the above activities could involve creative role playing in groups. For the artistic (everyone is artistic under the right conditions), ask group members to draw a picture of a person who leads the most ecologically sound lifestyle—one that makes the least negative impact on the environment. This activity provides much enjoyment, as the participants consider such things as how the person is to be dressed, what the person is doing for fun or work, and what that person uses for transportation. In addition to drawing the most ecologically sound person, a montage can be developed from magazine clippings to show how each person presently makes an impact on the environment, and another one showing how each person wishes to be. These activities are one way of moving from awareness to action with regard to environmental impact.

"We all live under the same sky, but we don't all have the same horizon."
(KONRAD ADENAUER)

#11—Environment Survey

This strategy offers a structure for you to capture your observations about the environment. After filling out the following survey form, you might want to discuss the items from a values perspective.

(1) The most numerous objects in view are _____.
(2) The most powerful force in the environment is _____.
(3) Something that I would like to add to this environment is _____.
(4) This environment is similar to _____ (an animal) because _____.
(5) This environment is similar to _____ (a machine) because _____.
(6) The funniest thing I see around is _____.
(7) This environment makes me feel _____.
(8) The most predictable thing about this environment is _____.
(9) If I could plan an ideal environment, it would include _____.
(10) Something I would change in the environment to make it better is _____.

As mentioned at the beginning of this section, the purpose of these activities is to invite you, staff, and program participants to use indoor activities to explore your values—and to value—the environment.

#12—Defuzzing Wheel

Many values-loaded words are fuzzy concepts—they mean many things to different people. In order to become aware of and explicit about your own definitions, thoughts, feelings, and associations around values-rich issues, we invite you to use the defuzzing wheel . . . "Ride on!"

To start your ride, draw a circle with spokes coming out from it. Place the word or concept to be defuzzed (e.g., racism) in the center of the circle. Now, freely associate to this concept by placing any thoughts, feelings, behaviors, individuals, conditions, etc., on the spokes leading out from the circle. Please feel free to jot down anything that comes to your mind—individual words, phrases, complete sentences, pictures. It is important for you not to censor or prejudge any of your ideas—there is no right answer to this.

The defuzzing wheel is an incredibly flexible vehicle. For instance, you could use it to focus on such concepts as: sexism, competition, wise use of resources, drug abuse, citizenship, or good camp. It is an excellent way to open up an area for exploration.

#13—Think and Listen

After completing your wheel, you might find it helpful to join with one or more people to share your ideas. If one of your partners has an association with which you agree (but you initially did not include it on your wheel), go ahead and add it to yours. Avoid arguments over "who has the best wheel" or over specific ideas—the intent of this sharing is to expand your thinking repertoire and to encourage peer teaching. We have found it helpful to have each person, in turn, be the "focus person." This means that each participant would have a specified amount of uninterrupted air time to share ideas.

#14—Prioritizing

Of all the data now on your defuzzing wheel (your original wheel plus the added ideas from your partners), what stands out the most for you? Which spoke of your wheel seems to get at the heart of the concept, which association seems to cover the most ground? Place an asterisk next to that spoke, and note (either in your mind and/or on paper) what makes that association the most significant one for you.

#15—Whip

Here is a chance for you to share a great deal of significant data with others in a short time. Seat yourselves so that everyone can see everyone else's face (circular seating—such as around a campfire—seems to facilitate this). Announce the "theme" of the whip (e.g., the priorities from our defuzzing wheels, something that you appreciate about yourself with regard to competition, etc.). Then, each person who wants a turn can briefly respond to the topic. In using a whip to follow-up the defuzzing wheel, we have often found it helpful to record on newsprint the ideas generated. This can lead to identifying the major themes on which the group would like to focus in addressing a particular topic—this is one way of developing a program around the interests and priorities of the participants.

#16—Learning Journal

Here is a chance for you to reflect on what you have learned through a written log. Complete the following kinds of statements:

—I learned that I . . .
—I relearned that I . . .
—I noticed that I . . .
—I became aware that I . . .
—I was pleased that I . . .
—I was surprised that I . . .
—I hope that I . . .
—I will . . .
—I want to learn more about . . .
—The strongest feeling I have is . . .
—With regard to (the topic at hand, e.g., racism), I appreciate the fact that I . . .

#17—Values Metaphor Hunt

Nature abounds with metaphors for values issues. One way for you to tap this metaphorical gold mine is for you to think of examples of the values issues you face in the world of nature (or in your local community, if that is your immediate environment). To do this, go on a "scavenger hunt in your mind," and locate things to complete the following: _____ from the world of nature is like (or reminds me of) *the values issue at hand.* For instance, if citizenship is the issue at hand, you might have a metaphor hunt inventory that would include: a hive of bees, a colony of ants, the eagle, etc. This activity is a way of physicallizing the defuzzing wheel. You could certainly follow it up with Activities #13-16.

#18—The Sense of Wonder

There are, indeed, at least six senses. In addition to sight, sound, touch, smell, and taste, we have the sense of wonder. And it makes a great deal of *sense* that *wonder* is at the heart of all learning. One way of discovering how wonder-full you are is to complete the following sentence stem: "With regard to *the values issue at hand*, I wonder . . ." You can use these wonderings to keep you from wandering: they can serve as the guideposts for you to focus on the particular values area.

Here are some examples of wonderings generated by people in their teens:

—*With regard to racism, I wonder:* What steretypes people have; how to reduce suspicion; how to avoid prejudices; about the pros and cons of interracial dating; how Whites would feel about attending an all-Black school or camp; how I can be proud of my heritage without being subject to attack; how we can make people more sensitive to the impact of racism; if the younger generation is any less racist than the older; could a war break out due to racism in the near future?

—*With regard to sexism and sex roles, I wonder:* How to bring it to a personal level, and not to a national level; what I can do at home and school to confront sexism; what kinds of fears other people have; how to break sexism handed down by parents; is it greater in some geographical areas than others; how I can recognize sexism; what is the relationship between sex and trust in a meaningful relationship?

—*With regard to work, I wonder:* If I should have some direction in vocation before college; what it would be like to work for myself, not someone else; why some work becomes monotonous and less self-satisfying; what my cutoff is between work and pleasure; if I will have to compromise myself by doing work I don't like in order to support myself or my family; why I fell I'll never be content with one occupation for my life but will try many; how to work to live, not live to work?

—*With regard to war, I wonder:* Why it exists; whether I or anybody else should be forced to support them; will war always be a part of us; if there are any feasible alternatives; if I am against all wars; why people feel it is necessary to kill others; if ideas and money are as important as human life?

—*With regard to family and lifestyles, I wonder:* Can I be open with my relatives when I haven't been especially open up to now; why I don't show more appreciation to my family; is it okay to have a family, given the world population situation; what will become of my family when I leave home; what role children should play in the family; how can I get back with my family; how much a family should demand conformity to one lifestyle?

—*With regard to drugs, I wonder:* Are drugs really a cop-out or just an occasional pleasure trip; how to resolve the inconsistency between believing in my body and mind being directed by myself and my liking to do some drugs; how to relate to people who do drugs when I don't do it myself; why I first tried drugs; why people make something as unstable as drugs a crutch?

—*With regard to money, I wonder:* How can it best be used; how can I give some up for others who don't have as much as me; can I get everything I want from life without it; how much will I sacrifice for money; why does it destroy so much; why I think of it as a means to an end instead of a real goal in itself; how important it is for me to feel successful?

#19—Think-and-Listen-to-Yourself Solo

Any one of the above wonderings, or any of the wonderings you generated for yourself, could lead into a full values exploration unit. This activity provides a structure for questioning and thinking to yourself.

Survey your immediate environment. Find a spot where you will be alone, undisturbed, and peaceful for a period of time. Using a journal, jot down significant questions and thoughts you have with regard to one of the values areas. Interview yourself, using nonjudgmental clarifying questions. This is one way of recognizing and tapping your own resources. When you return from the solo, you might choose to join with others and share through a think-and-listen format or through a whip.

#20—You Are Resource-Full

Not only are you wonder-full, you are also resource-full. And so are the people around you—both the staff and participants in your program. Here is an opportunity for you to build on these resources while also tackling important social values issues. Take a look at the list of people below:[3]

(1) Ms. Lee Sure: An expert in helping you to use your leisure time in the most enjoyable ways. She is sure to relax you and fill your life with fun.

(2) Dr. Santa Tation: Guarantees a pollution-free life for you. An advocate of "clean living," he will insure that you use intelligent means of waste disposal and that your environment is free of air and water pollution.

(3) Noah T. All: Has an incredible reservoir of knowledge that he can give you. He can help you in becoming a walking encyclopedia, with intelligent ideas always at your fingertips and on the tip of your tongue.

(4) Dr. N. R. Gee: Is a bundle of excitement. She can transfer to you a delight-full ability to energize those around you. As an energy source, you will have a magnetic personality that draws people to you.

(5) Bill D. Body: An outstanding athlete, Bill can help you develop your physical capacities and will guarantee that you will be in shape for the rest of your life.

(6) Prof. Hugh Manistic: Is a very compassionate, caring, and understanding individual. He has the ability to help you become incredibly empathic and comforting—someone whom people feel free to turn to in times of stress and distress.

(7) Dr. Neural Plural: Has the amazing trait of being completely open-minded. She never puts down anyone or any idea and has the nifty ability to accept and see the worth of different people, ideas, and lifestyles.

(8) G. Clef: An outstanding musician, Ms. Clef can help you develop your musical talents to the nth degree. She can also aid you in your growing appreciation of the arts to the point where you could be termed a connoisseur.

(9) Warren Peace: A renowned authority on conflict resolution, Warren can guarantee that your personal life will be a peaceful one. He also will make sure that your environment will be filled with harmony.

(10) Connie Sumer: An expert in consumer affairs, Connie will guarantee that you will make wise choices in the purchase and use of materials and services. You will never have any hassles with stores, and you will never be "ripped off."

Here are some ways to use this list of resource people: (a) In your journal, write down whom each of the above people reminds you of—this could be a chance for you to identify the resources of staff and participants in your program; (b) Place a " + " next to three of the names—these would be the people who remind you of skills that you have—allow yourself the luxury of bragging for just a moment (for instance, if you see yourself as enthusiastic, you might put a " + " next to Dr. N. R. Gee); (c) Place a " ✓ " next to three of the names—these would be the people who have skills that you would like more of in your own life; (d) Rank from one to ten these people as if they were applying for a job in your program: Your ranking will reflect what you value; (e) If you want a real challenge, join together with a group of five other people (staff and/or participants), and try to reach consensus on your rankings. By consensus, we mean that everyone would agree with the group's decision, and would be willing to publicly affirm it. In other words, consensus does not mean "voting," "railroading," or "taking an average of the rankings"; (f) Feel free to add (or to have staff and participants add) to the list of people—it might be fun for you to create your own list. Think of ways you could adapt this activity for the participants in the program—e.g., rank-order your preferences for whom you would like as a cabin mate, or as a counselor.

#21—Moral Dilemma Story

Each of us faces moral dilemmas every day of our lives. Here is an example of one story which you can use as a vehicle to clarify your values with regard to social issues:[4]

Once upon a time, there was a school called American High. *Bill*, a black junior at American, wanted to set up an Afro-American crafts and folklore program on Monday afternoons during the first semester. This was the best time for the fifteen black students who were interested in the course, and also the only time that Bill's outside resource people could be of help. Since they hoped to show films during the course, the students needed to use the school's audiovisual room (which has only one projector).

Bill approached the *vice principal*, explained his course, and asked to be able to use the A-V room every Monday afternoon for the semester. The vice principal okayed the program, and gave permission for use of the room.

The following Monday, Bill and the other fourteen black students arrived at the A-V room after school only to find it occupied by the players on the football team, who were watching their game film from Saturday. The forty-five white football players and coaches refused to leave the room, even after Bill explained that he had permission from the vice principal. In fact, *Art*, one of the players, blurted out, "Why don't you niggers wait until the end of football season to have your course—football is more important to this school than studying about artsy-craftsy junk and stories about niggers."

Tempers flared, and a big argument ensued. *Ernie*, another football player, felt strongly that the black students should have first priority to the room, and was appalled by Art's outburst. But Ernie did not say anything at all.

Bill charged back to the vice principal. After hearing of the conflict, however, the vice president rescinded permission for use of the A-V room. His reasons included: Forty-five students is more than fifteen—we have to respect the rights of the greater number; the football team provides a service for the school—your course would not; you can postpone your course and have it next semester.

A week rolled by, and next Monday afternoon came up. It found Bill and his fourteen black friends occupying the A-V room, and not letting anyone in. Bill told the football team that his course would be using the room for the rest of the semester. Upon hearing this, *John*, one of the football players, proceeded to break into and steal from some of the black students' school lockers. John felt that "some of my best friends are black, but those people occupying the room are being insensitive and destructive."

Suzanne, a black sophomore who was occupying the A-V room, was infuriated when she found out what had happened to the black students' lockers. She later went out to the parking lot and slashed the tires of the coach's car. That's the end of the story.

Are you ready for the next step? Try to rank-order the above six characters in the story from the one whose *behavior* you consider to be most humane to the one whose *behavior* you consider to be least humane (in other words, we are asking you to make a value decision on their actions, and not on their worth as people). Jot down the criteria you used in making this decision. Now, if you are brave, you could join up with four other people and try to reach consensus on your rankings. At the end of the discussion, it might be helpful to identify and summarize the major values issues around which the decisions were based.

Here are some of the values issues which one group of young people considered in seeking consensus:

(1) Responsibility, taking the initiative (Bill)
(2) Going through proper channels (Bill)
(3) Use of racial slurs (Art)
(4) Speaking out on one's convictions and beliefs (Ernie)
(5) Courage, decisiveness, considering alternatives (vice principal)
(6) Violence against material goods (John, Suzanne)
(7) Violence against people—physical and non-physical
(8) Acting on emotions (Suzanne)
(9) Who could have acted differently to prevent this from happening? Who was in the best position to avoid and/or deal with the conflict?
(10) Whose behavior caused the most hurt to people? In the short-run? In the long-run?

Finally, you might want to consider the following questions (in your journal and/or with the people in your consensus group): (a) Would your ranking have been changed if Bill's group had been a branch of the Sierra Club (rather than a black crafts and folklore group)? What if the group was focusing on women's studies? What if the group was a politically-oriented, anti-nuclear power one? What if the group was an ecology club that was interested in performing service projects for the school? As you can see, these questions provide insight into ways that you could change the moral dilemma story to focus on other values areas; (b) How did you and your group operate in the consensus discussion as compared with your performance in the consensus discussion Activity #20? It is not often that we have a "second chance to go around in life". . . what goals do you set for yourself in future group discussions (whether it be with staff or participants in your program)? What can you do to provide more effective leadership in the task groups of which you are a part?

Keep your eyes open to "real-life" moral dilemmas that occur in your program—tapping them is an excellent way to help people practice skills in considering consequences, generating alternatives, listening to others, and respecting differences.

#22—Values Sheets

The formula for this activity is simple: all you need is a provocative stimulus (an object from nature, an excerpt from a book or magazine, an item from the newspaper, a song, a movie, etc.)[5] followed by a series of clarifying questions—questions that will help you examine how the stimulus relates to you, your personal life, your values. Here are several thought provokers designed to get your wheels turning:

VALUES SHEET A: Dead or Alive*

"The wise, old hermit lived in the woods outside a small midwestern town. The wisdom of this man was widely known throughout the community. Many of the young men in the town spent a good deal of their time trying to disprove his wisdom so that all of the world would know "he's not so smart after all."

One day, two young men sitting on the bank of the river were indulging in their favorite sport . . . looking for a way to trick the hermit and thus end this legend of his wisdom.

Suddenly, one of the young men reached out and trapped a sparrow that had perched on the limb above his head. "I know how we can out-fox the hermit," he said.

"We'll go to the hermit's cave and I'll hide the sparrow cupped in my hand so he can't see it. I'll ask him, 'What have I in my hands?' If he is able to tell me that it is a bird, I'll then ask him, 'Is it dead or alive?' If he says it is alive, I'll squash my hands and the bird will be dead. If he says it's dead, I'll open my hands and let the sparrow fly away."

Hurrying through the woods, they soon came to the hermit's cave.

"Old man," cried the tormentor, "what have I in my hands?" The old man looked at him thoughtfully and then answered him, "A bird, my son." "Tell me, old man, is it dead or alive?" For a long time the old man just looked at the boys, then answered, very slowly, very deliberately, "It's up to you, my son, it's in your hands."

To Think and Write On:

(1) Have you ever tried to prove that someone was not as smart as people said they were? If so, how did you do it? How did you feel afterwards?

(2) Would you try this same experiment with a bird in your hand? If the hermit had answered that the bird was alive, could you have crushed it to death? Have you ever killed a bird? a fish? or other small animal? How did you feel then? How would you feel now? Have you changed?

(3) Do you consider hunting a sport for you? Does the answer to this question depend upon what animal is being hunted? Is hunting the protected whooping crane the same as hunting the more abundant white-tailed deer?

(4) How much power do you think you have in your hands when it comes to protecting wildlife or saving open space from development? Have you ever done anything to accomplish these goals?

---

*Albert Piltz and Robert Sund, *Creative Teaching of Science in the Elementary School*, (Boston, Allyn and Bacon, 1968), p. 186.

VALUES SHEET B: Where Have All the Buffaloes Gone?

Directions: Read the quote and answer the questions in writing. There are no right and wrong answers to these values questions.

"The buffalo is gone, and of all his millions, nothing is left but bones . . . The wolves that howled at evening about the traveller's campfire, have succumbed to arsenic and hushed their savage music . . . The rattlesnakes have grown bashful and retiring. The mountain lion shrinks from the face of man, and even grim 'Old Ephraim,' the grizzly bear, seeks the seclusion of his dens and caverns."

(Francis Parkman, 1892)

To Think and Write On:

(1) As long ago as 1892, people noticed that some wildlife were vanishing. Have you thought much about rare and endangered animals? Would it *really* make a big difference in your life if one of these animals became extinct because of man?

(2) Do you think that Parkman is sorry to see that buffalo, wolves, rattlesnakes, mountain lions, and grizzly bears were disappearing? What words led you to believe how he felt about them?

(3) All the animals mentioned, except the buffalo, are predators. This means that they kill and feed upon other animals. Do you like plant-eating animals better than meat-eating animals? Does it make a difference? Can you explain why many stories show predators such as wolves, rattlesnakes, and bears to be villains?

VALUES SHEET C: The Vermiculite Controversy

A volcano erupted millions of years ago in Louisa County, Virginia. The volcano left a small 14,000-acre pocket of a mineral beneath the surface called vermiculite. Vermiculite comes from the Latin word "vermis" meaning worm. When the mineral is heated it expands into wormlike shapes. It is used for cat litter, in insulation products, in concrete, and in agricultural soil conditioners. The big issue in Louisa County is whether to mine the vermiculite deposits or not. There are people on both sides of the controversy. There are strong reasons to support each side. Here are some pro's and con's.

Pro Mining

(1) Some landowners want their land mined so that they can make money.
(2) The mines would attract industry, create new jobs, and raise the tax base in the county.
(3) Vermiculite is a very useful product.
(4) It is wasteful not to use the vermiculite by developing the area. Progress must come if the people are to raise their standard of living.
(5) The Board of Supervisors voted five to one to rezone the area to allow mining and changed the county ordinance to allow mining almost anywhere, no matter what the zoning.

Con Mining

(1) The United States Department of the Interior declared the area a National Historic Landmark because of the colonial architecture.
(2) The mining would change the land by digging ten-acre pits up to seventy-five feet deep. Roads, settling ponds, and dumps would have to be built. Over 400 acres of land would be changed.
(3) The land was zoned for agriculture, not for mining, for many years.
(4) The Department of the Interior believes that the mining operation would harm the scenery of the area.
(5) Some landowners want to preserve the "unspoiled" and historical values of the land.

What other pro's and con's can you think of? Do you think the area should be mined? If you owned land in the area and could become rich by mining the vermiculite, would you sell or lease your land? Would you vote to change the zoning from agriculture to mining use? Who should have the say in how the land is used, the local people or the federal government?

VALUES SHEET D: No Quiet Place*

Directions:
Read the quote and answer the questions in writing. There are no wrong or right answers to these questions.

> "There is no quiet place in the white man's cities. No place to hear the unfurling of leaves in spring or the rustle of insect's wings. But perhaps it is because I am a savage and do not understand. The clatter only seems to insult the ears. And what is there to life if a man cannot hear the lonely cry of the whippoorwill or the arguments of the frogs around a pond at night? I am a red man and do not understand. The Indian prefers the soft sound of the wind darting over the face of the pond, and the smell of the wind itself, cleansed by the midday rain, or scented with the pinon pine."
>
> (Chief Seattle, 1854)

To Think and Write On:

(1) Chief Seattle wrote this on the occasion of the transferral of the ancestral Indian lands to the federal government. Even in the year 1854, the cities were noisy. Would you rather live in the city or country? Why?

Rank in order of preference the sounds you like to hear most:

_____ the sound of a train whistle
_____ the sound of the wind in the trees
_____ the sound of trucks and cars

(2) The Indian preferred the smell of the wind to the smell of the city. Which smells better to you?

List three things that smell good to you.

List three things that smell bad to you.

(3) Chief Seattle said that he did not care for the sounds of the city because he was a red man and did not understand. Are there things in other cultures that you do not understand?

What is an example?

---

*Kathleen Sauvage, Lorado Taft Field Campus, Northern Illinois University.

VALUES SHEET E: This was our land . . .

Directions:

Read the quote and answer the questions in writing. There are no right or wrong answers to these questions.

"This was our land—the land that the mountain needed in order to rise in majesty—the land that my people needed in order to roam its secrets in reverence. This was the land of our great waters—the beating heart of nature flowing through time. This was our land—the land that provided everything good for my people. This land was always our land, and the sun set upon it. The rain washed, and the fire was kind in its fury. It was so for all time. Then the land was taken from us. It's your land. Do you know how to speak to the land, my brother? Do you listen to what it tells you? Can you take from it no more than what you need? Can you keep its secrets to yourself? Sell the land, my brother? You might as well sell the sun, and the moon and the stars."

(From the Taos Indians)

To Think and Write On:

(1) During the 1800s, much land was taken from the Indians. Because of the values of the Indians, the land was pretty much as it was in the beginning. When the white man moved in, the demand on the land changed. Do you think you would like to live as the Indians did and only take from the land what you needed in order to survive?

Rank in order of preference what you need to survive:

_____ television
_____ forests
_____ open land

(2) The Indians listened to the land. In what ways does the land speak?

If you were going to chop down a tree, what would you need to say to it, if anything, before you chopped it down?

What do you think it would say to you if it could speak?

(3) "Sell the land, my brother? You might as well sell the sun, and the moon and the stars." What do you think the Indians meant by this?

If you were going to sell some forest land, how would you decide on a price to charge for it?

VALUES SHEET F: John Muir—A Person Close to Nature*

(1) John Muir was happiest when he could share his love of nature with others. What is something that makes you happy when you share it?

(2) John Muir collected plants and flowers and pressed them between two pieces of wood. Do you collect anything? If so, what?

(3) When John Muir was a boy in Scotland, he decided that disobeying his parents and going to an old castle was more important to him than staying home and playing in his yard. Have you ever felt so strongly about something that you broke a rule?

(4) John Muir won a prize for his inventions. He invented a machine to wake him up that told time, rang a bell in the morning, and even shook his bed. He also made a thermometer as tall as himself. He made a desk that opened and closed books so he could read faster. What is something you would like to invent? How would it be useful?

(5) When John Muir was a young man, he was blinded by pieces of flying metal while working in a factory making wagon wheels. John was blind for many weeks. When he was able to see again, he believed that he had been given a second chance to see all the trees and flowers he had read about. If you knew you were going to lose your sight next week, what would you want to look at carefully so you could remember?

(6) John Muir walked from Indiana to Florida with only a few clothes and a compass, collecting plants along the way. Have you ever felt so strongly about something that you would walk many miles for it. What was it?

(7) When John Muir walked from Indiana to Florida, he said, "I am wild and free again!" What is something that you like to do that makes you feel wild and free?

(8) John Muir lived in a place called Yosemite Valley. A famous scientist said that the valley was made by great earthquakes. John Muir said that it was made by glaciers. The scientist laughed at Muir. A few years later Muir found evidence that the valley was really formed by glaciers. Have you ever had someone laugh at you because he thought you were wrong? How did it feel?

(9) John Muir and his friends formed the Sierra Club to help save wild places. Have you ever belonged to a club or organization? What were some of your reasons for joining?

(10) John Muir wrote, "We are all part of the wilderness, and the wilderness is part of us." How much of your thoughts and travels are related to the wilderness? With your pencil shade in the part of your life circle that is wilderness.

*Information from *John Muir* by Glen Dines. New York: G. P. Putnam's Sons, 1974.

VALUES SHEET G: Values and Actions

"They came for the Panthers and I said nothing because I was not a Panther. They came for the Black man and I said nothing because I was not Black. Then they came for the students and I said nothing because I was not a student. Then they came for the liberals and I said nothing because I was not a liberal. And when they came for me, I looked around and said nothing because I was alone."

(Elaine Brown)

To Think and Write On:

(1) Do you identify with any of the people or categories above?
(2) What are some things going on in your world right now about which you would like to speak up?
(3) Just how does one go about "speaking up?" Which ways are the most comfortable for you? the most effective? What advice would you give to the Ernies (see Activity #21) of the world?
(4) But why stick your neck out? Why not?
(5) When was the first time you "spoke up" against a racist, sexist, or ethnic joke? If you are unable to do it, who should?
(6) Would you use a few moments of silence to work out a plan by which you could, indeed, speak up about something important to you?
(7) If you could send a telegram to the director of this program about an important issue to you, what would you say?
(8) Some people say: "We need to value what we do and do something about what we value." Do you agree? If so, could you relate something you have done about something you valued?*

---

*Adapted from Merrill Harmin and Sidney Simon, "Values in the Classroom: An Alternative to Moralizing," in William Rogge and G. Edward Stormer, *Inservice Training for Teachers of the Gifted* (Champaign, IL; Stipes Publishing Co., 1966).

VALUES SHEET H: Clarifying Your Conservation Philosophy

Read the following poems* and answer the questions:

A Conservationist's Lament

The world is finite, resources are
   scarce.
Things are bad and will be worse.
Coal is burned and gas exploded.
Forests cut and soils eroded.
Wells are dry and air's polluted,
Dust is blowing, trees uprooted.
Oil is going, ores depleted,
Drains receive what is excreted.
Land is sinking, seas are rising,
Man is far too enterprising.
Fire will rage with Man to fan it,
Soon we'll have a plundered planet.
People breed like fertile rabbits,
People have disgusting habits.

Moral:
   The evolutionary plan
   Went astray by evolving man

The Technologist's Reply

Man's potential is quite terrific
You can't go back to the Neolithic.
The cream is there for us to skim it,
Knowledge is power, and the sky's
   the limit.
Every mouth has hands to feed it,
Food is found when people need it.
All we need is found in granite
Once we have the men to plan it.
Yeast and algae give us meat,
Soil is almost obsolete.
Men can grow to pastures greener
Till all the earth is Pasadena.

Moral:
   Man's a nuisance, Man's a crack-
      pot
   But only man can hit the jackpot.

—Kenneth Boulding

---

*William L. Thomas, Jr., ed., *Man's Role in Changing the Face of the Earth* (Chicago: The University of Chicago Press, 1956), p. 1,087.

Questions:

(1) In one sentence for each poem, summarize the main ideas.
(2) Do you place yourself in either of the two schools of philosophy?
(3) Using pluses (+) and minuses (−), mark the statements or phrases that you agree with (+) or disagree with (−) in both poems.
(4) Can you identify any inconsistencies in your conservation philosophy? Explain?

VALUES SHEET I: Change

"Ills exist in society. Victims press for change. Or perhaps the advantaged person feels guilty and feels things should be changed. But change is difficult. Sometimes it means changing habits or giving up some personal advantage, or just hard work. Part of us doesn't want to change. We may be content with merely expressing our concern, merely taking a picture of the problem, merely writing a report. But if someone is hungry, he will continue to be hungry. Social injustices do not go away just because we think about them."*

Questions:

(1) What are your reactions to the above?
(2) Do you see yourself as doing something about some of the ills of society? What? When?
(3) Do you believe that "if you're not part of the solution, you're part of the problem?"
(4) What could others do to support you if you were to try to change a habit? What habit would you like to experiment with giving up? What habit would be hardest for you to give up?
(5) Write a dialogue (or role play it) between the part of you that wants to change and the part of you that prefers not to change.
(6) Do you see any injustices in your school or camp? If so, what might you *do* about them?

---

*Adapted from Merrill Harmin, "Hunger Doesn't Go Away When You Take a Picture of It," Southern Illinois University at Edwardsville.

VALUES SHEET J: Dream-Building

When a man starts out to build a world,
He starts first with himself . . .
Then the mind starts seeking a way.
Then the hand seeks other hands to help . . .
Thus the dream becomes not one man's dream
But a community dream . . .
Not my world alone,
But your world and my world,
Belonging to all the hands who build.

(Langston Hughes)

Questions:

(1) What is something which you have "started out to build" in your own life?
(2) What ways have you found to be effective in "inviting" others to share your dream?
(3) Are there any dreams which you now have that you would like the staff and/or participants of this program to share in?
(4) Do you have any ideas about how to build a better sense of "community" in this program?
(5) Martin Luther King had a dream, which he did not live to see fulfilled. What dreams do you want to realize in your lifetime?

VALUES SHEET K: Conflict

"Beetles don't argue with butterflies."*

Questions:

(1) What does the above quote mean to you?
(2) Where have you experienced or observed conflict in your life? What conflicts have you noted here in this program?
(3) How do you usually handle conflict situations? when you are a participant? when you are an "outsider?"
(4) What is your reaction to this statement: "without conflict, we cannot grow."
(5) What guidelines have you used in resolving conflicts in your own life that our nation might want to apply? If you were to send a telegram to the President with your recommendations, what would you say?
(6) Which of the following describes how you usually deal with conflict? Which would you like to have describe you? If there's a gap between what you're *likely* to do and what you'd *like* to do, what can you do to close the gap?: (a) avoid conflict at all costs; (b) negotiate; (c) nonviolent direct action; (d) physical force; (e) withdraw from conflict; (f) give in; (g) stand firm, no-budge.
(7) What recommendations do you have for resolving conflicts in this program?
(8) What other examples from the world of nature can you find that illustrate conflict or the lack of conflict?

---

*Merrill Harmin, "Beetles Don't Argue with Butterflies," Southern Illinois University at Edwardsville.

#23—Bill of Rights Revisited

The Bill of Rights lies at the heart of our nation's values around liberty, justice, and the pursuit of happiness. Ironically, as reflected in several recent studies, this document would probably be rejected by Americans if put to a vote today. Let us now use the Bill of Rights to help you clarify your values related to social issues: (a) First, try ranking the ten amendments in the order of their personal importance to you. You might also want to rank them according to which rights seem closest to being abridged today and which are most secure.[6] With regard to your own program, which rights are most important—this might suggest another ranking for you to do; (b) It might be intriguing to join with staff and/or participants to discuss or seek consensus on these rankings; (c) Take some time to reflect on how you might expand the Bill of Rights—what other "rights" do you think are crucial to people in our country? in the world? in your program?

For your interest, here are some "rights" generated by a group of elementary school students:

(1) Right to more field trips, since "we would learn more and understand more of our studies by seeing the things that we are studying;"
(2) Right to play sports with mixed teams (boy-girl);
(3) Right to one's own thoughts;
(4) Right to eat—being able to choose among cafeteria foods;
(5) Right to earn money by working;
(6) Right to privacy, being alone when one wants;
(7) Right to one's own feelings—"nobody can tell you how to feel";
(8) Right to personal property.[7]

A group of high school students suggested these rights:

(1) Right to a good education;
(2) Right to be responsible;
(3) Right to be able to distribute political literature;
(4) Right to voice opinions with no penalty;
(5) Right to evaluate staff;
(6) Right to express oneself emotionally;
(7) Right to freedom of learning;
(8) Right to be seen as human;
(9) Right to not be put in a category;
(10) Right to dress as one wants;
(11) Right to have staff have confidence in us.

This particular activity can help you, staff, and participants in your program to establish a just community, based upon a mutual understanding of one another's rights and responsibilities. At the same time, this activity could serve as a microcosm for creating a just "world community" and for negotiating the attendant values issues.

It might be interesting for you to take an inventory of the rights/rules/laws of nature. What parallels do you see between these and human rights/rules/laws? What "rights of the natural environment" do you want to preserve/protect in the rules of your program? Perhaps you could title your list an "Ecological Bill of Rights."

"We need to have people who mean something to us, people to whom we can turn, knowing that being with them is coming home."   (H. COOKE)

#24—Action Research + Action Search

This strategy is designed to help you act on your good intentions. Start by listing examples of injustices, oppression, and/or violations of your or your program's bill of rights. For instance, you might come up with such items as:

(1) Textbooks which exclude or distort minority contributions to America;
(2) Hiring standards for camping programs which are culturally biased;
(3) Forbidding girls to play in summer baseball leagues;
(4) Pollution of streams by local industry;
(5) People who consistently tell ethnic jokes;
(6) People who constantly litter.

Now it is time to search for actions to speak to the problems which your research has uncovered. Taking one problem at a time, brainstorm what you can *do* to address it. First, a word about "brainstorming," which is probably one of the most frequently mentioned and oft-misused techniques for generating alternative solutions. What we suggest is that if you fly with the DOVE, then your brainstorming sessions will also soar:

D: Defer Judgment—All ideas are acceptable; avoid killer statements like "that's stupid," "it'll never work," "people won't like you for that," etc.; take a positive focus on every idea that comes up (your ideas as well as others' ideas); hold off on criticisms—don't "drive" with your brakes on.

O: Off-beat—Try to generate as many weird, strange, different ideas as possible; use metaphors and analogies to help break out of traditional ruts; try to make the familiar strange; off-beat ideas can lead to humor and laughter (haha), which, in turn, can spark creative ideas (aha).

V: Vast Number—Seek as many ideas as you can—the more ideas, the better chance you have of finding good ideas; go for quantity—the quality check will come later.

E: Expand—The object in brainstorming is to piggyback or hitchhike on your own ideas and on the ideas of others; try to build on the contributions of your peers; cooperation and synergy, rather than competition, are encouraged.

Following the DOVE guidelines, generate a list of possible solutions to the problem at hand. When you have your list, take a moment to analyze it by using the following coding: place a "T" next to those actions which you would feel comfortable/effective in *t*rying; place a "C" next to those actions which you would *c*onsider pursuing; and put an "N" beside those behaviors which you would prefer *n*ot to try at this point in time.

In order to increase the probability of success in carrying out your good intentions, you may find it helpful to commit yourself to writing a contract with yourself (and/or with another person, who could support you as you seek to implement your contract). The contract might include the following elements: (a) Completion of an "I will . . ." statement—worded to focus on action; (b) Specification of a date—to serve as a timeline for yourself; (c) Your signature; and (d) Your support partner's signature along with the specific ways and timeline for his/her support (if you extend your contract to another person).

Examples of contracts might include:

I will write a letter to the local paper and to my representatives making them aware of the pollution caused by the local industries. I will write these letters by next Tuesday. Signed, Gail . . . I will support Gail by gently nudging her—I'll do this by kidding with her whenever I see her (like asking her if she's written her "smelly" letters yet). Signed, Helen

The next time I see someone litter, I will pick up the object dropped and present it to the litterer, saying, "You dropped this." Signed, Betty . . . I will support Betty by having someone else purposely litter in front of her sometime—I will then check back with Betty about what she did. Signed, Dick

This action research/search sequence is significant because it allows you to be divergent in seeking alternative ways of responding to injustice and oppression, and to be convergent in choosing behaviors that make sense for you personally. It also provides a structure in which you can *act* on what you value. We believe it is vital for us to value what we do, and do what we value.

#25—It's Your Choice

If you want some food for thought regarding social values issues, then chew on the following questions (by yourself and/or in a group). Be sure to take note of the values underlying your choices.

(1) Would you rather live in a commune or in a condominium?
(2) If your neighbor dumped trash in your yard, would you pick it up or tell him to pick it up?
(3) Would you rather smoke or have a car with a bad exhaust system?
(4) Would you live near a nuclear power plant if it significantly decreased your taxes?
(5) To help poor people, would you rather give up fifty percent of your salary to charity or work a year for VISTA?
(6) Would you rather live in a big house with a little land or in a small house with a lot of land?
(7) Would you rather be wealthy and lonely or poor and have many friends?
(8) If you were a parent, would you rather have your children be totally honest with you or not give you all the details?
(9) Would you rather have your children have a good job or a good marriage?
(10) If you had just been picked up hitchhiking after a long wait and the driver started telling sexist jokes, would you get out of the car or stay in?
(11) If you saw someone steal something, would you ignore it or confront the thief?
(12) If you were eating in a room where many people were smoking, would you eat elsewhere, stay and try to bear it, or confront the smokers?
(13) If you saw a child shoot a bird with a BB gun, would you praise the child, chastise the child, or ignore the situation?

(14) If you heard one of the staff members put down another, would you stand up for that person, leave the room, or join in?

(15) In dealing with social issues, do you see yourself more like a rock or leaves in the wind?

(16) If you had the money, would you have your house air conditioned or not?

(17) When you die, would you rather have a traditional funeral, be cremated, or donate your body to science?

(18) When you become old, which do you think you will fear the most: poverty, death, loneliness, lingering illness, or being a burden to your children?

(19) Would you have a mildly disabled parent live with you at home or put him/her in a nursing home?

(20) Would you impose your own lifestyle on your children for as long as possible or allow the children a free choice from the beginning?

(21) Would you go out of your way to share your Thanksgiving dinner with people in need or take care of just your own family's dinner?

(22) Would you sell forty acres for profit as a subdivision for tract housing or would you sell it at less profit as a wildlife refuge?

(23) What would be the worst thing you could find out about your teenage son: he wants to work in a weapons factory—he's a persistent litterer—he's an avowed racist—he pushes hard drugs?

(24) Respond to the same question for your daughter.

(25) Are you more of a spender or saver (of time, resources, energy, money, etc.)?[8]

(26) Would you rather install and maintain a car pollution device or pay more for gasoline?

(27) Would you rather see billboards and directional signs or see only wilderness scenery?

(28) Would you rather smoke cigarettes for enjoyment or not smoke and increase your chances for better health?

(29) Would you rather use styrofoam tableware or increase labor costs and disease probabilities by washing regular tableware?

(30) Would you rather use pesticides in fruit or avoid their use and eat blemished and wormy fruit?

(31) Would you rather use plastic garbage bags or increase the amount of flies and other pests?

(32) Would you rather vote for a needed sewage treatment plant or maintain low property taxes?

#26—What Do You Wanna Be When You Grow Up?

Young people are not the only ones who ask this question. There are many adults who are wrestling with tough issues related to work and leisure. The following Favorites Grid may help you, staff, and participants to sort through these issues.[9]

Divide a large sheet of construction paper into four squares, and then respond to the questions for each block:

(1) (a) When you were young, did you have a favorite place, a place you could call your own, perhaps a secret hiding place? (b) What was it that

made this place your favorite? (c) Do you have a favorite place now? (d) What makes it special? (e) How does it compare with your first favorite place?

(2) (a) Who is your favorite person at work, school, or camp? (b) How long has this person been your favorite? (c) What is it about this person that you enjoy? (d) Can you think of ways to enjoy this person even more? (e) Who else does this person remind you of?

(3) (a) What is your favorite activity at work, school, or camp? (b) What is your favorite leisure activity? (c) Do the two have anything in common? (d) What skills do they call upon? (e) Does either of them involve your favorite person or place?

(4) (a) When is your favorite time during the week? (b) What makes it special? (c) What are you usually doing or looking forward to at that time? (d) Are there any ways you can think of to have this kind of time occur more frequently during your week? (e) List the names of the people with whom you've shared this favorite time.

This activity seeks to build on your strengths, resources, and interests. Identifying and sharing favorites can have a nourishing effect on our lives, especially if we can develop ways of maximizing the frequency and intensity of those favorites. Asking, "How can you get more of what you want from life?" is a first step in doing what you want to do as you "grow up."

#27—Are You Someone Who . . . ?

Money is a values area that is full of conflict and confusion. Here is an activity to help you determine what that green picture of George Washington means to you.[10]

Divide a sheet of paper in half. Further divide the right side of the paper into two columns, A and B. For each of the statements that describes you, place a check in column A. There are no right or wrong answers—just descriptive data about you for your study. If you are interested, you may also want to discover how other people see you. You can do this by asking someone you know—friend, family member, co-worker, participant in your program—to put checks in column B next to each item that he or she thinks describes you (you will have folded over column A). You might be in for some interesting feedback and discussions.

Are you someone who . . .

(1) would change to a job you didn't like if it offered $10,000 a year more than you now make?
(2) would change your lifestyle if your income doubled?
(3) is more of a saver than a spender?
(4) wants something badly now, but can't afford it?
(5) would give money to a beggar?
(6) gives money to charities?
(7) thinks children should have to work for their allowance?
(8) has ever shoplifted?
(9) gives money to environmental action groups?
(10) believes in a lifestyle of voluntary simplicity?
(11) will never want much money?
(12) will never get as much money as you want?
(13) would spend more than five dollars at a carnival?

Of course, as with the other activities, you can adapt "Are You Someone Who . . . ?" to speak to other areas of values interest. Are you someone who will do this?

#28—Holiday Autobiography

More and more people seem to feel that holidays "happen" to them. Much of the meaning and value underlying holidays has either been lost or clouded. Holidays can be times of celebration of what is important to us, rather than times in which we go through meaningless motions. If we are to take charge of our lives and our holidays, however, we must be clear about what we value. Developing a deeper self-understanding can help you put the value back in your holidays. Start by taking an inventory of some events from your past. Your autobiographical sketch might be formed around the following kinds of questions:[11]

(1) Recall as many Thanksgivings as you can. Where did you have dinner each Thanksgiving? Did you ever invite anyone outside the family to dinner? Did your family have any rituals on Thanksgiving? If so, what values were reflected in those rituals (or lack of rituals)?

(2) Recall all the holiday presents you have given your parents in the past five years. What presents did you receive as a child that stand out in your mind? What was special about those presents? Which presents have you enjoyed giving the most? What was it that was enjoyable about giving these particular presents? If you could choose something from nature to give as a gift to your parents/children/friends/participants in your program, what would you pick? What gift from nature would you like to receive? What does it signify?

(3) What did you do on your last five birthdays (your own personal holiday)? In what other ways has celebration entered your life?

(4) Recall all the ceremonies in which you have taken part.

(5) At five-year intervals (from age five to the present), list your favorite holidays. Analyze what was special about the holiday for you at each age. Underline those items that still retain their special meaning for you. If this special flavor is missing from your holidays now, you may want to consider making a self-contract to build this special quality into the holiday.

(6) What rituals or ceremonies would you like to see in this school or camp/outdoor education program? What are some ways you think "celebration" could be incorporated into this program? If you could imagine an "ideal day" for you in this program, what would it look like? What can you do to make it a reality?

#29—Epitaph

The goal of this activity is not to have us dwell in morbidity, but rather to reinforce the notion that we are each responsible for the quality of our lives. It is based on the assumption that we all have a lot of living left to do.

"On the whole, I'd rather be in Philadelphia." That epitaph is attributed to W. C. Fields. It supposedly captures some of the essence and meaning of his life. What would you want engraved on your tombstone? What would be an accurate nutshell summary of your life? What object from nature would you want on your tombstone—what does this metaphor stand for?

Whenever something appears in your epitaph that has not appeared yet in your life, it should be noted. This could represent a potential goal toward which you might work.[12]

#30—Where Do You Draw the Line?

It is very appropriate for people to suppose (wonder) and to expose (share) their values. However, it is sometimes difficult to draw the line between growth-enhancing values exploration (supposing and exposing) and inculcation/moralizing (imposing and deposing values).

This activity invites you to take note of the strength of different values issues for yourself, which, in turn, can help you to clarify your boundaries with regard to supposing/exposing/imposing/deposing values. Take a sheet of paper and draw four columns with these headings: (1) I value and act on this; (2) I'm happy that others value and act on this (although I do not act on it); (3) I am willing to tolerate this; (4) I will actively fight and oppose this. Place each of the following items in the appropriate column:

(1) Cheating on income tax
(2) Reporting the cheater to the Internal Revenue Service
(3) Vice principal who makes a student kneel in order to check her dress length
(4) College student pushes drugs to raise his tuition
(5) Joining segregated swim club
(6) Littering
(7) Telling racist jokes
(8) Killing whales for profit
(9) Company dumping toxic wastes in rivers
(10) Mercy killing
(11) Developing nuclear plants
(12) Shoplifting
(13) Writing letters to the editor
(14) Voting in national elections
(15) Having a curfew for teenagers
(16) Camp director who paddles campers
(17) Making your own gifts
(18) Watching television
(19) Smoking
(20) Giving money to charity
(21) Decriminalizing marijuana
(22) Sending child to an alternative school
(23) Sending child to camp each summer
(24) Experimenting with being a "househusband"
(25) Recycling paper and glass

One way to springboard off this activity would be to note the criteria you used in placing each item in the appropriate column—how did you know where to draw the line? You may also want to do an alternative search (see Activity #24) for some of the items—e.g., brainstorm ways of opposing racist jokes, brainstorm ideas for gifts which you could make, etc.

Being clear yourself is the first step toward being able to work with others on emotion-full values issues. This activity is designed to help you explore your values "space," and to aid you in giving others space to explore their values.

#31—Making a Difference

What is values exploration all about? Making a difference. Making a difference in the quality of life . . . making our lives more value-able. In order to do that, we need to move from "I understand" to "I take a stand."

This activity suggests a seemingly simple (to understand), but oftentimes very difficult (to do) way of taking a stand: writing a letter to the editor.

Think about an issue of importance to you. Express your thoughts, feelings, values around this issue in a letter to the editor—of your local newspaper, a camp newspaper, a school district newsletter, or a magazine. You may want to turn the letter into a petition—it could be a values clarifying experience for the staff and participants in your program to be presented with the option of signing their names to it. You may want to encourage the staff and participants to come up with their own letters as well. As our nation moves into its third century, we will need active, thinking, and questioning citizens if we are to survive and grow. We will need people who have the courage to address important social values issues, who have the courage to take a stand, who have the ability to make a difference.

Outdoor Activities

The indoor lessons described above often use paper and pencil activities and group discussion to achieve their objectives. While these approaches are effective, they can be supplemented by valuing reinforcement outdoors. This section presents specific methods to become involved—both mentally with the valuing processes and physically with the manipulation of related materials and objects. We present them as suggestions—as a beginning.

KNAPP

#32—Object Ranking

Select a twig or leaf from each of the three most useful trees in the area. Rank the twigs or leaves according to usefulness to you. What criteria were used to determine usefulness? Select specific standards of usefulness (such as toolmaking, shelter making, survival food or drink, game equipment, and animal food). Select and rank the twigs or leaves according to beauty. Try this with plants other than trees.

#33—Nature's Substitutes

Find or make the best natural substitutes for the following items: a cup; a plate; a spoon; a candle; a nail; a fish hook. Select other useful items and invent substitutes for them. Use some of the items for a day and evaluate their effectiveness and beauty. How much energy and natural resources could be conserved by using these substitutes? Why do you think more people do not use them?

#34—What Is Noise?

Sit quietly for five minutes. On a pleasant-unpleasant sound continuum, place words or other symbols which describe the sounds you hear and their origin. When all the sounds are placed on the continuum line, mark the point at which noise begins for you. Does this point on the line vary with where you are and how you feel at a particular time? Compare your sound continuum with those of others. Would it be difficult to agree on the definition of "noise" in your group?

#35—Looking Around

Rotate your body slowly in a circle with your eyes directed above you at a 45-degree angle. Record all the sights that are pleasing to you during a 360-degree rotation. Do the same thing with your eyes straight ahead. Finally, repeat this with your eyes directed toward the ground at a 45-degree angle. In which of the three eye positions did you record the most pleasing sights? Were they natural or made by people or a combination of both? Do your perceptions coincide with those of others?

#36—Place—Thoughts and Feelings

Here is an opportunity for you to note the impact of the environment on you. Divide an index card into four columns. In column one, write down five words which describe your thoughts and feelings about a place. Move to three other places and do the same thing in the other columns. After being in four different places, examine the sets of five words. What do you notice about the effect of places on your thoughts and feelings? If you wish, share your descriptions with others. What can you learn about others? about yourself?

#37—Feeling Places

Here is a chance for you to legitimize and identify your feelings as one data source in dealing with values. Mark off an area about fifteen meters square containing as wide a variety of environments as possible . . . e.g., forest, field, pond, stream. In a group setting, ask people to go to the spot which makes them feel the most comfortable, least comfortable, most curious, most angry, most excited, etc. Form clusters of people after each movement and take some time to share your experiences about these places.

#38—Dollar Values

This activity provides you with an opportunity to use a fiscal yardstick to measure what you value in the environment. Find objects in the environment and place dollar values on the three most valuable items. Do this privately, and then share your assessments with others. On what objects was there the most agreement? most disagreement? Did you find some objects could not be judged in monetary terms? What terms can be used for those items? How can the degree of value be measured or communicated to others?

#39—Eye/I of the Beholder

Evaluate an area by walking over it. Use the viewpoints of different animals (e.g., deer, rabbits, snakes, squirrels, owls, robins, fox, mice, beaver, and bear). Examine food, shelter, water, space, and other aspects. Evaluate the same area from the human viewpoints of a building contractor, farmer, lumberman, hunter, naturalist, artist, and teacher. Does this role playing cause you to view the environment differently now?

#40—Litter Line

Find at least five pieces of litter and arrange them in a line on the ground according to the most offensive to the least offensive. Then arrange them according to the most biodegradable to the least biodegradable, and finally according to those containing the most abundant natural resources to the least abundant. Can you reach consensus with a group on these rankings? What can you determine about the personal values of those who littered?

#41—Mother Nature Speaks

Here is a chance for you to step into Mother Nature's shoes—an opportunity to develop empathizing skills. In a group setting, have people pair up. Imagine that a dam is to be built and the immediate environment will be flooded and covered with water. Each pair selects an object within everyone's view that they would like to save. List as many reasons as possible for saving that object. Have the members of each pair then tell the rest of the group what it is like to be that object—becoming the voice of the object, defend its right for existence above water. Have someone else role play the dam builder and have a dialogue.

#42—Cover Up

Survey an area and note the major ground surface cover in each place (e.g., cement, asphalt, grass, leaves, gravel). After listing the ground cover types, rank them according to the following: soil erosion prevention; variety of living things; comfort for sleeping; pleasing color(s); moisture-holding capacity; most acid; most alkaline. How have people affected the ground surface cover? Predict how the surface cover will look through the seasons of the year.

#43—What Is a Weed?

A weed is a plant out of place which is considered to be undesirable. Survey the area for weeds and state the reason(s) for labeling them weeds. Is it possible for some people to consider a plant a weed and others not?

#44—Changes

Find three changes people have made in the environment. Will these changes still be visible in five years? How have these changes affected the environment? What things will happen because of the changes? How can people improve the changes? Find evidence of natural changes. How do you feel about change in the environment? Find two changes that animals (other than people) have made. Take ten steps. Can you see more changes made by animals? Will these changes last more than five years? Will these changes affect other animals? How? How permanent are various changes?

#45—Texture Hunting

Texture in the environment can be discovered by touching objects or by placing paper over them and rubbing with a crayon or pencil. Find four different textures. How would you use these textures if you were a furniture maker? a clothes designer? a painter? a sculptor? What is one job you have thought about doing in your life? How could you use these textures in that job?

#46—Sniffing Around

Choose a partner and look around for three natural objects. Tell your partner which ones you chose. Then ask your partner to count slowly to ten while you describe how the objects might smell. Do this for each object. Next, pick one object and go to it. Sniff very carefully, noticing how it smells. Then give two descriptive words about the smell. Next let your partner select three natural objects and do the same thing. If you wanted to develop a sharper sense of smell, what are some ways you could do it? Do you both agree on "good" and "bad" smells?

#47—Sketching Progress

Locate a natural area containing as little development as possible. Is such a place hard to locate in your area? Sketch the scene carefully on paper. Then, one by one, add the following objects to the scene by sketching right over the natural scene (do not erase, just draw over the natural scene): a road, picnic site, telephone and power lines, a restaurant, fire hydrant, and traffic light. How has the natural scene changed? How do you feel about the changes? Discuss the pros and cons of "progress."

#48—String Fence

Cut a 100-inch piece of string. Using the string as an imaginary fence or boundary, mark off an area that you would like to protect from destruction by urbanization.

#49—Mini-Trail

Take a 100-inch piece of string and select a miniature nature trail route which includes as many points of interest as possible. Guide others along your 100-inch nature trail.

#50—Pleasing Shapes

Make sketches of three aesthetically pleasing tree shapes that you can observe. What characteristics do these trees have in common? Can you find pleasing shapes in other objects?

#51—Shelter Models

Using objects found in the area, build a model of a shelter that incorporates one or more of the following: protection from wind, rain, and snow; visual harmony with nature; human comfort, convenience, or warmth; ease of outdoor viewing; energy conservation; and other important design elements.

#52—Eco-Change

Find five plants or plant parts that can be picked without signficantly disturbing (changing) the ecology of the area. Arrange them in a row according to the one that disturbed ecology the least to the one that disturbed ecology the most. What other plants or plant parts were *not* picked because they would have significantly disturbed the ecology of the area? What implications does this activity have for your daily life?

#53—Historical Landmarks

Landmarks are chosen and set aside because of their importance to the history of the area. Select one historical landmark (natural or human-made) which should be preserved for its historical value. Share this landmark and its historical importance with others.

#54—Values Theme Hike

One way of making hikes more value-able is through use of theme cards. Each time you (and/or a group) goes on a hike, take one theme card with you. Three-by-five-inch cards can be used to capture such themes as: pleasant sounds, beautiful colors, graceful movements, good changes, useful plants, harmony in nature, ecological balance, eye-catching patterns, peaceful places, happiness, etc. As you walk, look for examples of the theme you carry. Another approach to the values themes might be to look for the opposite of each of the above "positives"—e.g., noise, ugly colors, clumsy movements, bad changes. This is a good way to keep your eyes open to what you value.

#55—Partner Scavenger Hunt

Here is a modification of the old, but still popular, scavenger hunt. This version is conducted in pairs, so that you can interact with a partner—as a way of encouraging cooperation, keen observation, and values decision making. As with the previous activities, feel free to modify the form below for your own setting and group:

Directions:

This scavenger hunt is different because before you can locate the items on the list, you and your partner should agree on what to select. Please do not pick any living plants unless there are hundreds more in the immediate area. If you cannot bring back the actual object, make a sketch or describe it with words. Enjoy the hunt, but most important, enjoy each other.

(1) Two stones that fit together like puzzle pieces
(2) Two leaves that fell last year from the same tree
(3) A picture drawn on sandpaper by both partners using only pigments from nature
(4) A natural object that both agree is the most beautiful in the immediate area
(5) Something green or brown that both of you can carry back together
(6) A poem that you coauthor based on a common experience outdoors
(7) Find natural objects and use them to create music together
(8) A crayon or pencil rubbing of an interesting texture
(9) Make some improvement in the environment together and share it with others
(10) Select three highlights from the time you spent together

#56—Litter Locations

Walk to a relatively undisturbed area outdoors and assign groups of participants to various spots. Give each group a quantity of a specific type of

---

"The appearance of things changes according to the emotions and thus we see magic and beauty in them; all the while, the magic and beauty are really in ourselves."   (KAHLIL GIBRAN)

trash (i.e., empty soda cans, toilet paper, can tab tops, plastic six pack rings, bottle caps) and ask them to distribute the objects as though they were litterbugs. Allow them ample creative license for deciding how to litter the area. Upon completion of the littering in various locations, gather the group together and have the litterbugs lead the group to their location. Ask the entire group of students to record the answers to the following questions at each location:

(1) On a scale of 1 (not at all) to 10 (very much), indicate how much this scene bothers you.
(2) How could this scene harm wildlife?
(3) About how long would it take for these objects to decompose and the area appear natural again?
(4) What are some reasons a person would throw away this type of litter in the woods?
(5) How could we solve this type of litter problem elsewhere?

After these questions are answered and discussion is ended, the whole group picks up every piece of litter at that location. The trash may be saved for use with other groups. After visiting all litter locations, further analysis of the data may occur to assess the values of the students in regard to littering.

#57—"Tree mendous" Trees

Select a tree and give it a name based upon something that the tree gives to the world (i.e., shade, lumber, fruit, wildlife shelter). (The name should not be the species name.) Using the "Tree Conversation Sheet," ask them to hold a conversation with a tree and record the imagined answers on a tagboard name tag. Be sure that they number each answer to correspond with the questions. After finishing, have them tie the identification tag around the tree trunk showing the tree name and the answers written boldly with a magic marker or crayon.

Tree Conversation Sheet

(1) How are you doing today . . . . . . ?
    (tree name)
(2) About how long have you been standing there?
(3) What gifts do you give to the world?
(4) Are you more useful to the world dead or alive?
(5) May I cut you down?
(6) Why or why not?
(7) What are three words that describe you best?
(8) When will I see you again?
(9) What else would you like to say to me?
(10) May I draw your picture?

After you have recorded the imaginary conversation with a tree, reassemble the group and walk from one tree to the other to share answers to the questions. (If the group is large, sharing may be done in small groups.) This technique is an excellent way to assess your values toward particular trees.

BROWN

#58—Animal Place Value

You will have an opportunity to closely examine a place where a certain animal lives. To find that place, throw a coat hanger bent into a circle wherever you want. You may aim the toss or throw it randomly. When you have found a place to examine, follow these instructions.

(1) Choose an animal that might live in that place.
(2) Can you find any evidence of that animal or the animal itself? (It is not essential to find the animal or its evidence to do this activity.)
(3) What conditions within the circle are necessary for the survival of that animal?
(4) Imagine each of the life supporting conditions being removed or polluted one-by-one. How would this affect your animal?
(5) What could you do to each circle place to make it better suited as a home for your animal? Do it if you can.

When you have completed these directions, share your answers within small groups of three to five participants.

#59—Beauty Seekers

Beauty exists everywhere in common objects if we take the time to find it. Select an object such as a plant, rock, area of soil, or piece of wood and carefully examine it for ten minutes. An excellent method for examining detail is to sit comfortably with the selected object in view. Then, draw every detail observed with a pencil *without looking at the paper*. Do not take your eyes from the object throughout the drawing process even if you pause. It does not matter what the drawing looks like because this is an exercise in observing detail and *not* in producing a replica of that object. (Many people are pleasantly surprised at the beauty of the drawing, too.) After the ten minute observation period, answer the following questions;

(1) What is beautiful about your object?
(2) Is it hard to believe that no other object in the world is exactly like this one?
(3) Can you do something to your object to make it more beautiful? If so, what?
(4) Examine your object for one minute more. Can you find more beauty in it?
(5) Do you believe that "beauty is within the eye of the beholder?" If so, how are you like the object you observed?

#60—To Pick or Not to Pick . . .

Some plants can be picked with no danger of becoming scarce in an area and others cannot. Many believe that good conservation practice involves maintaining a variety of plants in an area. In order to decide whether to pick a plant or not, a number of questions can be considered. Distribute the "Picking Questions" sheets. The purpose of the sheets is to provide some ideas to ponder before picking a plant. If the answer to a question is "yes," the plant may probably be picked for a particular reason. Decide how many "yeses" are needed in order to pick that plant. Go outdoors to select a plant and ask the questions. Decide whether to pick the plant at the end of the questioning process. (Caution: If there are rare or protected plants in the area and you do not want to risk them being picked, take your group to them first and go through the questions to illustrate why that plant should not be picked.)

Picking Questions

(1) Are there more than 100 other plants or plant parts of the same kind in the area?
(2) Can you learn something important from picking it that you could not learn by leaving it?
(3) Can it be made into a useful product that will benefit people in some way?
(4) Will the plant be as beautiful as it is now after it is picked?
(5) Will the whole plant survive even if I just pick a part of it?
(6) Will the area be improved if I pick this plant?
(7) Will the plant be saved from destruction if I pick it?
(8) Will the plant die soon and decay?
(9) Is the plant safe for me to pick?
(10) Is it all right to pick this plant even if the answers to all of the above questions were "yes?"
(11) What will you do now? To pick or not to pick, that is the question.

When the group comes together again, the participants' values may be assessed from their responses to the questions and from the discussion that follows.

#61—Action Learning

Action learning means becoming involved in meaningful group projects that provide opportunities to act upon important values. They deal with felt needs and desirable values in the camp or school setting. Once a list of desirable values is made, action learning projects can be planned cooperatively with participants and staff. Examples of values and related projects follow:

(1) *Value:* Rare and endangered plants and animals should be protected.
   Project: Identify plants to be protected along a nature trail.
(2) *Value:* Local plants and animals and their habitats should be studied in ways that lead to knowledge and appreciation.
   Project: Set up mini-habitat terrariums showing some of the local environments to explore.
(3) *Value:* People should preserve the natural beauty of the area by doing conservation and beautification work.
   Project: Do a service project to correct an environmental problem.
(4) *Value:* Ecological diversity should be maintained or increased whenever possible.
   Project: Attempt to increase the plant and animal life through plantings and management practices.

(5) *Value:* Local streams, lakes, and other water supplies should be protected from contamination by pollutants.
  Project: Monitor the water for pH, temperature, animal life, etc., over a period of time to detect pollution.
(6) *Value:* Natural materials should be used to enhance the aesthetic environment.
  Project: Gather natural materials for table centerpieces in the dining hall or cafeteria.
(7) *Value:* Collections of natural objects should be limited by abundance and the human populations using the area.
  Project: Make a display of natural objects that can be collected and used in various craft projects.
(8) *Value:* Human activities should be restricted to those which have the least long-range ecological impact on the environment.
  Project: Conduct a survey of the area and make recommendations about human uses.
(9) *Value:* Conserve energy in as many ways as possible.
  Project: Plan and cook a nutritious meal that wastes as little energy in the food web as possible.

Action learning has been a part of many camps and outdoor education programs for a long time. Camp leaders could examine the projects that are done now to uncover the underlying values. The list of important values could be expanded, and new projects implemented to address these values.

So What's the Score?

Looking to the outdoors is an excellent way for us to gather insights about what is inside us, about what we value. It is crucial—for us personally and for our society—that we link our "inside" world and "outside" world. We hope that the aforementioned activities give you a taste for some practical how-to's and stimulate you to create your own.

We have just presented you with over three score ideas for valuing activities that focus on important environmental and social issues. We sincerely hope that you do not limit yourself to the ideas presented here. It is crucial that you tap your own creativity, and the ingenuity of the staff and participants in your program, in stretching the activities presented in this section. If you do, your score will grow, and everyone will come out a winner.

Here are some questions that may provide you with ideas for next steps—where do you go from here?

(1) Rank-order the activities in terms of their usefulness to you. Think about the criteria you are using in this ranking (e.g., activity speaks to an issue of real personal concern, activity is one that staff and participants could engage in together, activity could fit easily into our program in an on-going way, activity seems to spark a lot of energy and fun, etc.).
(2) Take each activity, one at a time. Brainstorm ways that you could make it work for you in your setting. How could it be modified, rearranged, combined, or extended to better fit your needs?

(3) Which activities will you do just by yourself? Which ones would you like to share with staff, with participants, with staff and participants together, with friends, with family?

(4) List the objectives for and strengths of each activity. Are there other ways, new activities which you could generate, to speak to these same objectives and strengths?

(5) In what ways could you employ nature and your immediate environment in the activities?

(6) How can you change an activity so that the process will remain the same, but the content of the activity would be different (e.g., using the process of the moral dilemma story with different values issues)?

(7) What will your first steps be in springboarding off the ideas presented here? Make a contract with yourself and/or another person (see Activity #24). What is your action plan?

Footnotes

1 For elaboration on this, see Joel Goodman and Marie Hartwell Walker, "Affective Ed—A Means, Not an End," *Learning*, January 1976, p. 52.

2 For a thorough look at clarifying questions, check Louis Raths, Merrill Harmin, and Sidney Simon, *Values and Teaching* (Columbus, Ohio: Charles E. Merrill, 1966), pp. 51-82.

3 Adapted from Joel Goodman, "You Are Resource-Full," *Toward a Quality of Living* (New York: J. C. Penny Company, 1976).

4 See Joel Goodman, Sidney Simon, and Ron Witort, "Tackling Racism by Clarifying Values," *Today's Education*, January 1973, pp. 37-38.

5 Examples of songs include: Buffy Ste.-Marie's "Where Have the Buffalo Gone" and "Universal Soldier;" examples of films include: "Black History: Lost, Stolen, or Strayed," and "The Friendly Game."

6 For additional ideas, see Robert C. Hawley and Joel Goodman, "Exploring the Great American Dream," *Scholastic Voice Teacher's Edition,* October 21, 1975, p. 15.

7 See Joel Goodman and Clifford Knapp's "Making a Difference; Values Clarification and Social Issues," *Turning Points: New Developments, New Directions in Values Clarification, Volume II* (Saratoga Springs, NY: Creative Resources Press, 1979), pp. 78-79.

8 Adapted from ideas generated by participants in a workshop on "A Humanistic Approach to Tackling Social Issues," Human Development Project, Peace Dale, R.I.

9 Adapted from Sidney B. Simon and Joel Goodman, "Values Clarification: Focus on Work and Leisure," *Today's Catholic Teacher*, September 1973, pp. 84-85.

10 See Sidney B. Simon and Joel Goodman, "Values Clarification: Focus on Money," *Adult Leader*, September-October-November 1973, pp. 21-22.

11 Adapted from Sidney B. Simon and Joel Goodman, "Values Clarification: Focus on Holidays," *Adult Leader*, September-October-November 1973, pp. 19-20.

12 Sidney B. Simon and Joel Goodman, "A Study of Death Through the Celebration of Life," *Learning*, March 1976, pp. 70-74.

13 Some of the activities appeared in Clifford Knapp's: (A) "Outdoor Environmental Values Clarification," *The Communicator: Journal of the New York State Outdoor Education Association* (Fall-Winter 1975) Vol. VII, No. 1, pp. 9-11; (B) "Impact on Teaching Values," *Fifty Years of Resident Outdoor Education* (American Camping Association, 1980); and (C) "Values that Make Better Camping," *Camping Magazine*, Vol. 51, No. 5, pp. 8-9ff.

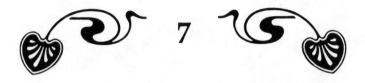

Making Friends with Yourself:
The Nature and Nurture of Self-Esteem

One day, Linus notes that Charlie Brown has been a really dedicated baseball manager, always giving 110 percent to the team. Linus suggests that the team show their appreciation to Charlie by giving him a testimonial dinner. Lucy responds by doubting that he deserves a whole testimonial dinner, and recommends instead that they give him a testimonial snack.[1]

Self-esteem. These two words have become one of the most popular couples in America today. Everybody likes self-esteem, everybody wants self-esteem. After all, how could you be against it?

In the face of the growing popularity of this dynamic duo, educators, camp leaders, parents, and helping professionals are beginning to explore the nature and nurture of self-esteem. This chapter will provide you with at least a testimonial snack, as we look at the what (what is it?), and so what (so why is it important—why do we need it?), and now what (now, what are some specific and practical ways to develop it?) of self-esteem.

What

Before plunging into enhancing self-esteem, it makes good common sense for us to first take a look at just what it is we are trying to enhance. The following anecdote illustrates this point:

An airplane pilot delivers this message over the intercom to the passengers on his flight: "Well, folks, we have some good news and some bad news. First, the good: we're making great time! Now the bad news: we're lost."

The first step we need to take is to set up our self-esteem "compass" which will help us find our direction(s). Take a few minutes to fill in the compass that follows—brainstorm all the associations, components, definitions you have for the concept of "self-esteem"—and place these on the points of the compass.

Charlie Brown notes that "in the book of life, the answers are not in the back." There is no "right answer" to the task you just completed—there are probably as many different self-esteem compasses as there are people. It might be an interesting experiment for you to check out your orientation with that of others. For starters, you can take a look at what we see self-esteem en-compassing:

(1) *Self-Esteem = Confidence + Competence:* This formula, although it appears to be simple, has important implications. It suggests that if we are to build self-esteem, we must provide opportunities for people to develop confidence (I think I can, I think I can) and competence (I can/do). These two factors are interdependent—the more competent I am, the more confident I feel, which helps me, in turn, to be more competent.

(2) *Self-Esteem = Successes + Strengths + Dreams:* This formula offers a three-dimensional view of self-esteem. The significant implication here is that we must provide chances for people to travel in time if they are to enhance their self-esteem. Identifying successes from the past can lead to feelings of being success-full (confidence). While growing up, we always heard the phrase "you have to learn from your mistakes." This is important—but it makes just as much, if not more, sense to learn from our successes as well. It is also crucial that we invite people to focus on their present strengths, to build on and maximize their abilities (competence). Finally, we need to support people in setting future goals in actualizing their dreams (confidence + competence).

(3) *Self-Esteem = Identify + Connectedness + Power:* This compass model also has three directions in which we might move. In helping people to move towards "identity," we seek to create opportunities for them to develop a sense of worth. If we want people to head towards "connectedness," then we need to provide an environment in which they can feel a sense of belonging. If "personal power" is the goal, then we need to seek situations in which people can experience a sense of agency. Of course, it is vital for us to remember that identity, connectedness, and power are interdependent.

So What

So what? What's the big deal? Why is it so important that we spend our time and resources in focusing on self-esteem? Haven't we got enough to do already without worrying about this? Are there any compelling reasons for us to commit ourselves to this goal? Yes, there are many.

(1) *De-valuation:* What we are talking about here is not monetary devaluation, although that may be a concern to many people. Rather, we are talking about the de-valuation of people. Anyone who works with young people (or adults, for that matter) cannot deny the epidemic of people not feeling valuable. This dis-ease manifests itself in a number of ways. Herbert Otto has found that young people can name seven times as many things that are wrong with themselves as things that are right.[2] On another level, suicides, drug abuse, vandalism, child abuse, dropping out of school, and increasing violence are manifestations of de-valuation. They are symptomatic of people who have given up, who have given up on themselves, who do not value themselves.

(2) *Killer Phrases:* How did this de-valuation come about? What causes it? Unlike the mysterious "Legionnaire's disease," we can quickly identify several culprits. The first one that comes to mind is the seemingly omnipresent "killer phrase." The killer phrase (or it could be a nonverbal look or gesture) serves to put-down another person, to kill a part of that person and his/her energy or ideas. Oftentimes, killer phrases are given unconsciously or unintentionally. Regardless of the motivation, killer phrases hurt.

What is ironic about killer phrases—and what makes it so hard to confront them—is that they seem to be imbedded in and legitimitized by our culture. You need only to turn on the TV to get a sniff of "up your nose with a rubber hose" or to see Don Rickles engaging in the "art" of one-downmanship. As you probably know, young people (and adults) are quick to pick up on this one-downmanship mentality. We recently asked a group of thirty junior high school students to generate a list of killer phrases that are a regular part of their vocabulary. Would you believe they came up with 200 different ones in a three-minute period?! They are constantly bombarded with "you're weird," "you turkey," "what an idiot"—is it any wonder that many people have been brainwashed to believe that they are not worthwhile?

(3) *Kookie Monster:* Perhaps the most insidious effect of the killer phrase is that it creates kookie monsters. This is not the Sesame Street variety—rather, it is the intrapersonal killer phrases with which we hit ourselves. Each of us probably has a little voice (or a big one) within us that at times says: "you're kookie," "you can't do it," "you're dumb," etc. What is insidious about the kookie monster is that we begin to believe him/her. And research has demonstrated the extremely powerful effect of self-fulfilling prophecies. It is crucial that we find ways to help people muffle their kookie monsters and to create positive self-fulfilling prophecies. Or, as Jack Canfield says, to help people become "inverse paranoids"—thinking that the world is out to do them good.

"I am larger, better than I thought. I did not know I held so much goodness."   (WHITMAN)

(4) *Achievement:* There has been a great hue and cry in the last several years over falling achievement test scores. Teachers and parents have been lamenting openly that "students aren't like they used to be" and that "students just don't have the basic skills anymore." As a result, many schools have picked up the "back to basics" banner.

This is an understandable, yet sad and ironic, phenomenon . . . sad and ironic because we could effectively get "back to basics" by going "forward to fundamentals." In this case, the fundamentals are focusing on those beliefs and feelings which are closest to each one of us—our self-esteem. For, as Canfield and Wells note, they "actually determine who you are![3] They also determine what you think you are, what you do, and what you can become!"

Extensive research over the past twenty years indicates a very strong relationship between self-esteem and academic achievement, task performance, and school success.[4]

BROWN

Now What

If one or more of the above "so what" reasons hit home for you, then you are probably reading these words. Given the nature of and need for self-esteem, what are some practical ways that teachers, camp leaders, helping professionals, parents, and young people can nurture their own and others' self-esteem? We believe that the road to developing self-esteem involves joining the A.A.A.—you'll be on the right track if you:

—have *A*ttitudes conducive to this goal;
—create an *A*tmosphere which encourages the development of self-esteem;
—provides *A*ctivities that en-compass the elements of self-esteem described in the "What" section.

Attitudes

The foundation of self-enhancing atmosphere and activities lies in the establishment of self-enhancing attitudes. These attitudes are the most important ingredients in nurturing self-esteem. We encourage you to change the amount of each ingredient in working with different people in different situations. In other words, feel free to tap your own flexibility and creativity in developing your own attitudinal recipes. Here are some ingredients to consider:

(1) *I Know You Can, I Know You Can:* Believing in people and in their potential is crucial. Having confidence in their competence will often build both their confidence and competence. This attitude can be the primary motivator to help others move from feelings of "I can't do it" to "I can (and will) do it." This attitude implies that you will stick with the person as she/he takes on new challenges and growth experiences.

(2) *The Message Is the Massage:* There is so much negativism in the world today, in the form of killer phrases, kookie monsters, and the news on TV which starts off with a barrage of crimes and distressing events. It has gotten to the point where many people are "numb" to feelings or seeing anything positive about themselves, others, or the world around them.

It is vital that we break through the wall of negativism by having a positive attitude and communicating it in a genuine (not saccharine) way. Hopefully, the positive message will massage the positiveness which lies numb or dormant in others. It could be as simple as telling a student or camper what you appreciate about him/her. Or it could be mailing a note to the parents, informing them of their child's achievements—sending them an efficiency report (or opposed to a deficiency report). Or it could be asking another person to focus on the positive—by asking, "What is new and good in your life?" It just makes good, common sense that positive, nourishing seeds—rather than toxic ones—are at the root of helping humans to grow, to learn, and to love.

(3) *1 + 1 Is Better than 1 − 1:* At first glance, most people would agree that it is better to build and to be synergistic, rather than to tear down and to be destructive. However, at times, there is a difference between what we would like to do and what we are likely to do. Enter the culprit: Yes, but . . .

> "*Yes,*" John has made a good point there, *but* it's not in the budget."
> "*Yes,* that's a nice idea, Betty, *but* we've already tried it."
> "*Yeah,* I could go along with you on that, *except that* no one else will like it."

How different it would be if we were no longer the but (sic) of killer phrases. Wouldn't it be nice if we had "but" butt out of our vocabulary? One might now say, "*Yes, but* what would replace it?" The word "and" could be a simple addition to our vocabulary to accomplish this purpose. Note the change in tone between the statements below and those above:

> "*Yes,*" John has made a good point there, *and* we need to explore ways of financing it."

"*Yes*, that's a nice idea, Betty, *and* let's take some time to generate new wrinkles based on our past experience with it."

"*Yeah*, I could go along with you on that, *and* we ought to figure out how to enlist others' support."

"Yes, and . . ." statements put the accent on the positive and on constructive problem solving. They add energy to a situation and to people. They motivate people to work together, to give support to one another, and to take their own creativity.

(4) *Beware of the Scylla and Charybdis of Self-Esteem:* In using our compass to chart our self-esteem course, it is vital that we be aware of two cultural obstacles: perfectionism and modesty.

Although many of us have heard the phrase, "No one is perfect," there is sometimes a tendency to attach a rider: "No one is perfect (but I should be)." Perfectionists are made, not born . . . a child brings home a paper with a "98" on it, and the parent asks, "What happened to the other two points?" . . . a young person playing in a little league game makes some good fielding plays, but the coach only remarks on the one error. Perfectionism leads people to drop out ("if you don't try, then you can't fail"), to procrastinate (in order to postpone coming to grips with one's imperfection), and to fall into the "winning is everything" syndrome (which makes people forget that "it's how you play the game" that is important). What we need to do is to combat the perfectionism syndrome by helping people develop the "courage to be imperfect."

At the same time, we need to be aware of a cultural norm that appears almost as an eleventh commandment: "Thou shalt not brag, because thou might become conceited, stuck up, and a snob." Unfortunately, many people have carried this to an extreme, where they are totally unable to recognize *any* of their strengths and good qualities. The modesty norm leads people to self-depreciating patterns (complete with kookie monster tapes) interpersonal relationships based on one-downsmanship (complete with killer phrases). The need here is to help people acknowledge, accept, and build on their strengths and to learn from their successes. Ultimately, this would lead people to believe and live by the following quotation: "You don't have to blow out someone else's candle to make yours grow brighter."

Atmosphere

We have confidence that you can identify many ingredients of a "nurturing atmosphere." Take some time now to do a memory scan of part of your own life. What are some occasions, times, places, or experiences in which you have flourished, grown, reached towards your potential? What was it like then? What in the environment/atmosphere contributed to your growth and self-esteem? Jot down some of the characteristics of the environment that you found nourishing:

In drawing on our own experience, we have also created a picture of a self-enhancing atmosphere. We invite you to expand your own picture by considering the following necessary, but not sufficient factors, which are ways of operationalizing the four attitudes presented in the last section:

(1) Success-full: Opportunities to succeed, to engage in risk taking, and to set important goals in taking on challenges are important elements in building feelings of success. If we maximize the chance of success for each individual, then we will have more "success stories."

(2) Respect: An environment that is full of wonder and that appreciates the dignity of the individual is a vital environment—and is vital to enhancing self-esteem.

(3) Comfort and Caring: Caring, mutual support, empathic listening, and genuineness are at the heart of enhancing self-esteem. If a person feels safe (physically and psychologically), if a person feels comfortable (able to comfort others and to be comforted), if a person trusts (self and others), then that person will be more likely to take risks and to support others as they take risks in growing.

(4) Democracy: It is important that democracy not be a "spectator sport" in our schools, camps, and homes. For us, democracy connotes shared decision making, having a sense of control over your own destiny, co-operation, pluralism, and equity. It seems clear that if people have chances to make choices freely, to make collaborative decisions, and to have some control over their destiny that they, in turn, will develop a greater sense of worth, belonging, and agency.

(5) Unconditional Positive Regard: We need to create an atmosphere in which people are appreciated for who they are, not what they ought to be. This has important implications for those of us who work with young people—we need to care by taking care not to impose our needs, values, and "should's" or "ought to's" on them.

(6) Touching Experiences: It makes sense to us to use common sense, that is, the common sense of touch to help people reach out to one another. We need to move gently, yet firmly, in this area—inviting people to literally and figuratively "get in touch" with one another. It could be as simple as a teacher making it a point to shake the hand of each student as she/he arrives in the morning, or the camp counselor placing a hand on the shoulder of a camper who is having difficulty.

(7) Making Lemonade: One of our favorite quotes is: "If life hands you a lemon, squeeze it, and make lemonade." What this means is that we need to avoid dwelling on mistakes, on the negative—and move on to focusing and acting on the positive.

(8) Different Strokes: Different people learn in different ways. Self-esteem is learned. Therefore, different people learn self-esteem in different ways. One implication of this inference is that the self-enhancing environment could be a "variety show," in which the pacing and spacing are varied, and in which people have opportunities to work and learn in different arenas (e.g., individual work, small group work, large group work).

(9) You + More: We find it helpful to take ourselves with a grain of salt. Humor frees our attention and frees us to appreciate ourselves more. Nourishing humor can be an excellent vehicle to help you feel more self-esteem, energy, creativity, and connectedness with others. We aim to create an atmosphere that is light and lively, informal, and filled with laughter.

(10) Encouragement: Encouragement is any action or statement that shows respect, trust, and faith in the person and his/her abilities, worth, and dignity as a human being. Encouragement emphasizes the process of

learning, at least as much as the product. Encouragement focuses on what a person can do, rather than what she/he cannot do—the glass of water is three-fourths full, rather than one-fourth empty. We look for the donut, not the hole.

We encourage you to play around with these ten guidelines—in doing so, you will be playing with a full deck in creating nourishing environments.

Activities

Each activity presented in this section is a way of putting into practice the attitudes and atmosphere described in the previous sections. They will help us to head in one (or more) of the directions on our self-esteem compasses:

(1) Helping people to develop self-confidence and self-competence;
(2) Helping people to identify and build on their successes and strengths in moving to actualize their dreams and goals;
(3) Helping people to develop a sense of worth (identity), belonging (connectedness), and agency (power)

These activities have been used and can be used in a wide variety of settings—schools, camps, with friends, and at the family dinner table. We invite you to adapt them for your use in other settings, too.

#1—The Magic Lamp

The Magic Lamp is a pantomime activity in which the participants act out one of their favorite activities or the thing they are good at doing. An imaginary genie's lamp is rubbed as each person in turn acts out something. When someone in the group thinks they know what the favorite activity or thing the person is good at doing is, he or she joins in silently and acts out the same activity, but extends the movements so that the originator of the idea knows that the activity has been guessed.

For some participants, this game presents problems because they can't think of their favorite activity or sometimes can't think of something they are good at doing. If this occurs, others in the group can whisper suggestions to the person. The game could become more complex if the participants act out something that individual staff members do well and then ask the group to guess who that action belongs to.

Further modifications of the game include acting out favorite animals, program activities, or any other category selected.

#2—Plaque, Not Flak

We have observed that people usually receive far more flak than plaques—even though the plaques are richly deserved. This exercise involves a "field trip"—venture outside and try to find something in the world of nature that would serve as a "plaque to yourself"—something that you could put up in your office, home, classroom, or camp cabin to remind you that you are lovable and capable. A variation of this would be for you to search for an appropriate "plaque" for someone else—a friend, a family member, a cabin-mate, a teacher, etc. This might even develop into a "good habit"—exchanging plaques with one another, rather than flak.

#3—Food for Thought

This exercise consists of two parts: a provocative stimulus (e.g., a quote from a book or newspaper, a film strip, a song, a picture, etc.) followed by a series of thought-provoking questions (which all have a form of the word "you" in them, and are nonmoralizing—there is no one "right answer" to the questions). We offer you a sample Food for Thought sheet which focuses on self-esteem—we hope it whets your appetite so that you will create your own. You can process Food for Thought sheets either individually (e.g., place them in a personal journal) and/or with others (their ideas might give you additional food for thought).

The human being is made up of oxygen, nitrogen, phosphorus, hydrogen, carbon, and calcium. There are also twelve and one-half gallons of water, enough iron to make a small nail, about a salt shaker full of salt, and enough sugar to make one small cube. If one were to put all of this together and try to sell it, the whole thing would be worth about one dollar.

(1) Do you believe that you are worth more than one dollar? Explain.
(2) When do you feel most worthwhile? With whom do you feel most worthwhile?
(3) Can you think of some ways to help others feel more worthwhile?
(4) Some people feel that they are not worth even a dollar. Do you have any ideas about how you might respond to them?
(5) If you were to create an advertisement that proclaimed your resources and strengths, what would it say?

#4—Self-Metaphors[5]

Metaphors are powerful tools which we can use to enjoy new and creative perspectives on ourselves and our world. This exercise seeks to help you reinforce feelings of "I like me" by asking you to complete an "I am like a _____ because . . ." statement. In essence, you have a chance to write a positive self-metaphor: what do you *like* about yourself, and what from the world of nature is *like* you? We have listed some responses from adults and young people who have done this—to give you some of the delightful flavor of this exercise.

I am like the edelweiss that grows high upon the mountain. People have to dare and risk hazardous trails to reach me. I grow above the tree line, in the soft spots between the rocks, in the cold air of eternal winter. But my petals, though strong as leather, are as soft as velvet for those who reach me.

I'm a leaf. Time brings about change. Sometimes I'm a leaf among many leaves. Life is full. The trees are in bloom. So am I. A part of it all. Fall is inevitable. At times I fall from the tree. Parting. Leaving.

Winter and I'm gone. The time when I still exist. Somewhere. But not where I can be easily seen. Spring comes. With warmth. And sun. And joy. And I grow and come out again.

I am a stream—I have a surface that everyone can see. But there are many things going on underneath that surface. I am one stream—within that stream are many different currents which flow at different speeds and in different directions. I hope to get in touch with my own flow.

I am like the wind. I can be as noticeable as a hurricane or as unassuming as a light breeze. I can go anywhere. It's my choice. People are concerned about me and like to hear the daily forecast, yet I'm unpredictable and like myself that way.

I am like a storm in the sense that I will work fast and furious for a given length of time on a certain task—and then die out and do almost nothing for a while. During periods of activity, I begin slowly, work gradually up to a fever pitch, push the project to completion, and then disappear from it altogether.

I am like a skateboard. My colors are sometimes bright and fascinating. Other times, I am colored in subdued hues. My wheels take me to many places at so many different speeds—weaving, turning, spinning. Sometimes, I just like to move quietly and slowly, my wheels hardly turning. I love to take people for a ride, even though they knock me over sometimes.

I am a volcano—sometimes I lie dormant, other times I erupt. I can get angry and erupt with red hot lava. Even when I am dormant, a lot of bubbling and turmoil is going on inside me. I am somewhat predictable and most of the time I am stable, just standing there. I try to take things in rather than erupt, but sometimes I can't take any more and have to shout back. I am part of the earth, which is always changing.

#5—Meeting of the Metaphors

The word "validation" is an important one for us. Validation involves accepting and appreciating yourself and others. If you don't receive enough validation, then you run the risk of becoming an (self-esteem) in-valid. Self-metaphors provide a vehicle for us to validate ourselves. We can springboard off that exercise, and call a meeting of the metaphors if we want to practice validating others.

The way it works is: you get together with others who have written self-metaphors. Everyone puts his/her self-metaphor in a pile. The metaphors are "shuffled," and then each person picks one. Take some time now to write a response, a validating response to this person's self-metaphor. Your validation should reflect empathic listening/reading on your part—try to express ways that you support, identify with, and/or appreciate this other person. Respond as if you are talking directly to the metaphor itself. When everyone has finished, put the papers back in the pile. Each person can then fish out his/her original metaphor.

Variations of this exercise include: having more than one person respond to each self-metaphor and having people read the self-metaphors and responses aloud to the whole group (some people are willing to take a bit more risk by guessing who wrote the metaphor and the response). We encourage you to evolve your own variations. In any case, the intent of this exercise is to help people to feel listened-to and validated, to help people build their validation muscles, and to provide a chance for people to be response-able. Below are the responses that were given to the self-metaphors above:

Dear Edelweiss,
   You sound worth reaching. You seem to have a nice combination of strength, support, and beauty. As a caterpiller, methinks I would enjoy hiking (or when I'm older, flying) up to meet you.

Happy Fall, Caterpiller

Dear Leaf,
   I sense a combination of moods in your poem. A concern with change from happy to sad, from sad to happy. I'm glad that after "falling off" and hibernating, you "come out again." I too am like a leaf. I think many of us are. Let's create our own Spring.

In spirit, The Stream

P.S. If you need a ride, you can float on me.

Dear Stream,
   It must be exciting to be a stream, to have the different speeds and directions to pick from. To choose what fills your needs, when you are needing. Getting in touch with your flow probably will make you more aware of what choices you have . . .

Smooth flowing! The Cocoon

Dear Wind,
   I enjoy the feeling your description of yourself imparts to me. I can feel your looseness and freedom and good feeling about yourself. You seem spontaneous and open and happy and have a clear understanding of yourself and your relationship to others. I like you, too.

Love, The Shoe

Dear Storm,
   I admire your task-orientation. Further, I can sympathize with your dormant periods. One who works at a fever pitch must also at times rest and replenish his stores of energy.

Sincerely, The Bee

Dear Skateboard,
   I admire your variety. It must be fun to be like the rainbow. Having the opportunity to be a variety of colors is so exciting. Traveling and seeing so many things is so adventurous. How much knowledge and fun you must have gained. You're lucky that you experience so many feelings. Weaving, turning, spinning, and then for the more passive end of it, going quietly and slowly. I'm glad, too, that you can handle people's indifference as well as their respect.

Have fun! The Fire

LESSER

Dear Volcano,

I, too, have sometimes felt blocked and then must explode or die, I think. Volcanoes can be a creative force—the islands of the Pacific are all formed by volcanoes, and think of Mt. Fuji—that volcano must have inspired thousands of paintings and poems. Can this frustration bubbling within you be used to motivate you to control some of the forces angering you? Can you decide to communicate your distress when you first feel it—not be afraid to reveal this inner you? Then, maybe your potential will flow more freely like lava.

With love, Afghan

#6—Validation Tag

Here's another exercise to limber up your validation muscles in a group setting. The object of this game is for everyone to get tagged—that is, to get tagged with a validation. One person starts off as the "tagger" (we try to avoid using the word "it"—"it" is such a de-personalizing word). The "taggees" start to run—in slow motion. When the tagger hooks up with a taggee, everyone freezes and listens to the tagger's validation of the taggee. The taggee then assumes the tagger's role and looks for another person to tag with a validation. The game ends when each person has had a chance to be tagger and taggee.

#7—Gift Giving

This activity is a good way to build on "I'm Okay, You're Okay" feelings. Divide a sheet of paper into ten columns: (1) in the first column, list ten persons who are very close to you—people who touch your life frequently and/or intimately; (2) note the last gift you have given each person—if you have not given a person a gift, then write "none"; (3) in this column, make note of a "gift" you think each person on your list has (e.g., ability to do carpentry work, wonderful sense of humor, easy-going, etc.); (4) what metaphor—what in the world of nature—would symbolize the "gift" in column three (e.g., carpentry work—a beaver; sense of humor—a monkey; easy-going—a leaf fluttering in the air); (5) list a "gift" that you would like to give each person (e.g., being able to listen better) learning to laugh more easily, being able to "flow" with what's happening); (6) here is a chance for you to choose a natural metaphor that would represent the "gift" in the previous column (e.g., listen better—rabbit ears; laugh more easily—a hyena; being able to flow—a stream); (7) note the gift that each person on your list might see in you (this is the flip side of the third column); (8) what metaphors would capture the essence of each of these gifts listed in the preceding column; (9) if you had to make a guess, what do you think each person would wish you had more of in your life; (10) what metaphorical gift could they offer you that would communicate the wishes in the ninth column?

This exercise helps you to generate a great deal of data about what gifts you have (strengths and successes) and what gifts you would like to receive (dreams and goals), about what gifts others have (validating them), and what gifts you might want to give. In looking at the mass of data, what clues emerge as to how to make gift-giving more meaningful in your life? What are your first steps?

How much joy can come from giving a gift that is valuable to the receiver, and from receiving a gift that you value. Indeed, the joy can be in both the giving and receiving. We present this ten-column grid as a gift to you—to deca the halls of your own life.

#8—Inquiring Reporter

Questions are powerful tools. We can use them to "get to the bottom of things"—to dig beneath the avalanche of killer phrases in order to uncover our strengths and successes.

Take some time now—either by yourself or with others—to brainstorm as many questions as you can think of that would invite a person to discover his/her "positive side." When you have finished, sort through your list and pick out four favorite questions for evoking a postive response—these could be the ones that would help a person to see him/herself in a new positive light, ones that would highlight his/her significant strengths and successes, or ones that seem to capture several strengths at once.

Now, what can you do with these questions? That's a good question. Here are some options: (1) Why not conduct a self-interview? Ask youself the very questions which you have generated. Who knows—this might even turn into an ongoing self-validating habit in your life; (2) In a group setting (e.g., classroom, cabin meeting, family room, staff meeting, etc.), take time to interview as many people as you can—using the questions you have chosen. This could be accomplished by having people informally milling around or by having a more structured environment (e.g., in pairs, each person serves as the interviewer for five minutes, and then is interviewed for five minutes—after which, everyone would change partners); or (3) It might be interesting to conduct some person-on-the-street interviews—either with people you know well and/or with acquaintances.

You might be interested in a couple of nine-year-olds who used this positive-inquiring-reporter idea in a neighborhood newspaper which they published for over 200 subscribers. Here are a few of the questions they asked to help people focus on the positive side of their lives—and the responses from their peers:

Q: What is your favorite hobby? Why?

A: Making models, like boats and airplanes. I think it's interesting and it requires skill. It's something to be proud of when you're through.
A: Carving is my hobby, because I like to create things.
A: Archery—it's fun, it helps me physically and mentally.
A: Art is my favorite, because I like to use my fingers.
A: Collecting fossils and shells. They're interesting to study.
A: Horseback riding—because I like horses.

Q: Where would you like to go on your ideal vacation? Why?

A: I would like to go to Florida, because my grandmother lives there.
A: Washington, D.C.—my best friends are there.
A: Camp—because I want to go waterskiing.
A: Somewhere in Europe, because I've never been there before and I think it would be interesting.
A: Spain—I've learned the Spanish language, and I think it's very interesting.
A: Disneyland—because I've read a lot about it, and it's exciting.

Although these questions are seemingly simple, they are not simplistic. They invite people to focus on their strengths, interests, and goals. Here are some additional questions—these were generated by a group of teenagers with whom we worked:

(1) What do you like to do?
(2) What are your favorite possessions?
(3) What do you value more than anything else?
(4) What kind of lifestyle do you think you will follow?
(5) What is your philosophy of life?
(6) If you only had three minutes to give your autobiography, what would you say?
(7) What type of personal ideals do you hold?
(8) Who do you most admire?
(9) What makes you laugh?
(10) What beautiful thing have you done for someone?
(11) What makes you happy?
(12) Tell me about the person(s) you care for the most.
(13) What do you want to be when you grow up?
(14) What's your favorite part of people?
(15) I was the happiest person in the world when I . . .
(16) What do you like about yourself?
(17) What was the highlight of the last week for you?
(18) What dreams do you have?
(19) What helps to bring you up?

(20) Have you been doing anything interesting or fun?
(21) What metaphor would describe how you see yourself in the past few weeks?
(22) What is unique about you?
(23) If you could watch a movie of yourself in the last two weeks, what would you like about it? What might you change?
(24) What's been the most consequential, long-reaching thing you've done lately?
(25) Where would you like to live?
(26) What are ten things you most like to do?
(27) Who do you love?
(28) Who loves you?
(29) What do you do for recreation and relaxation?
(30) What do you look for in a good friend?

The role of the inquiring reporter is crucial in this exercise. The interviews will maximize positive sharing and growth if the reporter: (1) listens emphatically—honestly and warmly, letting the respondent know that this is not a hit-and-run job; (2) gives the respondent space—by this, we mean that the person being interviewed has a right to respond and a right *not* to respond (to pass on any question); (3) encourages the respondent to focus on the postive—killer phrases and the kookie monster are out of the question in this exercise.

We have used the postive questions generated by students and campers as the heart of numerous curriculum units and lessons. Again, it is such a simple—but revolutionary—idea that young people will have more energy, motivation, and commitment to working on questions that come out of and that affect their own lives. That is the power of a good question—it has a way of hooking people's interest.

#9—You Asked for It

What you are going to get is an interview—if you ask for it. We know of many teachers, camp leaders, and parents who springboard off the Inquiring Reporter by establishing the postive interview as a recyclable ritual.

For instance, Mary Ann Baker, a second grade teacher in Edgemont, New York, schedules interviews on a regular basis. Students volunteer to be interviewed by their peers by signing up on a schedule. The interviewee assumes a focal position in the room, and then responds to (or passes on) the questions from his/her classmates. When the interviewee chooses to end the session, he/she simply says, "Thank you for your questions." The questions are all aimed at values and value—helping the interviewee to clarify what he/she values and supporting the interviewee in seeing his/her own value.

We have also worked with groups of adults and groups of adults and young people together in which interviewing takes place in pairs or in quartets (in addition to the large group format). Following the interview, we find a review to be a nice way of reaching closure—a review of what the interview likes/appreciates about the interviewee and what he/she said. When done in a large group, this kind of "strength bombardment" can be very reinforcing.

Here are some potential interview questions generated by a group of adults with whom we worked. We invite you to use these—or better yet, to create your own. We hope these questions whet your appetite for making the family dinner table, the classroom, the camp cabin, or the office more nourishing places to be.

(1) When are you happiest in your job?
(2) What makes you feel successful?
(3) What would make you happier?
(4) What is important in the innersphere of your life?
(5) What inspires you? When was the last time you were inspired?
(6) Why did you decide to go into your work?
(7) What do you do for leisure? What do you enjoy about that?
(8) What do you feel you are doing to better this world?
(9) What do you want to do with your life?
(10) Who are some people who have positively influenced you?
(11) If you could change your age, what age would you be?
(12) What is one thing you like about yourself?
(13) What would you do if you won the lottery?
(14) What is one wish that you have?
(15) What do you see yourself doing five years from now?
(16) Are there some things that you do now that you would like to change?
(17) When you are at home and no one else is there, what do you really like to do?
(18) What kinds of vacations do you like?
(19) What are the good qualities of your job that make you enthusiastic?
(20) What do you like to do for fun?
(21) If you could do only one thing today, what would you do?
(22) Who/what was the guiding force in shaping your ideas about raising your children?
(23) If you had one day left to live, what would be the first thing you would want to accomplish?
(24) Who do you admire? What values do they have that you think are important?
(25) What is the best time of day for you? Why?
(26) Who are you?
(27) What do you feel is the most important part of parenting?
(28) How would you personally define success?
(29) What has been the most important event in your life?
(30) What quality in yourself would you like to see in others? (generated by participants in a graduate course at Bowling Green State University)

Postive interviews can lead to positive intraviews—everyone can have the feeling of being on "meet the prez." If you elect to "meet the press" in your family, school, camp, or job, then you may very well become the "prez-elect." Do you want to have a self-esteem inauguration? Give yourself a vote of confidence today.

"If one advances confidently in the direction of his dreams and endeavors to live the life which he has imagined, he will meet with a success unexpected in common hours." (THOREAU)

#10—Can and Able

Here is an opportunity for you to gain confidence in your competence. Divide a sheet of paper in half—on the left, make a list of all the things you *can* do. Brainstorm—and post a "no trespassing" sign for the kookie monster. Now, fold the sheet over, so that only the right side shows. Give the paper to another person, and ask him/her to make a list of all of your *abilities* of which they are aware. At the same time, you could generate a list of -able words for your partner (e.g., lovable, enjoyable, music-able, sports-able, etc.).

It might prove interesting for you to compare your list of "can" and "able" words. What do the lists tell you about yourself? Are there any strengths that were hidden from you that your partner was able to see? Sometimes, it helps to have another person to point out or confirm our strengths—confirmation can lead to self-affirmation.

#11—Collage Degree

One way to legitimize your incredible competence is to give yourself a credible collage degree. This exercise makes use of the collage as a creative medium for patting you on the back. The only treble (sic) with collages is that some people are tired of the ol' magazine cut-and-paste route. So, for this exercise, we will strike a different note—be natural.

Go on a solo hike through your environment. Collect objects from the world of nature that reflect your cans and ables. These objects will serve as the instruments—take some time to orchestrate them into a collage. The end product could serve as your collage degree. It might be fun for others to try to guess what competencies your collage symbol-izes. This could even turn into an enjoyable guessing game—a la name that tune—a sharp way to drum up support for yourself and your strengths.

#12—Home Sweet Home

Here is a way for you to explore your own immediate environment—an opportunity to do a scavenger hunt for clues as to what enhances your self esteem. Draw a map of your local environment (it could be of an area as small as your home, or of an area as large as your neighborhood). Do not worry if your map does not look like the official Rand McNally version—just as long as you can understand it.

Take some time now to place the following symbols on your map: (1) a " + " next to the spot(s) where you feel nourished, where you feel yourself to be most lovable and capable (if you wish, you could even put sub-symbols—e.g., " + W" for where you feel a sense of worth, " + B" for where you feel a sense of belonging, and " + A" for where you feel a sense of agency); (2) a "T" for where you spend most of your time; (3) an "X" would mark the spot(s) which you would like to explore in more depth; (4) a "G" for those areas in which you give a lot of yourself, in which you give/ support/nourish others; (5) an "M" in the places where you would like to see more nourishment for yourself; (6) an "H" on the spot where you experienced a high point in the past week; (7) a "T" for those places which are toxic to you.

Here are some questions to guide your study of the map and symbols above—we hope they will aid you in tracking down ways of enhancing self-esteem: (a) In looking at the symbols you have placed, do any patterns emerge? What do the patterns tell you?; (b) What characterizes the spots where you have placed " + 's"?; (c) Are there ways you can re-arrange your life so that you could spend more time in the " + " places?"; (d) Is there anything you can do to affect the environment in the places where you placed an "M" or a "T"?; (e) Will you choose to spend less time in the "M" and "T" places"?; (f) Is there anything you can do to make more "high points" occur for you in your life?; (g) What do you think would happen if you were to place a "G" in the areas where you have marked an "M" or "T" (in other words, if you sought to reach out to others and offer them nourishment)?; (h) What does "home" mean to you?; (i) What helps you to feel "at home"—with yourself and others?; (j) How does your map compare with others who share the same environment with you—do any patterns emerge in looking at each other's maps? Are there any goals you want to address as a group?

This exercise seeks to put the cart-ography before the horse—we hope that your map will help you to create environments that will enhance self-esteem. We think that this lesson in top-ography will pay off—in helping you to feel "on top of things."

BROWN

#13—You-Turn

We turn now to an activity that will help you to focus on your dreams and goals. As you look ahead to them, we also encourage you to use your rear-view mirror—to learn from and build on the turning points in your life to date. Inevitably, up the road "a piece," you will encounter choice points and potential turning points. Learning from your past mistakes, and more importantly, from your past successes, may give you some clues about which way to turn.

> Two roads diverged in a yellow wood,
> And sorry I could not travel both
> And be one traveler, long I stood
> And looked down one as far as I could
> To where it bent in the undergrowth.
>
> Then took the other, as just as fair,
> And having perhaps the better claim
> Because it was grassy and wanted wear;
> Though as for that the passing there
> Had worn them really about the same.
>
> And both that morning equally lay
> In leaves no step had trodden black;
> Oh, I kept the first for another day;
> Yet knowing how way leads on to way,
> I doubted if I should ever come back.
>
> I shall be telling this with a sigh
> Somewhere ages and ages hence;
> Two roads diverged in a wood, and I—
> I took the one less traveled by,
> And that has made all the difference.
>   (Robert Frost)

In a sense, every moment of our lives is a potential turning point. Take some time to think about, write about, and/or discuss the following questions: (1) How many major turning points can you identify in your own life?; (2) What made them turning points—and what "trail markers" do they leave to help you identify future turning points?; (3) Did you know that they were turning points at that time—or only in hindsight?; (4) If you had to project, what choice points will you be facing in the future?; (5) What from your previous experience will help you when you encounter them?; (6) What might you begin to do now—or continue to do—to prepare for these future turning points?

The point around which this exercise turns is that you have control (and responsibility for) over what happens to you. You can be *conscious* and conscientious in taking charge of you and your life . . . we urge you to continue to engage in dream of consciousness exercises—you can make your own luck. This sense of agency is an important ingredient of self-esteem.

#14—Pollution Alert

This is an invitation for you to establish a tradition, a commitment to patrol and "clean up" the human environment. Your job, if you choose to accept it, Mr./Ms. Phelps, is to identify and weed out killer phrases, kookie monsters, and structures which are toxic to human growth. Your patrol may want to make a regular report to others on examples of human pollution which you have discovered.

You might record the number and kinds of put-down phrases that exist in a particular area (e.g., home, classroom, camp cabin, with friends). Note the effect the killer phrases have on the people who receive them and on the group as a whole. Perhaps you could even engage in an alternatives search to explore ways of avoiding/minimizing killer phrases.

#15—Moratorium on Bad Breath

Here is an action project that is very simple to understand, but probably very difficult to do. How long can you go without saying a killer phrase? How long can your group avoid uttering put-downs? How long can you go without hearing mutterings from your kookie monster? What we are asking you to do is to challenge yourself—to see how long you can hold your breath when it comes to levying killer or kookie monster phrases. This moratorium could be a matter of life and breath.

#16—You're Something to Brag About

One way to combat killer phrases and kookie monster phrases is to add humor to your life—by participating in a bragging practicum—a chance to salute yourself in raising your own brag. It may feel funny at first, and you may be bombarded by the kookie monster telling you not to root for yourself, but we encourage you to stick with it—to give it a fair chance, to give yourself a fair chance. We invite you to root, toot-toot your own horn.

Here is a good way to do it: the next time someone gives you a compliment/appreciation, take it in (rather than fending it off or denying it), and say something like:

> "How perceptive of you to notice!"
> "Could you repeat that three times!"
> "And that's only one of my many strengths!"
> "I sure am a wonderful person!"
> "You're certainly fortunate to know me!"

We hope this action projects a-peals to you. Don't be surprised if it evokes peals of laughter from you—keep it coming—you can laugh all the way to the bank of self-esteem. Open up your humorous and playful savings account today—it will bring your self-esteem a great deal of interest.

#17—Plus Sign

This is a new sign of the times. In fact, we encourage you to use the plus sign three times. Here is how and when: the next time someone presents an idea (e.g., in a meeting, in a classroom, at a party) to you, try to think of three things you *like* about the idea *before* you allow yourself to think (or verbalize) anything negative. Again, this seems like such a simple idea, but it is one that can be very difficult to implement—no thanks to ingrained killer phrases.

Or, try this one on for size—the next time you think of an idea, generate three things you like about it before you allow yourself to kill it. This action project is good practice for those who would like to maintain a postive outlook—and to communicate that outlook to others. It is a way of looking-out for each other: sharing plusses can keep us from becoming non-plussed.

#18—World Book of Records

Another way of increasing your sense of agency (and hence, your self-esteem) is to set a record. Get a copy of *Guinness' World Book of Records*—look through it and pick a record you (and/or others) would like to challenge—or create your own challenge. Then go ahead and try to break the record. At the very least, it should be a novel experience. And if you are very successful, someone may even write a novel about your experience.

#19—Fametags

One way of helping people to focus on the positive is to turn nametags into fametags. Take a 5 x 8 card and print your name in big letters on it. For each letter in your name, identify at least one positive adjective that reflects an ability or quality you possess—these would be abilities or qualities for which you are "famous"—the ones that people will remember you by. Be sure to allow yourself the "luxury" of bragging. After completing your card, take some time to mill around with others—feel free to "tag" each other with additional positive adjectives.

#20—Ten You're

If you have tenure, then you have job security. If you receive "ten you're," then you will be more secure with yourself. Here is how this ritual works— each week, someone from your group is designated as "person of the week" (or "camper of the week," or "student of the day," etc.). Place a sheet of paper in a prominent place with a picture of the "person of the week" on it. Head the paper with a title like "Ten Things You're Good At" or "Ten Things We Like About You." During the week, anyone can sign up an appreciation at any time. Of course, the end result is that the person takes away from this ten commanding reminders of his/her lovability and capability. You and your group will probably want to come back for "seconds" on this nourishing course of action.

#21—Construction Paper

A popular myth in our culture is that people grow best through constructive criticism. Actually, "constructive criticism" is just a euphemism for negative feedback. It is our culture's way of legitimizing killer phrases. We would much prefer to build on people's strengths and successes, rather than to focus on their "weaknesses."

This ritual invites you to carry out the "ten you're" idea on a daily basis with everyone simultaneously. In this case, everyone puts up a sheet of "construction" paper with his/her name (or picture) on it. Anyone can place a validation on anyone else's sheet at anytime. You may also want to structure in some time specifically to work with the "construction" paper.

There are numerous variations of this activity. Some teachers, camp leaders, and parents we know have set up "validation envelopes" and "nice things boxes" for people to exchange appreciations.[6] Others have set up a postal system for delivery of "positive" letters between people. Another idea is to create bulletin boards with such themes as: "I'm proud to be me . . ." and "I like the way you . . ."

#22—MALS Book

We are all probably familiar (too familiar) with the age-old slam book— the book which is passed around from person to person—with each one writing disparaging remarks about the individual(s) being "slammed." How simple it would be to turn this into a pro-cedure, one in which only "pro" remarks would be made about a person. And what a surprise it would be to present the entire book to the person as a self esteem present. Do you like our pro-posal?

#23—You Are Resource-Full

We may not always see ourselves as "experts," but we certainly do have a lot of expertise. It is a crime to waste the resources within us. Here is a way to help yourself and others to tap these natural resources: hang up a shingle, set yourself up as a consultant on a particular topic or area. You can "learn as you go"—teaching others is one of the best ways of learning for yourself.

In order to help students increase their sense of competence, one teacher we know asked her students to set up a placard on their desks announcing an area or skill which he/she saw as an area of expertise—one on which he/she would be willing to serve as a consultant to other students. Of course, a student was free to change the placard at any time.

This structure led to many beautiful "each one, teach one" situations. Not only did it help students to feel more competent, it also had the fringe benefit of encouraging cooperation and peer teaching in such areas as: math skills, writing skills, reading, athletic skills, and drawing horseheads. Yes, drawing horseheads—each student was able to carve out his/her own bailiwick.

#24—Friendship Circles

Meals can be wonderful occasions for nourishment—physical, emotional, spiritual. You may eat as many as 75,000 meals in your life— that's a lot of opportunities for "food for thought." Friendship circles can "serve" a number of purposes—enhancing self-esteem and developing a sense of community.

There are several ways you can set the stage—and set the table—for your friendship circle. Some people start each meal by joining hands and taking a moment of silence. Others will have someone share a poem, song, or thought that is important to him/her. Another option would be to have a "theme" of the meal (perhaps one of the You Asked for It questions in Activity #9), which everyone could address.

What other ideas can you cook up for friendship circles, for making meals meaning-full experiences (as opposed to eat-and-runs)? What courses do you want to prepare as a self-esteem gourmet? Wouldn't it be nice if every meal—all 75,000 of 'em—could be a testimonial dinner/lunch/breakfast—a testimonial to you and those sharing your table?

#25—Weekly Pro-Action Sheet

One of the strategies from the field of values clarification is called "the weekly reaction sheet." This strategy invites people to inventory their values as they react to the previous week. We would like to present a complementary ritual—the weekly pro-action sheet.

Here, you have an opportunity to inventory the positive actions you took in the past week and to set goals for positive behaviors in the upcoming week. We posit that it would be a positive experience for you to share what you have written with others. You may also be able to draw some interesting conclusions by looking for patterns in your sheets every month. Sometimes you can "make a difference" by identifying similarities.

We encourage you to create your own weekly pro-action sheet. You might want to springboard off the following kinds of items:

(1) Ten things I did last week that I feel good about . . .
(2) Three people who helped me feel more lovable . . .
(3) Three people who helped me feel more capable . . .
(4) Three people I helped to feel more lovable . . .
(5) Three people I helped to feel more capable . . .
(6) What others did to help me feel more lovable/capable . . .
(7) What I did to help others feel more lovable/capable . . .
(8) The high point of the week for me . . .
(9) My autobiography for the past week . . .
(10) One thing I would like to work on/get better at . . .
(11) A success/achievement/accomplishment for me in the past week . . .
(12) In the past week, if I had received a telegram that would have made me feel really good, who would it have been from and what would it have said . . .
(13) If I had an Aladdin's Lamp last week and could have made three wishes . . .
(14) Two ways I celebrated last week . . .
(15) One value I acted on in the past week . . .
(16) One value I would like to act on in the next week . . .
(17) In the past week, I was like a _____ *(metaphor)* _____ because . . .
(18) Last week, I wondered . . .
(19) My favorite "direction" in the past week was . . .
(20) Last week, I felt confident when . . .
(21) Last week, I felt competent when . . .
(22) Last week I felt close to people when . . .
(23) If I had had the last week "off" (with no responsibility), I would have . . .
(24) One way I interrupted a killer phrase . . .
(25) I have a dream . . .

#26—Comfort and Caring

Every single meeting, class, or workshop which we facilitate begins with "comfort and caring." This is a structured time set aside to deal with questions related to the comfort and caring of group members. People may raise questions ranging from "Where are the bathrooms?" to "When will we begin eating lunch?" to "Can somebody give me a ride home after the meeting?" to "Can I stay at someone's home after the workshop session today?"

Comfort and caring is a vital ritual—without it, we run the risk of having people stuck at the bottom of Maslow's need hierarchy: so concerned with physical and security issues that they do not have the attention to learn and grow and share with others. Comfort and caring is free—and it frees people up to participate actively and to move towards what Maslow calls "self-actualization."

#27—Validation Circles

Here is an opportunity for you to add-lib: adding to your self-esteem can be a liberating experience. Have the people in your group (e.g., class, camp cabin, family, office) form a circle. Each person, in turn (who wants a turn—the "pass" option holds here), gives a validation (to self or others) in twenty-five words or less. There are no comments or discussion—the validation circle is a moving experience—it moves quickly from one person to the next. You may choose to leave the validations open-ended, or to provide people with more structured (e.g., complete "I am proud that I . . ." "One thing I appreciate about _____ is . . ." etc.).

With younger children, we sometimes find it helpful to introduce this ritual by suggesting that they are leaning in the right direction for this exercise if they:

Listen exquisitely well
Each one who wants a turn can have one (also the right to pass)
Accept what others say (defer discussion)
No killer phrases or kookie monsters allowed on the premises

After everyone has had a turn, you may find it helpful to have someone in the group sum up the sharings—this can reinforce the listening norm.

#28—Do Your Own Think

We sometimes call this ritual "status quo-tations." That is because we place much value/status in using quotations as thought-provokers, feeling-provokers, and action-provokers. You might like to set up a "quotes wall" in the room, and encourage participants to create a quotes quilt relating to self-esteem.

You might choose to start your quilt by drawing from the quotes interwoven throughout this book. Or, the quotes that follow may give you some mind food. Of course, we encourage you to do your own think—to think up your own quotes and add them to the quilt.

To try and fail is at least to learn; to fail to try is to suffer the inestimable loss of what might have been. *(Chester Barnard)*

Just as we can throttle our imagination, we can likewise accelerate it. *(Alex Osborn)*

An oak is a nut that held its ground.

Behold the turtle—he only makes progress when he sticks his neck out.

Failure is the line of least persistence. *(Alfred Brandt)*

The best place to find a helping hand is at the end of your arm.

In the light of the influence of the self-concept on academic achievement, it would seem like a good idea for schools to follow the precept I saw printed on an automobile drag-strip racing program: "Every effort is made to ensure that each entry has a reasonable chance of victory." *(William Purkey)*

Luck is the residue of design. *(Branch Rickey)*

The surest way to corrupt a youth is to instruct him to hold in higher esteem those who think alike than those who think differently. *(Nietzsche)*

We found each other and we are beautiful/and/you go your way/and/ I go my way/You are not in this world to go my way/and/I am not in this world to go your way/You do not stand still/and/I do not stand still/and/If by chance or plan we meet again/LET US BE NOW! *(Dick Krajeski)*

People are like tea bags—they don't know their own strength until they get in hot water.

There are no errors when the game isn't played—but also no hits or runs either.

Fear will make people do great things. Love allows them to do the impossible.

If you hope to be somebody, be yourself.

There are no strangers in the world—only friends you have yet to meet.

Wishing doesn't make it happen, but it won't happen if you don't wish.

It takes 13 muscles to smile, 54 muscles to frown.

You'd better not compromise yourself—it's all you got. *(Janis Joplin)*

He who's not busy being born, is busy dying. *(Bob Dylan)*

I have never met a man who has given me as much trouble as myself. *(D. L. Moody)*

In a mirror, everyone sees his/her best friend.

Human beings can alter their lives by altering their attitudes of mind. *(William James)*

#29—Inverse Paranoid Projects

Here are some unique and enjoyable action projects that aim to create more inverse paranoids in the world—people who think the world is out to do them good. By creating some positive self-fulfilling prophecies, we can aid people in developing their own and others' self-esteem.

It might be helpful to have "teams" of people who carry out each project. They could then get together afterwards, and discuss their own and other people's reactions and learnings from the project. Here is a taste of some positive seed-planting activities you could undertake:

(1) Verbally validate (appreciate) five or more people in your school, camp or program;

(2) Plan a meal for someone new (to your school, camp, or program);

(3) Find in your wallet one symbol of a "success" you've had—and see what others have found in their wallets;

(4) Clip out or draw a cartoon that you think will make someone laugh— and give it or send it to that person;

(5) Send a special greeting card to someone who might not expect one from you;

(6) Write a letter to the local newspaper (or school or camp paper) commending somebody for doing something good;

(7) Do something nice for someone and keep it a secret;

(8) The next time someone brings up a new idea in a discussion, try to say "yes, and . . ." rather than "yes, but . . .";

(9) Sing or play a recording of your favorite song to someone;

(10) On the turnpike, pay the toll for the car in back of you;

(11) Give an apple to a toll collector;

(12) In a classroom, build in a ritual for a "secret friend" or "secret Santa";

(13) Send someone an anonymous positive note;

(14) Say hello to ten strangers in one day;

(15) Help carry packages at the grocery store—for free;

(16) Throw a surprise "unbirthday" party for someone you know;

(17) Make one positive phone call per day;

(18) Say "thanks" five times each day;

(19) During a conversation with someone else, say "to be perfectly honest with you . . ."—and complete the sentence with something positive rather than negative;

(20) Have participants in your program lead activities which the staff would sign up to take;

(21) Bring in a favorite possession and keep it around for the year;

(22) Ask each participant to bring an article from the newspaper which contains some good news;

(23) Make a tape recording of everyone's individual contribution to the rest of the group—and then play it for them;

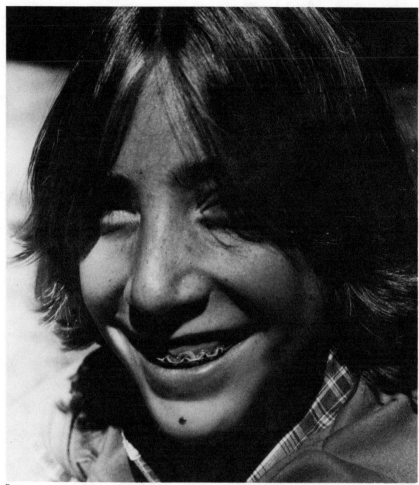

BROWN

(24) Have a special "good deeds" day in which the participants do helpful
things for others; and
(25) Create twenty-five more "inverse paranoid projects"—and carry them
out.

#30—Left-Handed Complements

When it comes time to say "good-bye" to people with whom you are
close (e.g., when camp ends for the summer, when the school year comes to
a close, when a visit from friends or relatives is over), you may want to find
a ritual that brings closure and that brings you closer to the people.

We have to hand it to you . . . our left-hand, that is. One light and lively
way of saying good-bye is to extend to each other left-handed complements.
Unlike left-handed compliments (which leave kookie monster crumbs all

over you), left-handed complements leave you feeling more complete.

If you gotta go, you gotta go. It's better to go feeling complete. So, extend yourself and your left-hand . . . while you are shaking hands left-handed, share an appreciation/validation with the other person that will leave him/her feeling more complete. Shaking left-handed may lead you to shake with laughter—sometimes it's fun to do things differently—it can play an important part in adding lightness to departures.

Footnotes

(1) As quoted in Donald Read, Sidney Simon, and Joel Goodman's *Health Education: the Search for Values*. Englewood Cliffs: Prentice-Hall, Inc., 1977.

(2) See Robert Hawley's *Composition for Personal Growth: Program Design and Evaluation*. University of Massachusetts, unpublished dissertation, 1972.

(3) Jack Canfield and Harold Wells, *100 Ways to Enhance Self-Concept in the Classroom*. Englewood Cliffs: Prentice-Hall, Inc., 1976.

(4) See William Purkey's *Self-Concept and School Achievement*. Englewood Cliffs: Prentice-Hall, Inc., 1970. Also, Ardyth Norem-Hebeisen's *Exploring Self-Esteem*. Saratoga Springs: NHEC, 1975.

(5) Adapted from Joel Goodman's (editor) *Turning Points: New Developments, New Directions in Values Clarification, Volume 1*. Saratoga Springs: Creative Resources Press, 1978.

(6) See *Health Education: The Search for Values* (footnote #1 above).

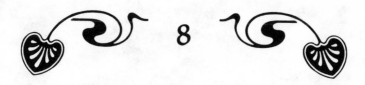

8

Adventure Learning: Personal and Group Challenges

The following case study takes the form of an interview between Joel Goodman and Jeff McKay. The discussion focuses on the principles and practical activities of adventure learning, as reflected in "Kids, Schools, and the School of Education," an undergraduate course at the University of Massachusetts. Jeff paints an intriguing picture of an ongoing course that uses adventure activities in the outdoors as the medium to integrate personal learning and professional applications (teacher training). In addition to presenting many helpful principles around which to organize such a course, he also provides details about specific activities to use. In fact, as a fun challenge, you might want to see if you can do a scavenger hunt in reading this interview and track down the following activities: Playpen; Stream Trust Walk; The Wall; Swinging Log; Beam; Spin the Stick; Electric Fence; Hug Tag; Flea Leap.

Jeff's course is a reflection of his attempts to synthesize experiential and humanistic education. His philosophy underlying the course is captured by Robert Frost:

> It takes all sorts of in and outdoor schooling
> To get adapted to my kind of fooling.

In the years that he has taught this course, Jeff has played around with many ideas. This interview provides an exciting look at the development, implementation, and evaluation of his experiential/humanistic synthesis, and challenges you to adapt and apply the principles and practice to your own situation.

Joel: I'm wondering, Jeff, if you could give us an example of an activity that might combine humanistic and experiential learning.

Jeff: One of the best ways for me to attempt to combine experiential and humanistic education is through the use of adventure games. These are

LESSER

activities which involve a group getting from point A to point B, over a wall, across a stream, or many other challenges.

For example, we have built a "playpen" at the University of Massachusetts. It's a series of posts sticking up from the ground, arranged in a circle. Some of the posts are straight up and others come up and then fork.

After asking people to pick a post, I define the purpose of the activity—for the group to get up on the posts. That involves some choice on the part of the participants. They need to decide which post to get on and whether to get up alone or with some assistance.

In many cases that kind of activity raises questions: "Why did I choose what I did?" "Did I help someone else?" "Did *I* need help? If so, how did I or could I have asked for help?" "How can I build cooperation in our group?"

Joel: From what you've been saying, several things jump out at me. One is that this actively involves people and the other is that people are given some choices. Participants are also given ways of learning from the experience by asking and answering questions. Can you give us some more details on the goals of adventure games?

Jeff: You mentioned some of the major purposes. Active learning is the key. It involves not only participating in the task, but also "spotting"—paying attention to other people so that they don't fall and get hurt.

It also involves participation in the sense of being aware of yourself and others. We've had people who could not physically participate for one reason or another who became involved just as much as those who were physically active.

The whole idea of choices is important. The participant needs to make choices: whether it be which post I choose to stand on; or—if we're working in pairs—which person I choose to work with; or, how I choose to go about negotiating an obstacle. If a particular experience brings up the question of who's talking and who's listening—then it's crucial to deal with that issue, rather than with some other issue that might be on my agenda, or something that has come up in the past with a different group but may not apply in this particular case. It's important to let the discussion spring from the activity.

The primary goal for me is to give people a chance to take a look at themselves through experience. I want them to look at how that experience and their view of themselves relate to their roles in teaching or working with others.

Joel: You're interested in a combination of personal and professional growth for people who are considering going into teaching.

I'm wondering how you came to choose humanistic education and experiential education as the two fields to synthesize.

Jeff: A couple of things happened pretty much at the same time. One was coming to the University of Massachusetts and getting involved in a variety of ways of looking at education, particularly, the humanistic education movement. I began to see some applications for myself as a teacher and a teacher-educator. At the same time, I became involved working with

Tunner Brosky, a teacher at the university who uses adventure games with prospective physical education teachers.

It struck me that what I was learning in humanistic education and what I was learning with Tunner had some connections. I see humanistic education as an effective way of helping people to take a look at themselves. It seems to be that to learn about the external world and not learn about oneself is not a full education.

Outdoor or experience-based education lends itself to a learn-by-doing approach.

I'm hoping that the participants in the course will get a strong experience in active learning—and also, an experience in reflecting upon and sharing their learning. I hope that if we can share those kinds of experiences as learners, then later, when many of these people go on to be teachers, they will be able to provide others with meaningful learning experiences .

Joel: I've certainly been influenced by my teachers; and their models have had an effect on the way I teach. Another goal that I'm picking up is the modeling that takes place by the facilitator of adventure games . . .

Could you elaborate on how your synthesis of humanistic education and experiential education might supplement either field individually? What does the sum of the parts have that either one of the individual parts doesn't?

Jeff: Humanistic education has been very good for me. It has been an enlightening process.

However, I have found at times, that some of my experiences with it have been lacking in reality. Sometimes they're too nice. Perhaps only half of the picture. That's a major concern for me about humanistic education.

As far as experiential education is concerned, I think that approach to learning sometimes lacks some of the softness that humanistic education has. For example, climbing a mountain—to stress only the challenge and conquering of the mountain—may neglect some of the quieter, more reflective aspects of the experience. At times, I've found my experiences in the out-of-doors too harsh.

I've felt the need to combine these approaches—to add some content and some reality to humanistic education; and to add humanistic and process approaches to outdoor experiences.

One activity many people may be familiar with is a trust or "blind" walk which is usually associated with the humanistic movement. One of the trust experiences we do in our course is traversing a log bridge across a stream. The reality of actually crossing a stream adds something to a trust walk. It makes it a real experience. If somebody falls, the consequences are getting wet or cold. That's real, not imagined or simulated. So that might be one example of adding the reality of outdoor experience to humanistic education.

Another example might be providing students with the challenge of getting up over a fourteen-foot wall. This is about as close to climbing a mountain as you can get without really climbing a mountain. I attempt to enhance the value of this activity by helping students reflect upon and share their experience . . . to ask questions and to facilitate sharing of the personal and interpersonal issues involved. That might be an example of how a humanistic process can add to outdoor experiential learning.

BROWN

Joel: You're providing "real life" experiences where there are some significant consequences. I can see how students would have an increased commitment and investment in their learning if they perceive it to be a "real life" adventure rather than a simulation.

What you seem to be saying is that the wall is your co-teacher. What you're doing is having the wall provide the stimulus, with you assuming the role of facilitator. You are the bridge between the stimulus and the participants by asking questions and helping students to make sense of their experience.

Jeff: Experience as teacher . . . At times I find myself losing track of that concept, but activities such as the wall continue to bring me back to realizing that there's not a lot that I can teach someone. There may be many experiences that I can provide that will give students an opportunity to learn. That does allow me to be a link between the wall and the participants and to help them participate in and, to some extent, interpret and integrate that experience into their own general frame of reference.

The wall as teacher . . . That metaphor has helped me to move in some directions that feel good to me. For example, in many cases the function of the teacher, as I see it, is first simply to present the learning experience. "Here's the wall. The task is to get the group over the wall." Secondly, I define the safety guidelines. For example, in an exercise such as the wall, it's important that no one hang from the top upside-down.

Over a period of a couple of years, using these kinds of experiences as vehicles for learning, I've learned something about how to teach in a way that feels better for me. One is that, in many cases, it may *not* be necessary for me as teacher to define the task. In some cases, the task either defines itself or the participants can define the task.

Last spring we were approaching what we call the swinging log. It's about twelve feet long and it hangs parallel to the ground—about a foot high. It's suspended from a couple of trees by ropes.

I had half a dozen different tasks that I gave the group to do—get up on the log as a group, get up on the log individually, get up on the log and jump off, etc. Those had all been fine learning experiences in the past. As we walked up to the swinging log, one of the women in the group said, "Hey, can we try something else?" It struck me at the moment that all I needed to do was back off and let the group define their own challenges. They came up with a number of different activities—both individual and group tasks.

That kind of spontaneity and creativity on the part of students excites me. It's the kind of learning that really benefits me as a teacher . . . I can learn from students.

What I talked about in the example of the swinging log is the students taking responsibility for their own learning by defining the task. It's also possible in some cases for the students to take responsibility for how we go about the task.

For example, with the wall, the normal process would be for me to define the safety guidelines, because, very clearly, the final responsibility for what happens rests on my shoulders. On the other hand, to the extent that I can involve the students in that responsibility, I think we're adding something to the course.

Another activity involves a beam which is about eight feet high. The task is for the group to get up over the beam and down to the ground on the other side.

One day, a student who had a particularly strong concern for safety and spotting said something about safety precautions. It occured to me that this person, because of his awareness of the need for safety, might have an insight or two that he could share with the group. I asked him to express his concerns; and he came up with some really good safety guidelines. That led to other members of the group expressing concerns about safety in general, and specific guidelines for how we negotiated the beam.

"Man cannot discover new oceans unless he has courage to lose sight of the shore." (ANDRE GIDE)

What I learned was that students, in many cases, have more going for them than we're willing to give them credit for. This particular group was quite capable of suggesting many important safety guidelines. As the one ultimately responsible, I would supplement their guidelines with any that they had missed.

The combination of students taking more responsibility for defining the learning experiences and for *how* we go about the learning experiences is a significant addition to the adventure approach to learning. What's exciting is that it's something I've learned from students as we have gone along.

Joel: Such a simple concept—that the student can also be a teacher. It's encouraging to hear you talking about that actually happening.

We often hear how important it is for students to take responsibility for their own learning. It often gets left at the rhetoric stage. It seems to me that the course you're involved in speaks to that very directly.

The notion of helping people learn how to learn is something that's translated in your course by having students define tasks and by having them establish the safety guidelines. I see some direct parallels between that and what could go on in classrooms. There's no reason why students couldn't have a part in establishing some of the classroom rules or guidelines—just as they can establish safety guidelines in an adventure learning course.

Another basic principle is that it doesn't make sense to cram a lot of information into students—especially before they've even asked the question.

Your course seems to help students create and participate in their own learning. They're the ones asking the questions, and out of that comes some motivation and interest in whatever it is they're going to learn.

Jeff: The phrase you used—that the student can also be a teacher—really gets at what education *can be* about. Teaching and learning are not processes that can be separated into two discrete roles.

For those who are going to be teachers, their experience as learners needs to include some experience in "teaching"—taking responsibility for what and how they learn.

The second phrase you mentioned that speaks to me is "learning how to learn." That's what it's all about. The kinds of skills that we, as teachers, need to provide for students are skills in problem solving, communication—the lifetime skills that are not only learning how to learn, but learning how to live. Those are not necessarily teachable in the traditional sense. They are, however, learnable.

Joel: The motto for your course, from what I've been picking up, could be "learning how to learn, learning how to live, learning how to teach." It seems to me the course encourages participants to take a look at themselves and their learning styles. It seems the course is also a vehicle for helping them to take a look at issues relating to teaching. Could you give an example of a typical class meeting?

Jeff: Yes. In any class meeting, it's important at the beginning to have some kind of experience which reestablishes our learning community. For example, we might play a game called Hug-Tag. Someone is "it" and everybody else tries to stay away from "it" by hugging each other. If you're hugging somebody, you're safe; but if you're moving from one person to another and you're alone, then you may get caught.

We also do an individual challenge in most classes—for example, jumping from one platform to another. We call that the Flea-Leap. Each individual "measures" the degree of risk—(for example, "Do I jump from the front or the back of the upper platform?") and then acts on that choice.

We also do an experience in a small group or in pairs, such as a variety of trust walks.

And then finally, some kind of all-group task which involves problem solving and initiative, such as getting over the wall.

Joel: Are there any other common threads that run through either a particular class or the entire course itself? Are there any "rituals" or traditions that you incorporate or that seem to emerge from the students?

Jeff: There are a variety of supplementary learning experiences: personal journals, a group log, readings, out-of-class experiences, and a major activity project. The purpose of all those parts is to integrate our experience in the course with some writing, reading, and outside experience.

For example, I ask students to keep a journal about their experiences each week. I'm interested in their actions, reactions, thoughts, and feelings. And, to a lesser extent, their observation of what went on in the group as a whole.

The group log is different. Each week one member of the group writes in a public group log. At the start of the next class, he reads his entry. I'm trying to promote an understanding that any individual's impression of what happened is true. If one person perceives an activity as x and other perceives an activity as y, that's fine. The message is that each person's perspective is valid.

Each week, I read (and I encourage students to read) a quotation or two that relates to our experience. For example, "If I give you a fish, you eat tonight. If I teach you to fish, you eat forever." The students enjoy the quotations, which often provide food for thought or a conceptual handle on our experience.

Joel: The group log seems to get at another of your principles: trying to get students out of the "right answer" syndrome.

Jeff: The right answer syndrome is a classic example of something worth unlearning. It comes up sooner or later, and in the middle, too. I've been asked many times: "How have other groups done this?" or "What's the best way to do it?" I do not answer that question, but respond, "What do you see as other ways of going about this task?" Occasionally, we'll do the same activity two different times in two different ways to help us see that there is no right answer. Gradually students become more comfortable with finding or creating a solution, and not necessarily "the" answer.

Joel: So there's more than one way to "skin the wall." That obviously has some implications for teaching, by helping people to expand their repertoire of teaching skills, and not getting stuck in the rut of "Here's the right way to teach a certain subject."

You've mentioned another medium to get across your message: assignments.

Jeff: One of the assignments we do is to spend some time with children outside of the classroom (e.g., ride the bus to and from school, attend recess, or eat lunch with children). My intent is to get students to look at learning a little bit out of the normal set or typical school environment. The other assignments are similar in that they are experiential (e.g., interviewing a student-teacher, attending a PTA meeting).

Finally, each student participates in a major activity project—volunteering at a mental hospital, serving as an assistant scoutmaster, working as a teacher's aide, etc. Once again, I hope the student will learn about education through actual involvement.

It's important that the student find his own activity project, rather than for me to set up an activity project for him. I give him some guidelines and possibilities, but it's his choice and responsibility. For some students that freedom of choice is difficult.

Joel: I would call that helping students to move from the "choose-one-of-the above" syndrome to "choose-one-*or*-none-of-the-above-and-create-your own."

Jeff: It goes back to the concept of un-learning. Let me talk about un-learning as it relates to these parts of the course.

For example, I'm aware that a weekly journal can become more of a "requirement" than a vehicle for learning. So I say: "At least once during the course, the log is going to be a burden rather than a learning experience; so don't do it." This surprises students a little. As I see it, *not* doing it is more valuable than doing it in that particular case.

I tell students that throwing a reading in the wastebasket is clearly irresponsible. On the other hand, reading it cover-to-cover because *I* gave it to them, or because it's a requirement of the course, is also irresponsible. So I ask them to start the reading and find out if it has any meaning for them. Also, to be aware if they're reading it for me or for the course. If they are reading it for me or the course, then they need to be aware of that and either work through it or lay the reading aside for a while. If, upon returning to the reading, the student still finds himself reading it for external reasons, it may be a learning experience for him *not* to read it.

I'm also interested in having students exercise some decision making regarding assignments. I say that if spending time with children on a bus or at lunch or recess doesn't have any personal meaning, then it's important to create an alternative learning experience. Over a period of time students start acting on those kinds of options, and that's exciting.

Joel: I personally agree with this approach. I can also imagine some teachers saying, "Hey, what are you doing? Are you saying that the assignments you give aren't important? Are you taking away the authority of the teacher using the assignment as a 'vehicle for motivation?'"

Jeff: One of the teachers who voices those kinds of concerns is me. It's very difficult for me at times to give students that kind of freedom. It raises the question, "Who's in charge here?" I recognize that. It is presumptuous to assume that, because something has meaning for me, it will have meaning for my students.

I don't see myself giving students the option to do *nothing*. I'm giving them the choice to do a, b, c, or a more meaningful experience of their own design. I ask them to check out that option with me if they have any questions or reservations about it.

Joel: You've given many details about the course components. Could you give a broader view of the fifteen-week course as a whole? How do you know what to put when and where and after what and for whom?

Jeff: For the first month of the course, we participate in a variety of experiences. I do not place much emphasis on educational issues. Rather I'm attempting to allow students the opportunity to experience many different learning activities and to talk about them. To the extent that those experiences raise issues, we deal with them.

Joel: What you're seeking to do at first is to get people actively involved and avoid intellectual head-tripping.

Jeff: Yes, I think that's necessary.

One concern I do emphasize, early in the course, is the concept of *un-learning*. For example, just recently in one of the classes, we were talking about different ways of learning. I said that one way to present adventure games would be for me to define the task, demonstrate or tell them how to solve the task, and then say, "OK, now go to it." One of the participants responded, "Yes, I know what you're saying, but if you had pulled that on us the first day, I don't think you'd have had any argument, because that's been our school experience."

That strikes me as a good example of why the concept and process of unlearning is necessary. As a teacher, I can unlearn a lot of my tendencies to tell students how to do it; and similarly, they can unlearn a lot of their experience which has said, "Teacher, tell us how to do it."

Joel: It appears that one of your major goals in the first part of the course is to have students change their "set"—not only of their role as students and the method in which learning is going to take place, but also of the role of the teacher. What you're trying to do is break them of the learning-by-rote method. You're trying to build in readiness, so that when you try a new approach, they're not going to tell you to "hit the rote" or ask you for the answers.

Jeff: I can give an example of altering our normal set of assumptions about teaching/learning.

One of the activities we do that is an experience in unlearning is called Spin the Stick. The student takes a stick about a yard long and holds it up over her head. She stands straight—arms over her head—with the stick pointing to the sky. When she has spun around ten times, she simply lays the stick in front of her and tries to step over it. At least nine times out of ten, the student falls to the ground, laughing . . .

There are different ways of looking at that experience. One is that there's no point to it at all. On that level, that's exactly the point. The experience speaks for itself. It's fun. On another level, the point is that Spin the Stick is an exercise in failure.

As an introduction to the course, the message is—"it's okay to do something that either has no point at all, or if it has a point, it's that it's fun, or it's acceptable to take a chance and to fall on your rear-end." Failure is okay. You have (what John Holt calls) the freedom to fail and (what Carl Rogers calls) the freedom to learn.

It's important that the student have the opportunity to try some new experiences and to risk to some extent. If it doesn't work, that's all right. That's a way of *un*learning.

Joel: It seems that the "fear of failure" is something that needs to be addressed—especially if you're talking about the kinds of physical challenges that are involved in adventure education.

In the process of breaking set or *un*-learning, people are risking extending their limits.

You say the first month of a semester-long course might be involved with experiencing or *un*-learning. How do you follow that up?

BROWN

Jeff: In the second month of the course, we begin to take a look at what we're doing and how it relates to the learning process. I'm hoping that—after learning how to *un*-learn, we can learn how to learn.

Let me see if I can give you an example. All different kinds of issues come up in the process of a group getting over the eight-foot-high beam. In most cases the group will explore alternatives. This is an aspect of learning—the process of problem solving and decision making.

In deciding how they're going to get over the beam, the issues of communication may come up. Who's talking? Who's listening? To what extent am I listening to what you have to say? To what extent am I trying to make sure that it gets done my way?

The task raises another issue—leadership and followership. Who is exercising leadership? To what extent can one move from leading to stepping back and following?

Those kinds of issues come up again and again. What I'm trying to do is to facilitate learning from their immediate experience.

Joel: It seems clear to me that the two components—the experiential (doing) and the humanistic (learning from doing), come together in this phase of the course: the experiential (the task of getting over the wall or beam) and the humanistic (the process of helping students to make sense of the experience). How about another example of a specific activity that would combine doing and learning from doing?

Jeff: In the Electric Fence, we string a rope about five feet off the ground and give the group an eight-foot pole. We ask them to get from one side of the rope to the other, using only the pole, without touching the "electric fence."

Once again, it's hard to guess what will happen, because it's almost a guarantee that, if I predict that x will happen, then y will happen. In general, however, the group needs to choose among alternatives.

It's interesting to observe *how* what happens, happens. I need to refrain from giving my observations to the students, and instead try to facilitate their awareness of the process of how they went about what they did. After the experience, I attempt to facilitate the discussion first on a factual level. "What happened?" "What did you do?" Then to the extent that it flows, I attempt to move the discussion toward personal values and feelings raised by the experience. Then I move to the question of learning—how does this relate to solving a problem and the process of learning in general?

Joel: Can you recall some of the statements that students have made in the past in response to "What has this got to do with learning?"

Jeff: I think there are some generalizations that can be made. Obviously, everyone's experience of an activity like the Electric Fence is different, and that's what makes it exciting. What's interesting is that after a month or so, students start to perceive the need for working together, the need for trust and support among the participants, and that leadership includes followership. Their awareness of these kinds of teaching-learning concepts develops gradually through experience.

Joel: One thing that stands out from the Electric Fence is that cooperation is built into the task. The task is defined so that the entire group has to get over the fence if they are to succeed. Do you consciously focus on cooperative tasks?

Another way of structuring that task would be to say: "Every person for themselves. Everybody over the fence as best you can." It seems to me the task—whether it be the Electric Fence or the Wall—is designed with a cooperative element. Do students ever say, "Hey, this isn't life. Life is competition."

Jeff: That's a significant question. Yes, many of the experiences are defined as group tasks. We do attempt to address the question of competition and survival of the fittest because certainly that's a reality in our educational system and in our society.

For example, one of the games I use has two parts. The first part is called Stand Off. Two people stand about arm's length apart and try to knock each other off balance by hitting hands. That is a challenging game and also a competitive game, as it is basically me against you.

Then we move from Stand Off to a different version of the game called Human Spring. The same people, rather than trying to knock each other off balance, extend their arms forward and lock hands as they spring forward and then backward. It's still a challenge, but now it becomes more of a cooperative effort, because the goal is to help each other maintain balance after springing off one another.

We spend some time talking about Stand Off and Human Spring, and how "challenge" is a common thread in both games.

Joel: I'm intrigued with the notion of challenge being the bridge between cooperation and competition.

How do you move from having students learning about learning in the second part of the course, to learning about teaching in the third part?

Jeff: It happens in a variety of ways. Over the period of a few months, my function as teacher, the wall's function as teacher, and the students' role as learner/teacher have a cumulative effect on the students' awareness of "teaching."

Another way that's more structured is to facilitate a discussion distilling the common elements of teaching/learning inherent in the activities. We talk about problem solving, cooperation, leadership-followership, communication, and related concepts. I ask them to speak about their experience as learners in adventure games so that we keep the process tied to real happenings. I also ask them to reflect upon and share their experience of me as a teacher.

The next step, and the most difficult one, is: "What are the elements of adventure learning that pertain to learning in general?" In many cases, it's possible to incorporate some of the elements of adventure learning into a more traditional environment—in elementary or secondary classrooms.

Joel: What you're doing is using your experiences in this course as the subject matter—as the textbook, in a sense, as they investigate teaching. It seems that the third part of the course invites them to read "the book" within themselves (helping them to develop self-literacy skills). They come up with their own answers to defuzz "teaching," and draw some implications as future teachers.

Jeff: Yes, I think the key word is "implication." Over a period of time those implications become more explicit. These awarenesses become more conscious through reflecting on what's going on and sharing with other members of the group and me.

Beyond the implications are the applications. "How does this approach to learning apply to you as someone who's interested in teaching?" "How can you incorporate cooperation into learning experiences you design for students?" "How can you provide learning experiences which ask students to define and solve problems so that the learning is real?"

Joel: You mentioned some specific questions that you might ask. I can see where students could make some direct ties between the experience and the implications and applications to teaching. What are some specific activities at this stage of the course?

Jeff: In the final phase of the course, we do some classroom-type experiences which spring from our outdoor experiences.

For example, if we're going to learn about different teaching styles, I present a lesson in different ways, and then ask them which method they preferred and why. Rather than telling them about different approaches to learning, I allow them to experience those different approaches.

Another example is an activity that's similar to a scavenger hunt. It's called a School Search, in which the students learn about a school by exploring. I might ask a question such as: "What indications are there that the librarian is attempting to motivate children to read?" The intent is to have the students search that out and then take a look at the educational issues involved.

Another example might be to have students interview a student teacher. Certainly it would be possible for me to tell them about student teaching. However, they probably would learn more by talking with someone who is presently in that role. In some cases, that requires students to risk—not climbing over the wall—but to risk contacting someone they don't know and interviewing that person to find out about student teaching.

I try to do a variety of indoor, nonphysical activities that incorporate at least some of the elements of adventure learning. Hopefully, my students make the transfer from adventure games to classroom teaching.

Joel: The sequencing in your course seems to get at a couple of things. One is that people are involved in and responsible for their own learning. Second, what you're doing is providing many different vehicles for students to get that direct experience which will be meaningful to them.

Jeff: I think that's a middle ground between teacher-directed, mandatory learning and no learning at all.

Joel: What you're talking about here is "structured freedom." It's not an authoritarian situation where there is order but no freedom. It's not a laissez faire situation where there's freedom but no order.

Jeff: Sure, I think there are a variety of alternatives between structure and freedom. For example, in another assignment, I might say: "Part I—This is required. Part II—pick A, B or C. Part III—Design your own."

Joel: I'm curious about evaluation of these kinds of experiences. What are some of the principles or beliefs you have about evaluation?

Jeff: Evaluation is a difficult question for me. I believe in process evaluation, because I don't think it's possible to quantify somebody's learning.
My primary concern is that evaluation spring directly from experience, rather than disrupt the flow of learning.
I use evaluation to improve the course and get more student input.

Joel: So what you're talking about is focusing on *im*proving as opposed to proving.

Jeff: For my purposes, the best kind of evaluation is self-evaluation. I ask students to look back at their commitment to and participation in the course, and to look forward to their next steps. I also ask them to evaluate me as a teacher and the course as a learning experience.

Joel: So the focus on evaluation is in terms of a "review, a view, and a preview." Having students review what has gone on for them, take a look at themselves now, and then preview what's coming up.
I've picked up two ways that you gather evaluation data. One is directly asking questions. The second is the group log.

Jeff: The log gives me a great deal of information about how and where to go the next week. For example, a student recently wrote about an activity, "I really thought the activity was too easy."
So the next week, we did some more challenging activities which the students really enjoyed. The journals and the group log often help me in my planning.

Joel: It's interesting that you legitimize students telling you "where to go." I imagine many people might be a little wary of that. You seem to take the data they provide you and use it in decision making.
Using some of those tools that you've described, I'm wondering what kinds of information you've picked up from students. Can you give us some examples of what they report?

Jeff: Some of the experiences we do are very difficult physically and, at first glance, they look like they might even be impossible. Students say things like, "Oh, we'll never be able to do that." Or, "I can't do that." Over a period of time, whatever it takes them to accomplish the task, they get the message that "I can't do it" is all in their heads. The experience of "doing it" helps students to feel their own power and skill and to learn from their successes.
When students negotiate a problem, that's a really strong learning experience for them. I can remember one woman last spring who looked at the fourteen-foot wall the first day and was scared. She said, "There's just no

way I'm going to be able to do that. I don't know whether the group's going to be able to get over the wall—but not me.''

A few months later, with a great deal of struggle, I think she had really learned from this accomplishment. A large part of the course is focused around activities that have success built into them in one form or another. There's certainly room for failure in the course, and I think it's really important upon occasion. In most cases, individuals and the group as a whole have some success.

Joel: What I'm picking up is that, in addition to learning by doing, you're also building opportunities for succeeding by doing. The act of courage at confronting that wall is something that can be encouraging. It seems like some of these experiences in a supportive, cooperative atmosphere could lead people to feel better about themselves. They might come out of a course like this with an attitude of "I think I can do it."

Jeff: There's a lot of truth in that. I think the key is that success is real and it's obvious. If the wall's there and you start on one side and you end up on the other, all you've got to do is knock on wood to realize that you have accomplished something.

Joel: What you have throughout the course is a built-in evaluation mechanism for the students. They get data: I either got over the wall or I didn't. At the same time, the wall for me is a metaphor for other walls that we encounter and can overcome in our lives.

Jeff: Let me conclude with some words from the students themselves—I think it's appropriate that they "get in the last word."

"I am immediately aware that I have unlearned a certain amount of the formalness of my previous education—at least enough to allow some self-directed learning and free expression."

"I used to think I learned when I did well on a test. Then learning seemed to be listening to what the teacher had to say. I think right now learning is being able to apply information to my life. Learning is living . . .''

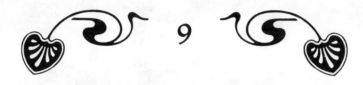

Playfair: Everybody's Guide to Noncompetitive Games

There has been a growing need and awareness in this country of the importance of helping people learn how to spend their leisure time. There has
been a concomitant interest in exploring noncompetitive forms of play and
recreation.

In 1975, Matt Weinstein and Pamela Kekich began to offer Playfair events
around the country. Each Playfair is a unique blend of noncompetitive adult
play experiences, audience-participation comedy, and newly-created group
challenges. Groups from ten to ten thousand have found Playfair to be enjoyable ways to focus on the nature and nurture of "play". . . in essence,
helping people to create their own re-creation in a constructive and cooperative mode.

In the following interview with Joel Goodman (a member of the Playfair
staff), Matt and Pamela offer insights on how to make games less competitive, less exclusive, and less demeaning—and how to build cooperation,
inclusion, and self-esteem into the larger "game of life." They also describe
a number of organizing principles for the Playfairs as well as a variety of
specific games they have created.[1] You might be on the lookout for games
with such intriguing titles as: 3-Way Tug-of-War; Imaginary Tug-of-War;
Big Ball Games; Blob Tag; Touch Blue; Incorporations; Big Wind Blows;
Three Positions; Introductions; Elbow Fruit Hop; Off-Balance; Human
Spring; Morra; and Wonderful Circle. On your mark, get set, go . . . !

J: Here's a very simple question to start: how did you ever get interested
in doing what you're doing?

P: When I started teaching and doing my master's in elementary
education, it seemed like there was a point when children changed the way
they played with one another and began to acquire physical inhibitions. So,
I started to look at "play." There are lots of books about organized sports,
but not many about play. I found out that there is a change in the way
children play with each other about the age of four or five. Then, by the
time they are six or seven, they have already learned the way we all know to

BROWN

play—through organized games that are competitive, uncreative, nonimaginative, and not physically playful. Before that, we all went through a stage of being inventive and fantasizing our experiences.

J: You made a distinction between play and sports. Can you say more about that?

P: That's an important question. Play does not necessarily involve rules that are set, and it is not necessarily organized. The way we played as young children was mostly by making things up and creating situations. In more organized sports, the rules are set. The acting out of those rules is more important than the creating of them.

J: Matt, how did you get interested in "play?"

M: I started working with games when I was training teachers in creative dramatics and theatre. What I became interested in was letting people have that experience of improvisation, of creating something together—but without so much of the stress on pantomime skills.

When Pamela and I got together, we thought that we could give people wonderful group experiences of a kind that no one has done—that concentrate on positive, exuberant feelings through playing with people. We had a feeling that that was a good direction to take. However, what we found is that the traditional games that everybody plays were not going to work for our purposes. They actually inhibited the playfulness in a lot of ways by

setting people against each other, or by setting up competitive win-lose and
"I feel-good-when-you-feel-bad" situations.

We did not want to abandon our idea that people could play together,
and have a unique, positive experience. So what we did was to abandon
almost all the games we knew as children—changed them around and invented
new games that worked for our purposes.

J: Would you agree that another distinction between play and sports is
that sports often results in one group of people feeling badly and one group
feeling good? The kind of play you're talking about doesn't have that happen.

M: Right, we avoid setting up direct confrontations like that. In our Playfairs, we used to have spoofs on that competitive feeling by having a tug-of-
war. That is a three-way tug-of-war, using two ropes tied together so that
there are three ends. It is very unlikely that one team could win against the
combined forces of the two other teams. So, we do play around with those
traditions, so that people can get a humorous look at them. For example,
you might also have a two-team tug-of-war with an imaginary rope. The
teams take their cues from a leader who directs the action and determines
who is winning.

J: There are a lot of adults and young people today who are saying, "Hey,
competition is great—in the kind of world in which we live, you need to learn
how to compete." What kind of response do you have to people who ask,
"Why do we need this?"

M: I think what you just said is true. But it's only true if you limit your
vision to saying that's the way the world is, and it'll never change. We think
that it can change, and that the world doesn't always have to be like that.
We are taking a small step to show people that there are other ways to interact. Hopefully, people will take this philosophy from the playing field and
see that it is possible to live lovingly and cooperatively.

P: People get lots of opportunities to find out what's wrong with themselves, but not many opportunities to find out about the joyful parts of
themselves. Those parts are really there all the time, and people can appreciate themselves and affirm each other's existence and humanness. There are
not many structures in our society for doing that and that's why we're
involved in creating and leading cooperative play opportunities.

J: Let's take off on this point of helping people to feel good and to
cooperate. These seem to be two of your main goals. Can you give an
example of a popular game today that goes against those goals?

P: We went to a party a few weeks ago that was specifically a charades
party. Before we actually started playing charades, I talked with three or
four of the people who seemed really friendly. We were having very nice
interactions. Then we started laying the ground rules for charades, and it
went from that into a whole evening where there was much tension. There
was one man, who, if I had not spent some time with him beforehand,
would have been hard for me to see as a kind, wonderful person. He was so
caught up in the game during the whole night. Husbands and wives, good

friends, coworkers were all lashing out at each other. It was amazing—there was no attempt to see each other as human beings and there was just such antagonism. Then, at the end of the night, after the game was all over, everyone immediately got up to go home and didn't interact with each other at all. It was so clear that there was so much pain involved in what was supposed to be a fun Saturday night. The intention was for them to all get together and have a good time, but the game pitted them against each other in such negative ways.

M: People in many traditional games situations exhibit behavior that is the antithesis of supportive. People are rewarded for pointing out other people's mistakes. A certain language of derision is the status quo in playing conventional games. People who are used to being really kind to each other lose sight of the fact that there are other human beings in the game and just humiliate other people and make them feel horrible.

What we try to do is give people a different kind of vocabulary for playing with each other, so they can realize that their purpose in coming together is not to play a game. The purpose is to use games as tools to reach out to other people and to exhibit the best parts of themselves—the joyful, playful parts, and to make contact with the same parts in other people.

J: So, people got so caught up in the charades game and its rules that they lost sight of themselves, others, and the original purpose, which was to have fun and interact with people. Given that type of situation—a game that seems to legitimize competition in a negative sense, legitimize putting each other down, legitimize putting the rules before people, what would you suggest? Would you suggest not playing that game at all, or is there some way of modifying it so that it could be a more positive, constructive opportunity for people to make contact with one another?

P: I think that many times you can change the game in a way that will make it more fun. We used to give people a chance to concentrate on "What are you liking about this game?", "How can we make that the focus of the game?", and "How can we do even more of that?" For instance, if what you like is getting up and running around the room, how can we build more of that into the game?

J: It seems that your objectives are to help people take control of the games they play, and, in a larger sense, to help them take control over their own lives by cooperating with others. Can you describe another game in which people have a chance to work with one another?

M: Big Ball Volleyball is played with a ball that is three feet in diameter, so that no matter what your skills are, it's almost impossible to do much by yourself. No one has the strength or agility to do it alone. So, by its very nature, it is cooperative. When that big ball is falling, you need many hands on it to keep it up in the air.

That particular game is usually the last one in a sequence in which we use the three-foot ball. We start with people passing it around in a circle to each other, then passing it over their heads, and down a line—where each person keeps running to the back of the line to keep the ball moving down the field. There's a lot of cooperative play with everyone handling the ball and giving it to other people before we start hitting it in the air. We first play with it in a way that everyone really can have control of it by giving it to other people.

Actually we don't play that game anymore mainly because of a personal choice we made to stop using any equipment. The reason for that is that when a game centers around a piece of equipment, it's much easier for people to forget that they've come there to be with other people, to make joyful contact with them. Instead they get sucked into "the game" by shoving people out of the way so they can get their hands on the ball. The big ball becomes the focus of everyone's attention, rather than each other. In lots of ways that's antithetical to our goals.

It's a tricky problem: playing with equipment like the ball or the three-way-tug-of-war rope is great fun, but it's difficult to facilitate the interactions that we want to see happening between people. When people come up to us afterwards and say, "Hey, that was wonderful, where can we get a ball like that?", we feel happy that they had such a good time, and yet disappointed that their attention is on the equipment rather than on the other people. So that's why we don't use much equipment anymore.

J: How do you spread the word on this new perspective about games and playing?

M: Playfair is the name of the games event that we present in touring colleges. It's about a two-hour sequence of facilitated games—cooperative ones, not competitive ones. The idea is that by playing together, people can get to know each other better. A feeling of community can arise out of a play situation. We're mostly brought in by colleges to work/play with a specific group of people—such as a freshman class for their orientation program or a student leadership retreat.

J: You talk about being invited by colleges to do most of your work. Are Playfairs adaptable for developing a community in camps, schools, or in family groups?

M: I think they have tremendously wide application. We've worked with a number of organizations, including senior citizens groups, schools, outdoor education programs, Campfire Girl counselors, and churches. For instance, one church was having their annual fellowship dinner and told us that it had always been a failure. The members always sat by themselves. The church leaders thought they would try a Playfair to mix the different people. By its very nature, Playfair gets people playing with other people. For the first time, members who were afraid to approach strangers were put in a situation where they were with people they didn't know—and got to know them.

I think it is important to develop a safe climate where people can interact physically with each other. By stressing the noncompetitive nature of the games that we play, we reach a lot of people who have stopped playing games in their lives, because they do not feel good enough to compete.

When I was in high school learning the trampoline, I didn't participate right away. By the time I got up enough nerve to try it, I was behind everybody else. They could do fancy flips while I was ashamed to admit that I had to learn the basics. The gap just got wider and wider, until it was impossible for me because of of peer pressure to ever get up on the trampoline. I think that is an important difference with Playfair. People can re-enter, safely and supported, into physical activity with us without having to worry about skill differences.

Also, we have been able to defuse some existing games that are predicated on skill differences and give people a chance to play them again. Tag is a good example of that. There are lots of problems with the old game of tag. One is that if you run fast, you don't get caught; and if you run slowly, then you're "it" for a long time. We've been able to do a lot of different things to tag to make it a number of different games, in which the tension about performance and skill is not there.

For example, to deal with the differences in speed and agility, we play a lot of Slow Motion Tag. In slow motion, you'll get caught sooner or later. Also, we play Blob Tag where instead of trying to get rid of "it," it's okay to be "it." In fact, everytime you tag someone, that person joins up with you and becomes part of "it," and the game ends when everyone is "it."

Often, we play Switch-Team Tag, where there are two opposing teams. When you get caught, instead of being penalized or eliminated, you move over to the other team. One team will eventually grow so big that it encompasses the other team, and the game ends when there is only one team, the winning team. In that kind of situation, where the only "penalty" is that you move from one team to the other, people feel the safety to experiment with new types of behaviors.

J: You have a commitment to providing opportunities for people to experiment and make games a laboratory for learning. It is also important for you not to eliminate people, so that in a game of tag, everybody stays in the game.

P: There are lots of opportunities during the Playfairs for people to do things that they ordinarily wouldn't try out. For instance, running in slow motion can be fabulous fun, but the average person doesn't usually get a chance to try it. Not only do we make that part of the game, but everybody does it. Nobody is watching you because everyone is doing it themselves. We work hardest at helping everyone feel included and helping everyone learn how to include other people.

J: Four principles were coming across very strongly to me in what you were just saying. One is the notion of equity—when you were talking about the guideline of everybody going in slow motion, there's a real feeling of equity. Second, it seems that people would be conscious of self, but not self-conscious. They are aware of themselves and their own experience of trying out new things, but the situation is safe enough that they don't feel self-conscious or that they're in a fishbowl. Third, you emphasize inclusion rather than exclusion. The fourth, I would assume, is that you're trying to get people actively involved in their own recreation, so that instead of watching the slow motion instant replay on a football game on TV, they experience slow motion themselves.

What are some of the other principles you use in designing Playfair experiences?

M: We start with games in which our leadership is strongest. We direct the participants in playful experiences, give them strong guidelines as to what they should do, and move them quickly from one thing to another. One of our principles is that we almost always play first and talk later. People's attention for hearing theoretical presentations and the philosophical guidelines behind our work is much stronger after they've played a little, loosened up a bit, and laughed. By playing first, and then talking about our philosophy and what we expect to do, we give people a common base of the Playfair concept.

Then, we let people think about their own particular histories of playing. We structure sharings where people talk one-to-one about how they grew up playing, about what kinds of games they played, and about pleasant memories they have of games. We move on from there to do some group games and then some partner games. We might teach ten different games in a forty-five-minute period to be played with ten different partners.

The progression goes from games where we have control to ones where the participants have more control and leadership. This is an important principle about the games we design. They are games in which we set up broad outlines of what can be done, but then we no longer give the commands or take over the leadership—it's open for anyone to take over. People then start coming out of the ranks, giving directions, and helping other people. There is an excitement not only about playing, but also about creating and leading at the same time. I think we've been very successful in developing those kinds of structures for games.

P: I want to address your initial question about Playfair principles. I want people to be up and moving right away. The first things they do should be physical, but not threatening.

Matt was talking about how we gradually let the participants take over the leadership. There's a game called Touch Blue that reflects this progression. When I first learned the game, it went like this: when the leader says touch "blue," everybody touches blue on another person: when the leader says, "touch red," everybody touches red on another person: the leader continues to give directions and everybody follows. That was the whole game. My first thought was that this was not very active. Why not let people move around in between, so there would be a locomotion element? I would then say "touch blue" followed by a command of how to move around (e.g., skip, hop, jump). The next step in the thinking was, "Why should I be the only one to dream up all the things to touch and the ways to move? I want to play, too." So I set up the structure to allow any of the players to say what the commands would be.

J: This seems to reinforce the principle of equity—the leaders participate as well—the leaders are players, even though at the beginning of the Playfair, you would offer specific structures so that people wouldn't flounder. I'm wondering if you could give some examples of some games you might play at the beginning—the ones that would have more specific instructions or directions—and then give an example of a game that might occur toward the middle—and then one that might be more open-ended and occur near the end.

P: There's a game called Incorporations, where the leader shouts out commands of kinds of groups for people to get into. The game is about forming and reforming groups. We might say, "get into a group of three," or, "get into a group of three plus one," or, "get into a group of people who were all born in the same month." People are told exactly what to do by the leader. We participate in the game, and also are the ones calling out the categories of groups. This game allows people to be with many different people, totally based on random categories that are safe and don't threaten anybody.

J: It sounds like one of those fast-paced games where people are up and moving. There's a chance for them to get to know other people who they might not have associated with before. When you get together with other people who have the same astrological sign or are wearing the same color, that's usually a random grouping.

M: There's another game that follows this same principle of grouping people in categories. In this game, the responsibility moves from the leaders to the players. The game is called Big Wind Blows. We play it with a parachute. It works like this: the group asks the question, "What does the big wind blow?", as they lift the parachute over their heads. One person calls out a category—for instance, "everyone born in May." Then, everyone born in May runs underneath the parachute and changes places with someone else before the parachute comes down.

Besides the fun involved in running underneath a billowing parachute, the game creates that same feeling of belonging with people. Other people clusters could be: "everyone who is wearing sneakers," "everyone who wears glasses," or "everyone who had scrambled eggs for breakfast." It is fun for people to see others who belong in that coincidental category with them. It is up to the members of the group to think of the commands to get everyone moving.

J: What happens if somebody calls out a random grouping that you might not think is positive? Is there anything you do to guard against that?

P: One of the most important principles is to tell people ahead of time that they may say something like, "everyone who is too fat." We tell them, "take charge of yourself, and don't do that. Remember that you want people to feel good about running under the parachute."

J: In other words, you would encourage people not to say something like, "everybody who thinks that they're ugly." Can you give us other examples of games that might be used near the beginning as loosener-uppers or get-to-know type games?

M: Three Positions is a good game at the beginning. What we do is divide the Playfair participants into three different teams. If we were working with a group of sixty, we would divide them into three teams of twenty. We would solicit from the group three different positions that any person could hold for a few seconds. The positions are physically simple enough so that everyone can do them (for instance, standing on one leg, scratching your kneecap, rubbing your stomach). With that repertoire of three different positions, each team huddles and picks one. Then, on a given count, they come out and show the position. The object of the game is for all three teams—without ever talking to each other—to do the same position at the same time.

One of the good things about starting with a game like that is it gives people a chance to talk with each other and make decisions. It gives people a sense of solidarity by doing something all together and working toward a common goal. There's also a great sense of joy, if after a few rounds, people figure out a strategy and all three teams do the same thing.

We also let people other than ourselves do the countdown. We have a lot of funny ways of counting, rather than just 1-2-3 . . . we'll do it on the count of "carrot"—and count off "soybean, potato, carrot." Other people pick up on that funny way of counting, and it gives people a creative way to announce to the group when it is time to show their position.

J: A couple of principles seem to be important in this game: a chance for laughter (from creative counting) and a cooperative goal structure (from having all three teams try to demonstrate the *same* physical position). This contrasts with a competitive philosophy in which one position is more powerful than another—as in the popular rock-scissors-paper game.

P: The counting method gives people the idea that we're playing around with game structures, that they are not sacred. It is another way of saying that "1-2-3" is not the only way to count—that sometimes you can count to "stringbeans." That's important to get across from the beginning.

J: How about another example of a game you might use near the beginning as an energizer?

M: One principle that we're concerned with is letting people know each other's names. Sometimes—and people love to do this—we have people go around and pretend they are the host or hostess at a party. Everyone here has been invited to the party, but no one knows each other's names. We give participants two minutes to introduce every person there to every other person. People are collaring people, finding out their names, bringing them over to someone else, introducing them. There's a lot of handshaking and laughing and people meeting their best friends as if they never knew them before. Playing Introductions is a real good way to have physical contact and an excuse to ask, "What's your name?"

J: When you say giving people an excuse, what you're really doing is giving people permission to do some things that, in many cases, they'd like to do, but are afraid to do. This seems to be an important Playfair principle. Can you give an example of another game that "gives people permission?"

P: Elbow Fruit Hop asks people to do things that are outrageous and silly. Usually, adults don't want to be silly, or they think they don't. It's a game in which one person gives a series of commands: a part of your body to touch, a category of objects that you would say over and over again, and a way to move around. For example, everybody might hold onto their stomachs, saying the name of a city while jumping, until somebody changes the three commands.

J: How does a participant change the commands?

P: We have a whistle that people come over and blow. Depending on the size of the group, we sometimes use it with a microphone. It is important that they know where to go for the whistle. It stays in one place within the playing area, so they don't have to run across the field to change the commands. People realize that if they're tired of hopping around, it is their responsibility to change the commands into something that they feel like doing.

It's loads of fun to see people walking or crawling around, holding their noses, and saying "asparagus" over and over. The basic principle is to establish a norm in which everybody gets to do it, so no one feels stupid. It's a way for people to be boisterous and not feel self-conscious about it.

J: What you're doing is legitimizing having fun, being "crazy," and letting the kid in everyone come out and play. I take it the name of the game comes from the three elements that the people would do: the elbow is an example of a part of the body, fruit could be one of the categories, and hop is one example of a physical movement.

P: Elbow Fruit Hop is also an example of a game in which we set up a structure for people to end it. We tell people at the beginning, "If you want to end the game, then the commands you call out are elbow, fruit, hop," so that the name of the game is the way to end it. That happens in a number of our games. The principle behind this is that people are likely to remember the name "elbow fruit hop" if they use it in the game.

I'd like to say something about "letting the kid come out and play." Being silly and laughing a lot may have the connotation of being "childish," but what we're saying is that it's okay to be like that, to do things like that when you're over thirty. Our hope is that people will not come away from a Playfair thinking, "Well, I acted like a kid today, now I have to go back to acting like an adult." We hope they will say, "I was an adult all day today, and I laughed and had a fabulous time with myself and others."

The intention is not to act like a child, but to be yourself and to experience a sense of your own playfulness.

J: I like the notion of focusing on the playfulness in us—getting away from the Peter Pan notion that when you reach a certain age, you lose your playfulness. You're not asking people to return to being Peter Pan, but rather tapping the play-fullness in them as older people. How about one more example of a game that brings out people's playfulness?

M: We've adapted a game called Animals, from the New Games Foundation. We solicit three different animals and the sounds they make from the group. We ask people to pick one of those, then with their eyes closed, to make the sound of the animal they picked. They then try to get together

---

He who binds to himself a joy
Doth the winged life destroy
He who kisses the joy as it flies
Lives in eternity's sunrise.
             (WILLIAM BLAKE)

with everyone else who has picked the same animal. Of course, we have a few people standing outside to stop people from walking away from the crowd and to help people get together. There's always great laughter accompanying that game.

J: One principle you mentioned is important: people "spotting" if games involve some sort of physical risk. To insure people's physical safety in Animals, some people should have their eyes open.

M: It is safer for the people walking around with their eyes closed if they know that there will be some people around with their eyes open to make sure that they don't walk into walls or poles. People don't have to worry that they're walking in the wrong direction and that people will laugh at them. A lot of these risks are eliminated.

J: The games you have described so far are for groups of people. I'm wondering if you can give some illustrations of cooperative games that two people could play together as partners and how they are paired.

M: It's fun and very important to invent nonthreatening ways to help people find partners. It's difficult to just say, "Okay, pick a partner," or "Pick the person you'd most like to play with," because that brings up all sorts of feelings of embarrassment and panic for people. We've thought of lots of good random ways to get people with partners, so there's little tension. For example, "Put from zero to five fingers in the air, walk around and see what everyone else is holding up. Pick a partner so that your fingers when added result in an even number." Or, "Find a partner who's wearing the same number of rings as you are." The list is endless.

It's also fun to adapt games that are usually played in groups to two-person games. Leapfrog, for example, can be played by two people, with one leaping over the other. We do many physical type games with partners. One, for example, is called Off Balance. The object of the game is for both people to support each other, and yet to be continually off-balance. There's a lot of movement, leaning on each other, pulling away from each other— but always as a coordinated type of movement exercise.

J: Unlike competitive arm wrestling, the object is to be off-balance and yet make a cooperative effort, so that one person isn't the "winner" and the other the "loser."

M: Both participants are off-balance the entire time, and yet no one falls at all. Both people support each other the whole time.

There's another game called Human Spring. Here, two partners stand about three to four feet apart with their palms out in front of their chests. They lean into each other, touch hands, and then spring back. The idea is for them to keep their balance. It's a coordinated springing back and forth, with the option of varying the distance between them.

There's also a partner game based on the Italian counting game, Morra. Each of the partners makes a fist. On a given count, each one can put out from zero to five fingers. The object of the game is to guess the total number of fingers that will be displayed. The total could range from zero to

Brown

ten, depending on what you and your partner put out. That originally is a competitive game, in which the first one to guess right wins. We usually play it so that when you and your partner have a total of three correct guesses between you, then you've both "won."

It's fun to add variations. You can play with two hands and get up to twenty possible numbers, or play with four people, each using one hand. The more people who play, the harder it is to make a correct guess.

J: How are the partner games usually played in Playfair situations? How do you structure them?

P: Sometimes we divide people randomly into pairs, and then ask them to label themselves (e.g., scrambled eggs and fried eggs). Then, we arrange the people into two concentric circles with pairs facing one another (e.g., the fried eggs on the outer circle facing in and the scrambled eggs on the inner circle facing out). We teach one partner game, and after playing it, we'll ask the fried eggs to move three people to their right. So, each person quickly goes on to another partner. Then we teach another game. People can learn eight different partner games quickly and play them with eight different partners. Then, we give people some free choice. Randomly matched up with a partner, they get to pick which of those games they want to play. People have a repertoire of games to play when they get together with that new person.

J: This sequence seems to use the principle you mentioned earlier. You provide some structure first and then give people a choice about which game(s) they would like to play.

The group games and the partner games would take place earlier in a Playfair. What do you do near the end to bring some closure to the experience?

M: We always give people a chance to talk with each other, sometimes to share highlights of what's happening to them there, sometimes to talk about what's good in their lives outside the Playfair. We always like to end by giving people a chance to verbalize their appreciations for how the day has gone. One game for doing that is called Wonderful Circle. People put their arms around each other's waists, and move in a circle, taking small steps. Whenever someone has something wonderful they want to talk about (e.g., something they appreciate about the leadership, something they discovered about their own playfulness), they can stop the circle and speak. The circle moves around to the left until someone says, "stop." That person would say one positive thing then say, "go," and the circle would move around to the right until someone else said, "stop."

P: When we work with smaller groups, we often use a different format for a closing. We ask people to sit in a circle and share one by one some specifics about what they appreciated during the playfair. We usually give

---

"In the child there is no separation between spirit, soul and body. Everything is reproduced in this inner being. He imitates his whole environment."
(Rudolf Steiner)

some pretty clear guidelines about what they could focus on—e.g., their own participation on interactions with other people, positive characteristicss of the group. We think it is important for people to say out loud what they felt good about.

J: In closing this interview, I would like to let you know that I really appreciate the creative perspective you bring to playing. I believe that if we can help young people and adults to play together positively, cooperatively, and joyously, we will have a significant impact on how they play "the game of life."

Footnote

(1) For more information about *Playfair*, and for descriptions of sixty exciting cooperative games (as well as the keys to inventing your own), see the new book by Joel Goodman and Matt Weinstein: *Playfair: Everybody's Guide to Noncompetitive Play*, published by Impact Publishers, 1980 (available through Creative Resources Press, 179 Spring Street, Saratoga Springs, NY 12866).

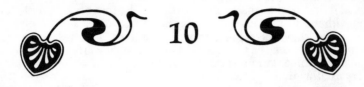

Creative Leadership:
A Humanistic Approach to Coaching

One of the most traditional forms of outdoor activity in our country has been sports. We need only take a look at baseball as "our national pastime" to realize how pervasive an influence athletics have been in our culture. The Monday night football syndrome, where meetings can't be scheduled on Monday night because they might conflict with the football game on television, is an indication of people's interest in sports. In what ways can we humanize some of the more traditional forms of outdoor activity?

In the following interview, Joel Goodman will be speaking with Jeff McKay, who offers a unique background. Jeff has been a successful coach on the college level. A significant part of his success comes from his effectiveness in applying humanistic education guidelines and principles to his coaching. He suggests a number of innovative approaches to mixing the following ingredients in athletics: challenge, cooperation, individual excellence, joy, and learning.

Joel: Let's start by taking a look at some of the roles you've had in coaching.

Jeff: When I was in college I worked for a man named Bennie Friedman who was a pro quarterback back in the old days. I worked as his assistant at a national football camp for quarterbacks and pass receivers for about six years. One of the things I learned from Bennie is the idea that a player needs to be his own coach. To me that's a nugget that's been worth developing.

My first formal kind of coaching experience in an institution was at a small secondary school in New York where I coached football and baseball. I was doing things in ways that my experience had taught me and it wasn't particularly enjoyable. Then I moved to California and coached football and baseball again. I remember that the football coach, Bob Schaup, was highly successful. One of the good things I learned from Bob was the idea of fun. The day before the biggest game of the year, the players were very tense over what would happen. Bob had them playing volleyball over the football goal posts. Part of me said, "That's crazy." But there was another part saying, "Hey, this guy's on to something."

I then took a year off from my involvement in athletics. As I look back on it, the time and space away from athletics allowed me to cast off many attitudes and approaches that were old for me. I came back to athletics a year later with more openness and freshness. I got involved at the University of California coaching the freshman-sophomore team. I started experimenting. I wanted to try some new things. So I started fooling around with coaching through experimentation—giving players a voice in how we practiced. It was a very exciting time for me.

At this point, two things influenced me. One was an involvement with Esalen Institute's Sports Center—where I explored the martial arts, talked about improving athletics as a human endeavor, and met Tim Gallwey who has developed the "inner game of tennis." The second influence was meeting George Davis, a beautiful man who at the time was coaching football in northern California. He used football as a vehicle for creating almost a pure Athenian democracy.

I've also spent two years coaching the freshman-sophomore team and one year working with the varsity at the University of Massachusetts. I've had a chance to further develop some of the directions that started in California.

Joel: If you had to summarize the kernel of your philosophy, based on these different experiences, what would it be?

Jeff: I see sports and athletics as a holistic experience that involves mind, emotion, and body. The possibilities for personal growth and learning in a traditional sense are almost boundless. I would like to facilitate in my athletes—a sense of personal growth and the ability to fully participate in a joyful activity.

Joel: I'd like to probe a little deeper into the philosophy underlying your interest in humanizing sports. What are your guiding principles in coaching?

Jeff: I start with what I call individual excellence. My feeling is that my first job as a player is to do my own best; and my job as a coach would be to help someone to move toward individual excellence. That means that individual excellence even comes before team, which is a little different from the way some coaches might think. I like to start out with the idea of individuals challenging themselves to achieve excellence, which has nothing to do with statistics. I also put a lot of emphasis on working together by stressing cooperation as opposed to competition. Even people trying out for the same position can cooperate and help each other to improve.

Joel: You're talking about dealing with cooperation and competition, not only interteam but also intrateam.

Jeff: I think competition is a loaded issue. There's the Vince Lombardi school of thought which says competition is everything and winning is everything. I don't buy that. There's another view which says competition is evil and winning is nothing. I don't buy that either. I feel there's a comfortable, healthy middle ground. For you and me to compete—where you do your best and I do my best—isn't necessarily evil at all. With my teams I try to emphasize *us* first, and to not concern ourselves particularly with the other team. Our job is to do our best whether we're playing a poor team or a great team, our job is still to do our best. Our motivation is not based on who we're playing. It's based on who we are. That has worked very well. To get a team up to play a really good team and to float through and play poorly against a bad team doesn't do anything for me.

I had an experience with the University of Massachusetts varsity in which we swept a doubleheader. The team we played wasn't very good. I talked to some of the players who felt that sweeping that particular doubleheader really was not a satisfying experience. I am saying that winning is not everything—it's the getting there that is really worthwhile.

Joel: Your emphasis is in moving from either hollow victories in which the focus is on beating the other team to taking a look at winning victories within yourself where you're competing with a standard of excellence within yourself or within the team.

Jeff: There are three levels of moving from your individual excellence at second base to the cooperation of you and someone else at shortstop to competing with the other team at another level of cooperation. Our team's job is to do our best, and your team's job is to do your best—that's a cooperative contract between us. That's a beautiful concept for me.

The problem is that, at times, this contract is taken too far, and becomes: "Whoever wins takes all the marbles, and the loser gets nothing." I've really thought a lot about winning because I think it's a crucial concept to address. One way most people judge success is to ask, "Did you win or lose?" I don't thing that's the only way. It's possible to play very well and not win. Think about the runner who finishes in tenth place but beats his/her best time. That's a win! If you do your individual best, and I do mine, then winning becomes irrelevant.

Joel: So you're moving from looking at winning in a reverent fashion to looking at winning in an irrelevent fashion.

Jeff: Another principle it has taken me a long time to learn: the idea that competitive sport can be fun. I think I had fun as a competitor; but when I first became a coach, I thought that fun had nothing to do with it. I thought that it was a choice between winning or having fun. I don't believe that anymore. I also thought that the fun came from the winning; and if you lost, then all you had done wasn't fun.

As a coach, I try to incorporate some fun into what we do. For example, we have relay races at the end of practice and a home run hitting contest once a week. I've tried to structure fun into our practices so that after we work very hard, the players and I have a release.

Many athletes have an inclination to fool around. For me it's imporant to separate the fooling around from the hard work. One way I can do that is to legitimize "fun" on certain occasions.

Joel: What you're moving toward is the concept of unconditional fun . . . fun that is not based on whether you win or lose, but on how you play the game. Do you have any other principles?

Jeff: One of the things I believe very strongly about athletics is that it should be an educational experience. That means that the player has a large say in what happens. When I get players coming from high school, in many cases, what they want to do is to perform for the coach. I try to help them see that they perform for themselves first, and their teammates and me second.

Joel: Instead of trying to psyche out the coach, each player is setting his or her own goals of excellence and trying to meet those and, at the same time, work cooperatively with teammates. What you're talking about is viewing the player as umpire, in the sense of making internal decisions and evaluations and judgments about certain issues.

Jeff: I am concerned about coaching individual people as well as coaching the team and allowing for individual people to have idiosyncrasies and to do things differently. I don't feel it's at all necessary for everybody on the team to look the same or do this the same or hit with the same kind of stance. It strikes me as counterproductive. Everybody's different physically. Everybody's different in their head. To the extent that we can take that into consideration in athletics, people will do better; and people will, more importantly, have a better time.

Joel: The times when I've played on coach-oriented or coach-disciplined teams, as long as the coach was there hanging over your head, you got down to it. But the norm that developed is that when the coach turned his back, that's when players started messing around. What you're talking about is—regardless of whether the coach has his eyes on you or not, you're your own boss and you direct yourself.

Jeff: Right. There are some implications of that, too, for the coach. For example, one thing that I work at—and I'm not sure how close to it I get—is to get away from being a coach all the time. There's a tendency for me, since I know how to grip a curve ball, to teach somebody how to grip a curve ball. I think in the long run, it's going to be much more successful if I can help that person experiment and have him learn how to throw a curve ball rather than to have me teach him how to throw a curve ball. My guess is that, when it's the bottom of the ninth, and the heat's on, he's going to remember it much better if he learned how to do it himself, rather than having me teach him.

And that's one of the beauties of this when we come back to the question of success. Yes, it does work; and I think, in the long run, it pays off. The player can learn a lot without my getting in the way. That's not to say that I don't need all the skills and all the resources in order to be able to help him, but that I use those when appropriate rather than always teaching and coaching in a dogmatic sense.

There's another part to it, too, and that's to try to help players to become their own coaches; that takes a while. My experience as an athlete and the experience of lots of the athletes I'm working with now is that they have their own "coach" and their coach is their head getting in the way of their body. Somebody is having trouble hitting; and he comes to me and says, "Is my weight too far forward? Do I need to cock my wrists a little more? Am I moving my head? Am I moving away from the plate?'' Can you imagine trying to remember all of those and hit the ball at the same time?

Joel: Zen and the Art of Archery—Revisited.

Jeff: I'm not denying the coach's need for knowledge in all those areas. It's just that, in many cases, we need to clear out the space inside the head to allow the athlete's body to perform naturally and then help with some refinements and some minor adjustments. The thought of being able to *teach* somebody how to hit is more than I can bite off, and more than most people can bite off.

Joel: You talked about coaching individuals. Do you also have a principle that relates to coaching a team? How do you help a group of individuals to get together into a team? Is that important to you?

Jeff: Yes, that's very important. One of the beauties of sport, to me, is the camaradarie—building a community. What I'm interested in doing is creating a team that is the players' team and not just my team. This is not that way-out a concept. What I'm concerned with is moving gradually from a coach-dominated team to a player-run team. My experience is that that has to be gradual because most players' experience has been: "Tell us what to do, coach."

One of the first things we do is to elect player representatives, which is almost the same as electing captains. The difference for me is that, rather than electing captains at the end of this year for next year, we'll start next year with who we have and elect from that group. It seems more present tense. Those player representatives get involved in such decisions as: "What do we need to work on in practice? Do we take a day off this week? When do we take a day off this week? Do practices need to be longer or shorter?" These kinds of decisions are normally made by the coach. In many cases, their decision is the same as mine; and in many cases, they have good ideas that I hadn't thought of. So, it's not a question of their taking over my responsibilities. It's a question of all of us being responsible.

I also have the players involved in decision making about rules and regulations. I can remember the first time we did this at the University of Massachusetts many years ago. One of the player representatives was a tremendous leader, so I turned the show over to him to develop the rules and regulations, the dress code, etc. He got up there and he started laying it on the team: "I think we ought to do this and that!" I was sitting in the wing saying, "Oh, my God." During a break, I pulled the rep aside and said, "Time out. The point of this is to not have *me* run your lives. And the point isn't either for *you* to run their lives." Athletes are not irresponsible. They just need an opportunity to take responsibility.

Joel: This is another example of your trying to move from an authoritarian setup where the coach rules to the democratic vision that you mentioned earlier where there's participation and sharing of the responsibility.

Jeff: Right. Another principle that's been particularly important is for me to learn from the players. I remember one day at California, I was walking out to practice and quite a few players were out early. One of the catchers was hitting infield to them. My first urge, as a coach, was, "Oh, you've got to get up there and take over for him because the coach hits infield." Then I stopped myself and said, "There's nothing wrong with him hitting infield. In fact, they're having a great time!" The enthusiasm and the motivation that was going on there was terrific. One thing I've learned from that is that player-run sessions—or, in a more generalized sense, player-initiated practice—is a tremendous idea. I've found that, to push the metaphor, they can take the ball and run with it.

Joel: A common stereotype in our culture is that of dumb jock. It occurs to me that one of the reasons that has developed is that in most sporting situations, the athletes are not allowed to think for themselves. They're always spoon-fed the directions from the coach—e.g., to steal or not to steal. What you're doing is having the athletes tap the information in their own computers and come up with the decisions for themselves.

Jeff: The final step for me in the whole movement toward self-discipline is a concept that I learned from George Davis, whom I mentioned before. He has been using sport as a vehicle for creating a democratic enterprise for over twenty-five years. The idea is, very simply, that it is our team; and the players need to be able to participate in that. So what we do first is to have people decide where they want to play. I make sure that everyone knows that he has a shot at the place where he wants to play. So if you want to play shortstop, fine, you try out for shortstop.

The next step is that everyone chooses the starting lineup. That's a big jump and a beautiful jump because what that says then is, "You are responsible for yourself and your teammates." Everybody on the team votes. The beauty of it is that it's a real strong message of, "Hey, my talk about it being your team is not just talk. Here you are." At first, the players find that a little bit difficult to deal with. Once they get used to it, then it really becomes a growth experience in democracy for them. This country is a democracy, and, as such, we ought to be doing what we can in education and in sport to really foster that idea.

Joel: The message that you're sending is that, literally and figuratively, they're responsible for the positions they're in and that you really do place faith beyond the rhetoric level in their ability to make decisions about which positions, either individually or as a team, they place themselves in.

Could you say more about the players' reactions? I can certainly imagine that, after years of being in an authoritarian, "coach-knows-best" system, there might be some chaos and havoc at the beginning. How do you move from that? And does it work? That's a basic question to which a lot of coaches would say, "Hey, you can talk all up and down about this democracy stuff and that sounds great, but does it work? Do I keep my job as coach if the players are making those decisions for themselves?"

Jeff: One of the exciting things is that it has worked. The first time I started the vote I was afraid. I thought the players were going to vote for their friends and not pick the "right people." So, the first place for me to start was to be reasonably comfortable with myself in trying this out.

I've had coaches say to me, "It all sounds nice, but aren't you really neglecting your responsibility? It's your job to plan practices." It is my job. The only thing I'm doing is involving the players in the planning of practices, too. It's ultimately my responsibility. I don't see myself getting out of the responsibility but taking on some more.

The same is also true of the vote. People may say, "That's really your responsibility to figure out who plays where and then who starts and who plays when." I don't think that's true. The vote certainly can be used in an advisory kind of capacity. But the point of it is that I think it takes much more guts on my part to say, "Hey, here's a large piece of the pie. You guys see what you can do with it," than for me to say, "Do this. Do that. You play here. You play there." I don't feel it a cop-out at all. I get angry when people say that I'm copping out. I also think that twenty people know better than one person. It's very possible that I may have a bias against a player of which I'm not even aware, so I write him out of the starting lineup. But when twenty people vote, these kinds of individual prejudices get cancelled out. That's a lot of what democracy is about. For me, it has worked very well.

Joel: You see democracy as a risk, build that into your program, and accept the responsibility for that risk. You also follow the old adage of "Two heads are better than one," (and twenty heads are better than one). You draw on the resources, thinking, and perspectives of everybody involved and do not limit your vision.

Jeff: Another concern that I have and that people have expressed to me is, "How about the players? Can they deal with this?" I've talked with people about doing this on the college level, but they say, "Sure, it works in college but it wouldn't work in high school or in the pros." I don't think that's right. It's probably easier, the older people get because they're supposedly more mature and able to take more responsibility; but this worked for George Davis in a high school situation. It has worked for me with college freshmen and seniors.

I don't think it's a question of age. I think it's a question of the coach being comfortable with it, and helping athletes to be comfortable with it. I like to challenge the athletes with: "Look, people have said to me that this won't work. The reason it won't work is that you're not mature enough and you're not responsible enough. And I say Hogwash! It's up to you. Here's the ball." And they take off running.

Joel: What about the people who are on a survivor level, who say: "This sounds great, but what about my job?" In other words, what kind of winning-losing record does this kind of system or approach produce? What has it produced for you?

Jeff: It has always been successful. When I was at the University of California with the freshman-sophomore team, we were twenty and thirteen playing Pacific 8 level competition, and that was without a pitcher who had an E.R.A. below three. At the University of Massachusetts, the first year we were ten and three; and my next year we were fourteen and four. So it works.

In baseball you either win a game or you lose it. And then there are some in the middle. You either win ten to two and bomb somebody or you get beaten eight to one. Those games are not the ones that matter. The ones that matter are the ones where it's five to five in the bottom of the ninth. Those are the fun games. Those are the competitive games. Those are the thrilling games; and those are the ones, if you want to be a champion, you need to win. I can remember my first year at California—out of those twenty wins, we won six in the ninth inning by breaking a tie or coming from behind. My feeling is that a lot of where that came from was the players' attitude of "We're in charge. We can make our decisions. This is our ball club." So, when it comes to the bottom of the ninth, it's not them performing for me or performing out of fear. It's them having faith in themselves.

Joel: Let me move into some specific scenarios and issues that would focus on the applications and implications of what you're suggesting.

Let's take a very typical thing that occurs during a baseball game and other sporting events: razzing going on between teams. How do you, as a coach, handle razzing?

Jeff: I'd like to start by going back to the idea that our job, first of all, is to be responsible for ourselves individually and to take care of ourselves. All we owe the other team is the respect of their being there. If a player on our club gets into razzing, I try to work with that person and help him not to do that. Our job is with us and our own excellence and our own competition. Razzing detracts from the game. It takes some energy away from us, and dissipates it in negative ways. We've got a full-time job of doing our best by putting all our energy and effort into picking ourselves up.

Joel: What you're saying is that players ought to be playing "pick-up games" rather than "put-down games."

Let me provide a second scenario. Let's say the focus in this case, is the umpire. The umpire has just made, from your perspective, an awful call. The players are upset. You're upset. How do you deal with that? Part of this relates to the issue of "sportsmanship."

Jeff: It's very unfortunate that we need umpires, first of all. If I were talking in a visionary sense, I would work to create a situation in which umpires are irrelevant. But that's not the reality right now. What I try to do is to ignore the umpires, and to just concern ourselves with ourselves. Now, I have fallen victim to arguments with umpires but I think I'm getting closer to a situation where I'm just going ahead and playing the game and letting the chips fall. The chips include the umpire's decisions—right or wrong—bad or good. I have felt the need at times to protect my players;

and that comes out of defensiveness and is something that I'd like to work through.

Joel: Here's another issue: should everybody get to play? Or should only the best play? If you have a vote and the object is to field a winning team, does that mean that some players will never get off the bench?

Jeff: That's a good, tough question—particularly for a competitive situation in which winning is something as opposed to everything or nothing. One of the ideas expressed by the Boston Celtics as much as anybody—is the idea of the whole bench being the "sixth man." I think that's a good concept. For me, that fits in with the idea of "pick 'em up."

Starting doesn't mean anything more than starting and probably playing a majority of the game—not necessarily all the game. I think when push comes to shove, then it has to be my decision during the game as to: "OK, do I give so-and-so a chance to play today?" Those are the kinds of decisions that I feel that I have to make—previously having had the players' input. But during a game, I can't take time out to have a vote. If the game is one in which we're way ahead, it's no problem putting people in. The question is how soon? To put them in in the ninth inning for a token appearance is better than nothing, but not much better than nothing. My inclination would be more to put them in during the sixth inning so they get a real bite of the experience—so they feel they can have some say in what's happening rather than to just show up at the end. Three plays at the end of the fourth quarter doesn't make any sense to me.

Where that's tough for me—and I think for other coaches—is the decision of when you take the risk. If it's five to three in the sixth inning, do you say, "Well, we're only ahead by two runs," so you don't put them in? Or do you say, "Hey, we're ahead by two runs"—so you put them in.

Joel: What about the morale of those players who are third-string catchers?

Jeff: One very helpful thing is that ninety percent of our practice consists of game situations so that they are involved in real doing as much as is possible. Prior to the game, when we take infield and outfield practice, everybody on the team participates, rather than only nine guys going out and warming up with the others being on the bench.

In practice, we might play a short game in which, when the ball is hit, everyone on the defensive team has to touch the ball before a putout can be made. The point of that, in one sense, is everyone is important, everyone participates, and on another level, it's fun.

This makes me think of another thing that helps. When I first coached, I think I fell into the tendency to spend a lot of time with the number one pitcher—and progressively less time with the number two, number three, and number four pitchers. It's really easy to slip into that. When I became aware of that, I made and continue to make a conscious effort to work with Joe Blow, who's the third-string catcher—if he's having trouble with his hitting, I'll work with him after practice. That's a clear message—not so much in words but in actions. This says to the third-string catcher, "Hey, he gives a hoot about me. I am a part of his team." I think that's really motivational.

Joel: So what you're really doing is providing equality of opportunity and equity in terms of your attention to players regardless of whether they're the star of the club or the third-string batboy.

Let me ask you this, Jeff. What gives you the greatest joy? What are some of the things that give you great joy in coaching? What's in it for you? What keeps you going and motivated?

Jeff: One of the major things is relationships with athletes and helping them to move toward self-motivation, self-reliance, and self-discipline. On a personal level, that has been a real good experience for me.

On another level, I get real enjoyment from being successful in the way I go about it. It makes me feel good to think that I can break some new ground in approaches to coaching and the game—and to be successful at that.

Joel: Let's imagine you could implement anything you wanted to in the world of sports or in the world of coaching. For instance, in baseball, how might you want to change the rules?

Jeff: One would be to change the game, so that the goal would be not winning. If two teams did their best and were of equal ability, the ultimate goal could be to end up in a tie. This smacks pretty hard against traditional views.

I hope some day to become a commissioner of a little league in order to effect some positive changes.

Joel: OK, Mr. Commissioner. What advice would you give to some of the coaches in your league?

Jeff: What would be necessary would be to find out where they are—each one individually. I would then try to help them move so that they take less responsibility and the children start to assume more responsibility. I would want them to realize that exerting pressure on a youngster, as I see it, rather than helping his performance, hinders his performance. The stereotype of the Knute Rockne speech to the little third-graders probably does more harm than good not only to the child but also as far as how well they do in the game. I shudder when I see young players whose knees are shaking, who are worried about, "Boy, if I don't get a hit, the coach is going to knock my head off." Sports ought to be fun.

I think that I would do a lot of crazy things—e.g., games in which you hit with the opposite hand, running around the bases backward, etc.

"You give but a little when you give of your possessions. It is when you give of yourself that you truly give." (KAHLIL GIBRAN)

Joel: Let me ask you to look in a broader sense, beyond little league to the future of sports in general, and more specifically, to some of the hopes or visions you have for sports—where we might be heading with sports—what sports might look like in the year 2000.

Jeff: Let me start off with where I'd like to see myself going, and then move to a more social vision. The score is tied two to two and it's the bottom of the ninth. One of our players hits a line-drive over the second-basemen's head. There are two out and, if it drops in for a base hit, we score a run and win; and if it's caught, the game's all over in a tie or we have to go extra innings. The other team's second baseman makes an incredible play; and our whole team applauds him. That's where I'd like to get.

I see the beautiful things going on in martial arts and in mind-body disciplines becoming more and more a part of American physical education: I see outdoor education growing by leaps and bounds. Lifetime sports and lifetime skills will also grow in popularity. I see some things coming out of the women's movement as being very healthy and exciting—less emphasis on winning, more concern for the person and how he or she feels, etc.

I also look at the other side of the coin: sports are becoming ultracommercialized, violence is increasing, football coaches teaching linemen to hold. I've seen that happen. Money is running the game right now.

Joel: In a recent "Tank McNamara" comic strip a sportscaster comes up with examples of how kids are now playing baseball. It's not actually playing the game of baseball, but they start choosing up, "Hey, I'll be the free agent. Hey, I'll be Reggie Jackson's agent. Hey, I'll be Fred Lynn's . . ."

Do you have any closing personal reflections or thoughts that you might want to share?

Jeff: I feel a need to make some kind of closing statement that refers to my personal experience and get off the cosmic pitch about what's right or wrong about athletics. Before I do that, I want to mention two books that have been helpful to me in moving in a direction that feels good to me. One is called *Zen and the Art of Archery*, which is about a German who goes to Japan to learn archery. He finds out from the masters that, to learn archery, he needs to learn Zen. There is a message in that for me—not only about a way of teaching—but also that archery isn't really what's important. What's important is what you can learn through archery about yourself and about others. I like to view baseball that way and to think that the other sports also have possibilities that help people move in that direction.

The other reference I want to mention is called *Democracy and the Football Revolution: The Fifth Down,* which is written by Neil Amdor, a former sportswriter for *The New York Times.* The first half of the book deals with the abuses of recruiting and the overemphasis on winning. The second half of the book is entitled "Democracy" and it's about George Davis. It's an answer to those abuses and describes how George went about his experiment in Athenian democracy with young high school students, using football as a vehicle. That brings it full circle to me, because the abuses outrage me. Now, I feel I've moved beyond awareness of the abuses toward solutions—through democracy and through working with individuals. That's a good direction. That feels good. What I want to do is to continue to move along those lines and maintain my awareness of what I feel is oppressive but put the focus on the beauty of sport. Sport can be an experience that helps people to learn about themselves and to move and to grow.

"A friend is one who knows you are as you are, understands where you've been, accepts who you've become, and still, gently, invites you to grow."
(EMERSON)

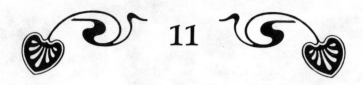

Human Relations Youth Adventure Camp: A Model that Really Works

The Human Relations Youth Adventure Camp (HRYAC) was founded in 1974 as part of the National Humanistic Education Center. The camp has been based on the belief that human interactions in a controlled setting can be influenced in a positive direction. Our purpose was to create a small and ideal community in the wilderness.

For three weeks in August, twenty-four boys and girls ages eleven to fourteen came together in a primitive setting in New York. They lived in tents, and shared the responsibilities of group living. The only building was a one-room log cabin and later a three-room building.

Some of our basic assumptions were: (1) Everyone has the ability to relate to others with love and caring; (2) Everyone has a zest for life which is sometimes hidden, but is always there; (3) Everybody knows what is good for them and they can learn to trust their inner wisdom; (4) Staff who have strong interpersonal skills will help campers develop theirs, too; and (5) Campers learn to act maturely by being given opportunities to control much of their own lives.

As this description of HRYAC unfolds, you will see how we integrated these assumptions into each day's activities.

Certain elements essential to building a close community were considered in planning each day. They were:

Trust and Caring—Trust, or a feeling of confidence in and security with people, must extend throughout the entire community for growth to occur. Campers must feel that the staff cares about them and there must be someone around for each person to count on. Campers and staff must be able to share concerns openly, and have confidence in their ability to work together toward common goals.

Respect for Self and Others—Each person, staff and campers alike, must feel important to the successful functioning of the community. Each person's individuality is accepted and appreciated. All members of the community are treated as people whose needs and feelings are important.

BROWN

Cooperation and Cohesiveness—Cooperation must be reflected in the camp program. If activities are structured to foster group cohesiveness the members will evolve into a cooperative community. This goal does not merely happen—it must be carefully planned.

Opportunity for Input—Everyone in the community must feel that what they have to say will be heard and considered. They must feel a certain degree of power and control in their lives. No one will be a fully functioning person without the chance to influence the future.

Problem Solving and Conflict Resolution—Problems and conflicts are natural and predictable occurrences in close living situations. They must be greeted with optimism that solutions will be found, and eagerly as a challenge to human intellect. A forum must be provided for problems and conflicts to be attacked with rationality.

In the Beginning . . .

Our opening activities were designed to help people get acquainted. To trust people you first must get to know them. Step one for us was to learn everyone's name. We accomplished this with forty people in about fifteen minutes with a pillow-throwing game. We sat in a circle and tossed a pillow around. The one rule was that before the pillow was thrown to someone, you must call them by name.

After learning names we went around the circle and each person answered a question such as, "If I could be magically changed into any kind of animal, what would it be, and why?" As people answered, they began to emerge as unique individuals.

An important concern at the beginning was, "Who will be my tentmates?" Instead of making assignments, we allowed the campers to group themselves. The process sometimes took a while but it always was worked out. The next problem was, "Which tent will be ours?" The tents were already set up and some sites were more desirable than others. Again, instead of telling the campers how to decide, we presented the situation as a group problem, and allowed the solutions of how to decide fairly to come from them. A more efficient method in terms of time and effort would have been to tell the campers what to do. Our thought was that by allowing the campers to make decisions important to their lives, we were demonstrating our confidence in their ability to think and decide, and building an atmosphere of trust and respect.

We believed strongly that campers should have a lot of input into their scheduled activities. However, because we were concerned with welding the group into a cooperative, caring community, we designed some activities for the first few days which included everyone. Each staff member and camper participated. One of these activities was a stream walk. We walked down the center of a rocky stream for about two miles. The water was often up to our waists and higher. Some of the smaller campers had genuine need for help from others near them. We walked as a total group with concern for the safety and feelings of each person. This was an authentic stress situation and the cooperation and caring needed to bring everyone safely back to camp created a feeling of cohesiveness important to the community.

Rules

The codirectors of HRYAC developed a minimum list of those rules deemed necessary: (1) for maintaining the health and safety of everyone; (2) for caring for equipment and the environment; and (3) for the perpetuation of the organization's reputation in the eyes of parents and the surrounding community. With these guidelines, a minimum set of rules was presented to the participants *along with* a reason or reasons for each rule. The consequences for breaking each rule were carefully described.

Many times rules did not have to be made beyond the minimum set until a problem arose which affected the community. A rule was most likely to be followed when everyone agreed with it. For this reason additional rules were developed by consensus of the whole group. Reaching consensus took time, but often resulted in greater cooperation with the rule. In reaching a consensus, everyone had to agree that they would be willing to follow the rule because it made sense to them.

Enforcing rules had to be consistent and direct. Community agreement on a rule made enforcing it much easier. The removal of privileges for breaking a rule was more humane than any form of punishment such as belittling or embarrassing the offender. Respect for human dignity was the overriding guideline in making and enforcing rules. There are no simple answers to rule-making and enforcing, but group discussion and problem solving so that everyone wins was the goal. The use of power by those responsible for the program was inevitable, but it was kept to a minimum in order to realize the goals of self-discipline and mutual respect.

After much debate and hard thought, we arrived at the following list of rules for our Human Relations Youth Adventure Camp:

(1) Saws and knives may be used only after skill has been demonstrated *because* misuse of them may cause serious injury.

(2) The roof of the log cabin is off limits *because* walking on the cedar shingles will break them.

(3) Smoking or striking a match is to be done only in the designated area *because* of the danger of fire in wooded areas and the fact that the actual smoke and the sight of people smoking offends others. (The effect of smoking on an individual's health was discussed but it was decided that a smoking ban would lead to sneaking and lying in some cases of persistent smokers.)

(4) Shoes are to be worn at all times outside *because* of the danger of cutting feet and the inconvenience of administering first aid.

(5) Participants will sleep in their own tents *because* of Health Department regulations concerning the number in each tent and the risk of damaging the reputation of the camp in the eyes of parents and others.

(6) Food consumption is for mealtimes only except when a snack is served during the evening *because* food quantities are purchased for meals and regular snacks only, and cleanup of utensils will be inadequate at any other times.

(7) Make sure that someone on the staff knows where you are going if you leave the immediate camp area *because* the staff is responsible for your health and safety at all times and it is dangerous to be alone if an accident occurs.

(8) Don't wash with soap in the streams and lakes *because* the pollution may destroy the living things in the water and make this area less attractive.

(9) Don't walk on the logs around the campfire circle *because* they roll and may result in an injury.

(10) All accidents—major and minor—must be reported to the first aid person *because* it is important to treat all injuries and the staff may be liable for negligence if a problem arises in the future.

(11) Meat must not be put into the compost pile *because* of the possibility of a dangerous animal coming into camp.

(12) No deep water swimming is allowed unless a qualified water safety instructor is on duty *because* of the danger of drowning.

Beyond these basic rules, campers had a wide range of choice in conducting their daily lives. It is always more difficult to extend a range of choices to campers, but the effort is worth it in building self-reliance and decision-making skills. Unless campers feel they have a strong opportunity for input, they often will be unhappy and rebel. We did not expect the campers to always choose what we wanted for them, but as long as no rule was broken, we let them go.

The enforcement of camp rules was done by all. It seemed like the power of a total community to enforce rules was much stronger than the power of any one person or small group of persons.

Rules differ from the personal prejudices of the staff in that there are usually no major consequences to the offender when prejudices are not heeded. Being in touch with personal prejudices, the opposite of value preferences, and distinguishing them from rules are very important. Knowing that a behavior of a participant is bothersome, but is not against a rule, may influence how the leader acts toward the participant. Sometimes a staff member will punish a participant for some offensive behavior that violates a personal prejudice and not a rule. The following section lists one author's personal prejudices that operate when he conducts a resident outdoor education program.

Fifteen Personal Prejudices

Cliff Knapp

(1) Telling "ghost" or other scary stories.
(2) Telling "dirty jokes or stories," making suggestive sexual references, or using off-color language.
(3) Permitting verbal or nonverbal put-downs of others and yourself.
(4) Playing traditional team sports (basketball, baseball, etc.) and other competitive games.
(5) Giving material awards and prizes to a select few in games, contests, or daily living activities.
(6) Permitting any kind of littering.
(7) Engaging in "horseplay" or physical "roughhousing" with participants.
(8) Making threats that are unwise to carry out or administering physical punishments (exercises, etc.).
(9) Allowing radios, TVs, stereos, or tape recorders to be played when they detract from the program.
(10) Permitting yelling, screaming, foot-stamping, booing, loud whistling, or other noises in inappropriate places.
(11) Permitting inconsiderate noise and disturbance in cabins or tents after "lights out" time.
(12) Drinking soda, eating candy, or having any special privileges in the presence of the participants.
(13) Giving special treats in the form of privileges or food unless everybody participates.
(14) Ignoring table manners, wasting food, or allowing contests with food or drink.
(15) Violating the rights of others as persons in any form (searching luggage, not respecting personal privacy, etc.).

What are your personal prejudices? Are they different from the rules you and your organization have established? Take out a piece of paper and make a list of your personal prejudices and rules.

"Why should we be in such desperate haste to succeed and in such desperate enterprises? If a man does not keep pace with his companions, perhaps it is because he ears a different drummer. Let him step to the music he hears, however measured or far away." (HENRY DAVID THOREAU)

Positive Focus

A primary goal for the three weeks was to increase both self-respect and respect for the other members of the community. We wanted our campers to like themselves and others better by the end of the session. One theme which influenced nearly everything we did and which built toward this goal was a focus on the positive. A camp norm was a ban on "put-downs" and "killer statements"—those actions and words which result in people feeling less of themselves. Once the campers learned to recognize verbal and nonverbal put-downs, they cooperated by checking themselves and reminding each other to stop negative actions.

A ritual which encouraged positive focus was called "new and goods." As part of each evening's program, we went around the circle and each person shared something that was new and good for them during the day. If someone could not come up with their own new and good, others were glad to help. Sometimes we did a "proud whip" in which each person completed the statement, "I am proud that . . ."

We structured many occasions for giving and receiving compliments or validations. As part of the evening closing, we formed a five-minute validation circle in which anyone who had an appreciation or compliment for someone in the community could speak out and share it with the whole group. One problem that arose was holding the circle time to only five minutes each night. Other validation techniques used at various times were:

Validation envelopes—Each person decorated an envelope with their name and artwork and hung it on the fireplace. A stack of scrap paper was left in a convenient place for use. Whenever people wanted to share a positive comment, they wrote it on a piece of paper, signed it, and put it in the person's envelope.

Validation book—Each person's name was written on a page in a notebook. The notebook was passed around, and positive comments were written on each person's page. At the end of camp each person was presented with his or her page.

Focus person—As a closing activity on the last night, each person had one minute when everyone in camp focused on them and showered them with validations. By limiting the time to one minute, each person was left with the feeling that much more could have been said if the time were longer.

Creativity night—This was a time when individuals could get up in front of the group in an atmosphere of support and encouragement and share something of themselves. Sharings varied from telling jokes, leading or singing songs, reading an original poem, or doing a skit. One boy who was to have his Bar Mitzvah in the fall, shared some of the chants from the ceremony. For some it was easy; for others it took great courage to perform in front of their friends. It was a time to focus on individuals, and both performers and audience saw themselves and each other in new, positive ways.

Focusing upon personal strengths was a theme which ran throughout the camp. One activity directed the campers to go outside and find something in nature which represented one of their positive qualities. When they returned they shared their discoveries with one another. Self-concept building was an important aim and we structured the program to accomplish this.

Trust-Building

We felt that learning to touch each other to demonstrate friendship and caring was an important factor in building closeness and trust. We started with such games as "People to People." In this game, the participants paired up and one person was chosen the leader. The leader called out the parts of the body the pairs must touch, such as "toe to toe," "finger to finger," "arm to arm," or "knee to knee." When the leader called, "people to people," everyone had to find a new partner. The person left over became the new leader.

Another touch activity involving a high level of trust was "People Pass." This activity required at least twenty people. Everyone stood together in a tight line with their arms raised. Each person in turn was then lifted, passed from the front to the back of the group, and gently lowered to the ground.

Massage was a popular activity. The campers divided into two groups. One group laid down on their stomachs with their eyes closed. The other group chose reclining partners and under the leadership of a staff member, gave head, back, or foot massages. After awhile the groups switched and the people chose new partners. Gentle touching is a way to communicate caring, which is turn promotes trust. In any of these activities, the option to pass, or not participate, was always honored without question, but few chose to exercise this privilege.

A "Blind Walk" is another activity we used to build trust. The campers paired off, and one in each pair was blindfolded. The sighted people guided their blindfolded partners and nonverbally shared the environment with them through senses other than sight. Sometimes the experience included a blind lunch. It took a high level of trust to allow someone to feed you an unknown meal.

KNAPP

Another technique we used for getting acquainted was small group sharing. We divided ourselves into groups of three or four and shared answers to questions such as, "What are some of the things I like about myself?", "What are my goals for the three weeks of camp?", "What will you like about me when you get to know me?", and "What fun things have I been doing this summer?" Because feeling listened-to is an important prerequisite to speaking freely, we used these small-group times to introduce and practice listening skills. The act of listening with interest while people talk about themselves is another method of promoting trust.

Campers had considerable input and latitude in deciding how to spend their time. If two or three campers had something they wanted to do and could find a staff member to do it with them, it was generally done. Campers built and labeled their own nature trail, constructed a tree house, a sauna and primitive shower, an underground fort, a raft, and a playground for tots complete with see-saw, birchbark slide, and tire swing for the staff's young children. One group of campers and staff put on a circus for the whole group. Another baked banana bread and made pizza for everyone. We all helped to cut down a giant birch that weighed hundreds of pounds. We hauled it several hundred feet, carved it, and erected it in place. It was such a highlight that we decided to name the session, "The Year of the Totem." The campers also offered their own activities for others to select. There was always an option to do nothing, but the offerings were so varied that boredom and nonparticipation were not problems.

There were no skill awards for excellence in any of the activities we did. We all did the best we could and that was good enough. There were many cooperative projects that built upon different individual talents. We had a thirty-minute community meeting each night after dinner. Any issues of concern to anyone in the community could be raised. To help the organization, a meeting agenda was posted all day so that any item could be written down for discussion that night. Campers usually led the meeting and made sure that only one person at a time spoke. Everyone, including staff and directors, had to wait to be recognized by the leader before they spoke. The community meeting was the foundation of much of the decision making and was an important part of the day to everyone. When asked what they learned from the community meeting, campers answered with three different types of responses:

(1) Most frequent were responses dealing with solving community problems. They recognized that problems can be dealt with openly and solved rationally by everyone.
(2) The next grouping of responses recognized how everybody's thoughts and opinions were considered and how people really cared about each other.
(3) The third grouping of responses dealt with speaking out and expressing feeling and problems in a large group of people.

These kinds of learnings alone made the community meetings worthwhile.

Problem-Solving

In any community problems arise and need to be dealt with directly. We tried to include everyone in the discussions and decision making, and come up with solutions which could be accepted by everyone.

One technique we used to deal with an all-camp problem was fishbowling. This involved two concentric circles of people. The inner circle discussed a topic for a period of time while the outer circle just observed and listened. Members of the outside circle were not allowed to interrupt. After a set time, the circles reversed and the outer circle became the inner one and discussed the same topic.

A problem for which we used this technique was the staff's growing dissatisfaction over picking up litter, equipment, and personal belongings of the campers. The staff went into the inner circle first, and discussed their gripes about picking up after the campers. The campers listened intently, and when their turn came to talk they expressed their feelings about the staff concerns. The whole group then divided into quartets to brainstorm ways of solving the problems brought out in fishbowling. This was a morning activity for the whole camp and was very necessary to clear the air before doing other things that day. It took a lot of trust for each group to express concerns about the others and not fear punishment or rejection.

We dealt with problems as a community, and with the exception of the areas of health, safety, care of property, and preserving the camp's public image, we allowed campers to influence camp policy. One time, staff-arranged groupings for an out-of-camp trip were challenged, and after considerable discussion, the decision was changed to allow the campers to group themselves.

At a group meeting, one girl broke into tears because her tent was scheduled to be moved for an overnight trip. She was a long way from home and had been on the move all summer. After she expressed her feelings, it was easy to take another tent and give her the stability she needed. It took trust to speak out against the plan to take her tent and it took trust to express feelings in the group.

In a primitive wilderness setting, chores are obviously important to the successful functioning of the camp. If water is not brought up from the stream, no one can wash. If dishwater is not put on to boil well before the meal, everyone suffers because dishes must be done before other activities can begin.

The method for assigning responsibilities was decided by the campers. One year a camper was appointed to design a caper or chores chart. Another year people volunteered for jobs for the next day at the beginning of each community meeting. People were on their honor to volunteer for each job. Staff did not supervise jobs with the exception of cooking and dishwashing, which were health matters. Staff signed up for jobs as well as the campers. With no one telling them when to do their jobs, people had full responsibility to see that they were done. It took a lot of trust on the part of the staff to allow campers this freedom, and we found that when we extended trust in areas of importance, our faith was justified.

Schedule

Given the above component parts of HRYAC, how did we put them all together? What follows is a sample calendar of the three-week program in 1978 to give a sense of the flow and overall organization of the program.

CALENDAR **********************

	Sunday	Monday	Tuesday
* Morning		9 AM Nurse Check-In (Songs while you wait (Unc and Manhattan) Rules & Policies #2 (Stream) Group Community Building (Clock, line games, people pass, snail, cookie machine)	All Community Stream Walk
* Afternoon	Arrival 4 PM-Community Meeting Tentmate Selection	Fire Drill Tour of Camp (All) Swim Tests Canoe Tests Beach Activities (Manhattan)	Validation Envelopes Skills Courses: First Aid Knife Safety Saw Safety
* Evening	Meeting Rules & Polices #1	New & Goods Calendar #2 Agenda "Getting to Know You" (Louisa)	Community Meeting Interviews #1

****************************Week #1

Wednesday	Thursday	Friday	Saturday
Guitar Chords (Anna B.) Knife Safety/ Saw Safety (Stream) First Aid for Everybody (Wanda) Canoe Skills (Vera, Boo) Weather (Unc) O.B. Course (Sunshine) Letters (Kara)	Backpacking trip —│ Hike (Sunshine) Cooking (Louisa) Raft Painting (Unc) Parachute Activity (Wanda) Golf Course (Manhattan)	Raft (Unc) Frisbee Golf (Manhattan) Sat. Dinner Planning (Anna B) Edibles & Blueberries Hike (Wanda, Sunshine) Candle Wax Melting (Vera)	Happy Birthday (Laura) Raft Painting II
Hike to Reservoir (Unc) Frisbee Golf Planning (Manhattan) Optional Swim Sychronized Swim Swim Test Special K (Kathy) Canoe Test	Singing Charades Cooking Mini-Hike	Wood Cutting and Raft Scraping (Unc) Frisbee Course (Manhattan) Body Painting (Anna B) Cookies & Dinner (Wanda) Macrame & Edibles (Sunshine) Canoe Tests (Vera) ARRIVAL OF THE BIG E Utensils Dinner	New Games (Max) Joint Dinner (Joy)
Name Drawing Interviews #2 Night Hike	Back Rub Introduction	Barn Dance	Special Campfire (Ernie)

CALENDAR********************

	Sunday	Monday	Tuesday
* Morning	Hey, Hey, Hey What About Me? (Big E) Raft Painting II	Off Today (Anna B & Sunshine) Raft Launching 10:30 Corn Bread (Man) Canoe Test (Boo) Macrame (Louisa) Car Wash (Vera) Raft & Service (Unc) Creative Writing (Wanda) Knife & Saw (Stream) Drama (Eve)	6:30 AM Early Birds (Barry) Blue Mt. Hike Lunch Pack (Vera, Wanda) Canoeing (Boo) Woodcarving (Stream) Macrame (Louisa) Song Writing (Manhattan) Guitar (Unc) Candlemaking (Sue) Drama (Eve)
* Afternoon	Hey, Hey, Hey What About Me? #2 (Big E) New Games II (Max & Co) Individual Time	Pre-rappelling, limit 6 (Boo) Candle Making (Vera) Wild Rodeo (Unc, Wanda) Macrame/Cookies (Louisa) Setup (Manhattan)	2-4 PM New Games Sagamore Visit Happy Birthday (Anna B)
* Evening	Movie—Bless the Beasts and Children Group Interviews #3 Beasts Discussion	Mini-Canoe Trip #1 (Manhattan, Louisa)	Mini-Canoe Trip #2 (Unc, Boo) Massage (Sunshine)

*******************************Week #2

Wednesday	Thursday	Friday	Saturday
Laundry at Old Forge Guitar (Unc) Bread Baking & Raspberry Hike (Vera) Choc Cake (Louisa) Blueberry Picking (Stream) Drama (Eve)	Off (Manhattan) Canoe Trip — — — Hike & Nature Crafts, Beaver Sticks (Wanda) Tie Dying Prep. (Vera) Drama (Eve) Hike (Unc) Ceative Writing (Anna B.) Pre-rappelling (Boo)	— — — — — — — — — Laundry at Old Forge Camp Empty: Inspector In-spects	— — — — —| RAIN . . . Sleep, Sleep . . . more sleep Branch Orifice (Unc) Meal Committee (Anna B.)
2 PM Jam Making (Trish) Cake Decorating (Robin) Happy Birthday (Kara)	Tie Dying (Vera) Swim (Anna B.) 2 PM Frisbee Les-sons, Ultimate Frisbee (Andy Simpson) Nature Crafts and Sketches (Wanda) Cake Bake (Kathy) Road Crew (Uncle Al) Pre-rappelling (Boo) Happy Birthday, Dean!	Cookout on Beach Manhattan Comes Back! Inspector Inspects	Good Deed for the Day (Louisa) 2PM Canoe Pickup Cooking (Wanda, Max, Sandy B.) Barn Busting (Boo) Tournament (Manhattan)
Acid Rain People for Dinner (Howie, Barb) Group Interview #4 Creativity Night	New Games Blob Tag Prui Killer Validation Circle	Magic Box	50's Night

CALENDAR************************

	Sunday	Monday	Tuesday
* Morning	Backwards Sunday Newspaper (Man, Anna B.) Tie Dying & Candles (Vera) Nature Crafts & Gift Ideas (Wanda) Rappell Intro.	Backpack Trip #2 Run & Dip Group Interview #5 Backpack II Hits the Trail (Vera, Wanda) Whistle Making (Stream) Rappell (Sunshine, Boo) Cookies (Louisa) Jell-O (Chuck) Community Newspaper (Man, Anna B.) Road (Unc)	The ManUnc Expedition Gifts (Anna B., Louisa) Bye (Chuck, Tisti, Uptown) Rappell Intro.
* Afternoon	Tie Dying Candles (Vera) Group Initiatives (Sue, Unc) Swim (Anna B.) Apple Luscious Making (Louisa) Hike for Nature Crafts (Stream) Uptown Takes Off! Drama (Eve) Crafts & Swim (Wanda)	Swim (Stream) Large Candles (Sunshine) Pre-Rappell (Boo) New Games (Tisti, Chuck) Cookies (Louisa) New Games (Man.) Drama (Eve) Lots of Fun— Group Initiatives	Return of Backpack II Return of ManUnc Rappellers Return Captain & Co. Visit Many Happy Returns!
* Evening	Group Interview #4 Vulture & Co. Story	Talkity Talk About Camp Tone (Uptown & Co. Sing)	Group Interview #6 Campfire

✱✱✱✱✱✱✱✱✱✱✱✱✱✱✱✱✱✱✱✱✱✱✱✱✱✱✱Week #3

Wednesday	Thursday	Friday	Saturday

Frisbee Golf Opening Ceremonies
Group Interview #7
Gift Making
  (Anna B.)
Warm Fuzzing
  (Sandy B.)
Roadeo (Unc)
Shell Painting
  (Stream)
Rappell Beg.
	Frisbee Tourney
	Newspaper
	  (Anna B.)
	Oh Phi Hole (Unc)
	Firewood (?)
	Strengths Game
	  (Manhattan)
	Your Choice
	  (Wanda)
	Help as Needed
	  (Sunshine)
	Drama (Eve)
		Last Night Comm.
		  (Wanda, Man)
		Rappelling (Boo)
		Breadmaking
		  (Vera)
		Newspaper
		  (Anna B.)
		Initiatives (Unc)
		A Bit O'Candles,
		  Macrame and
		  Lunch
		  (Sunshine)
		Drama (Eve)
			Kettle Circle
			Sierra Cup Ceremony
			Evaluations
			Dear Me Letters

2 PM Acid Rain Lab
  Visit
Swim (Stream)
Gift Making (Man.)
4:30 PM Group
  Initiatives
	Group Interview #8
	Sand City
	Options
	  Massage
	  Group Initiative
	Newspaper
	Firewood
	  Collection
		Group Pictures
		Drama
			Sad Hello
			
			Forevers!

Celebration Night	8 PM Square Dance Fireside All Night Vigil	Hambake Dinner Validation Circle	

Evaluation

A technique which we found valuable for introspection and personal evaluation of the camp experience was the "Dear Me" letter. This was usually a private letter written by each camper to him/herself. These letters were collected and sent to each person a few months later. Sometimes unfinished sentences are provided to give ideas for what to write in the letter. Here are some excerpts from "Dear Me" letters written at our HRYAC experience:

"My favorite part of camp was the stream hike. Or maybe it was going to Montreal and singing on the sidewalk. There are so many great things about camp, it's hard to choose.

The low part of camp I think was when it was raining for about the fifth day. Everyone was restless.

I learned at camp that it's not something to be ashamed of to show your emotions.

I felt happy and loved here and like I really belonged.

I relearned macrame. It has been a fun part of camp.

I think the unique part of camp is that a group of so many people can be so close. There weren't any splits in the group.

I appreciate the community for accepting me and loving me and helping me." Signed . . .

"I learned how close people can really be. I felt close and related to everybody. I relearned how to be a better person. I am concerned about people here, and I only wonder whether I'll ever be this close again." Signed . . .

"I learned that there is a lot more love in the world than anyone thinks. I have also learned to care for people more and to hug and touch them . . . I appreciated myself for being part of the community and fitting in pretty well. I appreciated the community for including me and caring for me. See you soon." Signed . . .

"I learned that I can be free with people and that they understand. I felt I have become a better person after I went to camp.

I need to know I'm wanted by people and that I can show my love for them.

I appreciate myself for loving and caring for other people. I appreciate the community for being a great place to live for three weeks." Signed . . .

At the end of our three-week camp, we did a survey to find out just what type of impact we had on our campers. It was a sentence completion-type of questionnaire with thirty-three sentence stems.

"You are richer today if you have laughed often, given something,
forgiven more
Made a new friend
Have taken time to trace the wonder of Nature in the commonplace
things of life."

(ANONYMOUS)

We Want to Know

Our camp has come to an end for another year. What you take with you will be yours for the rest of your life. Please complete the following sentences. Feel free to add more to each sentence if you wish.

(1) The best thing about the people at camp is . . .
(2) Living in the wilderness for three weeks was . . .
(3) The thing I enjoyed most about being here was . . .
(4) The thing that took the most courage for me was . . .
(5) One of the hardest things for me to do was . . .
(6) I did the following things for the first time in my life . . .
(7) One thing that helped me become more mature was . . .
(8) The most exciting thing that happened was . . .
(9) The scariest thing that happened was . . .
(10) One memory that I will keep for the rest of my life is . . .
(11) The people here who mean the most to me are . . .
(12) One thing I learned from the community meetings was . . .
(13) One thing I learned from the scheduled activities was . . .
(14) I got to know the people best when . . .
(15) The food was . . .
(16) If I were just starting this camp again today, I would . . .
(17) Sleeping in tents made me feel . . .
(18) The counselors helped me most when they . . .
(19) The thing that bothered me most about camp was . . .
(20) If I had the power to make one change in this camp I would . . .
(21) Deciding what I wanted to do each day was . . .
(22) The jobs of cleanup, water, latrine, and cooking were . . .
(23) Nature is important to me because . . .
(24) The activity that was the most fun was . . .
(25) The thing that I most want to say to Vera and Cliff (directors) is . . .
(26) If I could return next year it would be because . . .
(27) One reason I wouldn't want to return next year is . . .
(28) This camp is different from most camps I know because . . .
(29) Some new activities I would add to the camp next year are . . .
(30) The best description of what happened at camp if anyone asks me is . . .
(31) The hardest decision I had to make was . . .
(32) Two words which best describe how I feel about camp are . . .
(33) Some other sentences I would like to write about the camp are . . .

The completions for one sentence were very interesting because they revealed how the campers got to know the people in camp best. Knowing people is part of trusting them. The answers fell into four main categories: (1) one-to-one informal conversations; (2) small group camp activities such as trips, chores, or parties; (3) responses to people having problems or being hurt; and (4) whole-group trust activities such as the stream walk or massages.

A strong bond developed between many counselors and campers and the cement was trust and respect. In response to the question asking when the counselors helped the campers most, the campers' responses fell into three main areas: (1) verbal interactions such as talking seriously, joking, encouraging, or comforting; (2) conveying an attitude of respect, caring, or empathy by simply paying attention to them; and (3) physical contact such as backrubs, first aid care, or hugs. One camper said of counselor hugs, "It makes you feel really special and no one is telling them to do it."

Only one response indicated that the counselor helped them most by teaching an outdoor skill. That activity was rappelling. That is a powerful finding to us. Our counselors were most helpful to campers when they were just there for them, talking to them, paying attention, or touching them. That indicates that a lot more time should be devoted to developing human relations skills.

Another question asked the campers to use two words which best described how they felt about camp. Out of twenty-three different words used one year, just two words were used thirteen times. They were "loving" and "caring." No other word was used more than twice to describe their camp experience. Some of the other words used were: togetherness, understanding, community, mature, nature, homesick, happy, fun, very free, great, and beautiful. Something must have happened to those who chose the words loving and caring. They felt strongly about the people in camp. When we asked the campers about the thing they enjoyed most, over half mentioned the people.

HRYAC is an experiment in humanizing camping. Many of the program activities are repeated year after year because they work. New activities are tried each summer to continue the search for ways of promoting an ideal wilderness community in which good human relations and a joy for living are the main goals.

What follows are excerpts from my journal and other writings to give you more of a taste for the camp.

Excerpts from the Director's Journal

August 3—The question of why I'm running a camp for twenty-four kids faced me tonight. Fatigue is probably the reason this question comes to mind tonight. It seems like thousands of items are needed or wanted and most of it has to be carried into the cabin one by one. This is just plain hard work with pressures of great responsibility on my shoulders. Health problems have started already with Jay's sore throat and Judy's bee sting. Nothing serious yet. We ran one and one-half hours behind schedule due to a late bus pickup and heavy rains when the campers arrived. All cleared up and we congratulated ourselves on the first day. It is a temptation to tell the kids everything I think they should know to make our routines run more smoothly. It will take time. Establishing a community of thirty people is a big undertaking. The reasons I established this camp will undoubtedly become clearer as the weeks go by. Our problems seem to be with one girl who holds her right hand to her mouth and says she has a toothache, a boy who is scared of other kids, and another who would rather be alone tonight. Another camper seems to want acceptance so badly that he attracts attention by his continuous wisecracks. What will tomorrow bring? Tonight will bring needed rest, I hope. The mosquitoes and flies are the only obstacle to quiet sleep.

August 4—Larry conducted the "get to know" activities today. The pillow throw to each person while calling out their name works quickly. I read a list of about twelve rules to the group. Our first community meeting went well. Tomorrow we plan a stream exploration and nature awareness session.

The tent selections went smoothly for the most part. The campers decided on a system of requesting each of the nine tent sites in their group of three. If there was a conflict for a tent site, sticks of varying lengths were drawn to settle the conflict. Dawn, Jocie, and Beckie were the only ones who weren't satisfied with their site. Paul helped them pick a new place and they re-pitched their tent.

August 5—Today was the all-group stream hike. We drove the group to the crossing of a stream and a road and then walked downstream. It took about two hours at a slow, exploring pace. We waited for the tail end of the line every few minutes. We accomplished our purposes of nature awareness, adventure, and cooperation. We linked hands and arms and helped each other over slippery places and fallen logs. The winter wren, jewelweed, hornet's nest, crayfish, stoneflies, and the people in the group helped make the time enjoyable.

After the community meeting, we closed the evening with verbal appreciations for Paul and Kevin. We will do more each night. We need to pay attention to those who are so far quiet and hanging back a bit. The group of campers from last summer and the new ones are blending into one community as the special magic of group building begins. The campers are speaking out freely and enjoying the freedom to be themselves. Apparently, the rules made sense to them and they still see that they have many choices in their lives. I wondered about confronting some of them with the issue of sex. A few campers paired off today to form couples. It is difficult to know when to raise my concerns and when to keep my doubts to myself. I wonder where that issue will go?

There are so many variables to think about in operating a camp. There are facility variables like the broken gas refrigerator and the human variables of the staff and campers. I even have to think about my role as a father and husband. I will do the best I can with all of these responsibilities.

August 6—The community meeting worked like the textbook says it should. Many people voiced their gripes and suggested solutions. We used the newsprint a lot for meeting agendas, notes of things to do, and the day-to-day schedule. We have only been able to plan one day ahead as far as the program goes. There are still many little things to do to make our home in the wilderness comfortable. The mosquitoes for the first time are not over-whelming. Sue and Jenny took four campers on a night hike and we were not bothered around the campfire like the first night. A good staff armed with lots of talent, dedication, and the ability to work hard is surely the formula for success in this camp.

It felt good today and I know why I'm running this camp now. The "Death of a Wombat" story went over well tonight. Campfires and meetings seem to flow without strain. The campers love to sing, and Sue and Judy lead songs beautifully. The question of swearing and going out on a group overnight without adult supervision were discussed and cleared up for me. Swearing and off-color jokes *do* make me uncomfortable. Also going off in coed groups for an overnight is not allowed without staff being there. The campers did their Seton Watch (a time alone in the woods for reflection and quiet) today. I should have asked more of them for their reactions to this new experience. Some said they liked it. We need to share the results of our day rather than only gripe about community problems.

August 7—We need to plan the schedule a few days in advance to heighten the excitement for expected events and to show better where we're going. Everyone seems happy with the way our lives unfold, day-by-day. This is a hard way to make a living, but satisfactions are rewarding.

After the community meeting, we had time for some contributions for creativity night. We arrived at a consensus that our meeting would only last thirty minutes. I could have made that rule at the beginning, but it was better to have the whole group decide this after a few evenings of long, drawn-out meetings. A rule will only be followed when people clearly see a need for it and respect the rule makers as people. The need for the thirty-minute meeting rule was clearly seen after experience and was quickly accepted and held to.

August 8—The group this morning created many useful and beautiful crafts. A raft, bench, grass broom, birchbark basket, and a grass wall hanging were some of the crafts. The beauty of the morning was that I was there to help get what was needed and the campers did what they wanted to do. It was a good example of providing a rich environment and letting people go (or allowing them to go).

The community meeting went quickly despite a number of items on the agenda. Our creativity night was a rousing success. There seemed to be true appreciation for all of the offerings by everyone. The next one will be even better, I predict. We closed the evening with everyone sharing their "new and goods" of the day. Finishing the birchbark stitching, the good spirits of the group after realizing that they were lost, and personal satisfaction about overcoming difficulty were some of the highlights of the day. For me it was observing the morning happening in camp and building a tent fly over a holey tent.

August 9—This morning we offered sessions in tree-house building, bench building, and nature trail construction. The nature trail activity didn't attract enough interest but the other sessions did. Instead of doing the nature trail, I went with the creative writing group. It was another example of allowing things to happen without standing in the way of creative, able people. It also met my personal needs for creating and sharing. My guess is that all were happy with the morning because it was what they wanted to do and they had a hand in determining how they were going to do it. I'm glad I decided to have this camp because it reassures me that this is the right way to work with people.

We had a long, but productive community meeting which got out a lot of feelings. We closed with "new and goods" and a birthday celebration for Ann. The group is molding rapidly into a cohesive, loving community. As our meeting went on beyond nine-thirty, I had to get away for a walk alone. I can only take so much of any group before needing to get away. I have an ebb and flow of group intimacy and the need to be alone.

August 10—Today was the all-group trip to do the wash. After deciding to take fifteen campers in the morning and fifteen in the afternoon, the campers didn't want to cooperate. Being together in certain groups was

BROWN

more important than the numbers we had picked to fit in the vehicles. Chaos sometimes reigns when free choice is given to grouping, but resentment may reign when campers are forced to do what they don't want to do. What is more important in solving this issue? I ask myself that question continuously about many things. It takes time to sort out the pros and cons involved in each decision we make as a community.

I went fishing alone today and when I returned to camp everyone was involved in a massage activity. Everyone enjoys touching and being touched. It is now "legal" to rub backs and necks and heads while the meeting is going on.

We closed the evening with a discussion of the upcoming camping trip. Some expressed concern about the formation of camper cliques. The staff in private decided to break the clique up to force exposure to new people outside the clique. A clique shuts out others and we agreed this was not fair to them. We didn't anticipate the affect of our decision on the campers when we would tell them about the groupings for the trip.

At the community meeting, only one agenda item was written on the newsprint. The leader asked for other items concerning feelings people had. Kari started by describing how uprooted she felt because her tent was scheduled to be taken on the camping trip. She cried freely as she told of her travel-ridden summer. We were glad to arrange to take other tents and let Kari's stay put. Knowing about a problem is sometimes the hardest part in solving it. The next item on the agenda was the splitting of the groups for the camping trip. Some of the members of the clique felt very close and knew that after the next few weeks they may never all be together again. They couldn't understand our reasons for splitting them up. We had time to explore the feelings of some in the nonclique group too. They didn't seem to have any resentment about being excluded from the clique—at least no one expressed any. After everyone had a chance to express their feelings on the issue, I decided to allow the campers to regroup themselves according to the way they wanted. The only ground rule was that the numbers should be even. The meeting ended happily with the regrouping. The staff agreed to the regrouping when they saw how important it was for the clique group to stay together. Our plan to dictate the groupings for reasons of imagined or real hurts to the nonclique group didn't work. The issue was balanced almost equally between the pros and cons, so our change of plans was relatively easy. One good thing that came from the meeting was the expression of feelings about cliques and their affects upon others in the community. More thought is needed about when to structure the lives of campers and when to allow them free choice.

August 11—After an informal songfest, we had another community meeting. Some of the old campers expressed how they thought the camp was more strict than the previous year. The rules we made were for health, safety, care of property, and the perpetuation of the camp's good reputation. We ended the meeting with "new and goods" and a proud whip in which everyone mentioned one thing they were proud of about themselves. Dawn, Dean, and Jocie had difficulty in pinning down what they were proud about in themselves. Others in the group helped them when they couldn't come up with something to say. This camp community meeting structure provides a way for people to ask for what they need. There ought to be more ways to meet different human needs in this setting. For example, we need to develop structured exercises for people to request praise, alternatives for solving personal problems, better ways for using free time, empathy, and other needs. What are more of our human needs and how can this community help others in meeting these needs?

August 12—This morning we had a beautiful blindfold session. We started with everyone blindfolded and we took journeys by tuning into our five senses. We did a tree fantasy in which we imagined we were small and could travel inside the vessels of a tree. We did a partner blind-trust walk. For the most part it worked out better than I expected. The campers were really into the activities of the morning. To wind up the session before the blind lunch, most of the group played a game of passing objects in a circle while blindfolded. We left the blind lunch as optional and most people decided to participate. Feeding someone or being fed were new experiences for most of them. The most persistent thought coming from the morning was that the campers ranging in age from eleven to fourteen had abilities and sensitivities that I normally expected only from adults.

Before the community meeting, the campers had a rousing soap foam fight. My only objection was the possibility of injury and the angry feelings that were generated in a few. This "soap foam happening" provided a vivid example of the lack of consideration some had for others by forcing this messy game on them. If I would have stopped the game at the start, this learning opportunity never would have been available. We have not come down as typical authoritarians in this wilderness community, but we do lead and organize. Very few things the campers do have made me angry so far.

We really give the campers opportunities to determine their lives with us. We listen to them, help in solving problems, express our frustrations, and enjoy the benefits of community living. This is different from my experience in the public school.

August 13—Our group is going almost like an adult group would. In fact, I'm beginning to doubt if there really is a significant difference in human behavior just because of chronological age. Matt and Elizabeth have fallen in love and are inseparable. People get hurt emotionally and cry and feel good about one another. Campers are more into their own needs than adults when it comes to picking up after themselves and getting their chores done. Maybe adults have been caught up in the work ethic and don't know how to play as well as kids do.

August 14—We had a short community meeting led by Eve tonight. Swearing was discussed in detail. The campers agreed to check out the group before swearing. If anyone in the group didn't feel comfortable with swearing, it wouldn't be done. I wonder if they can stick to that arrangement?

August 15—The group that stayed back at camp today decided to dig an underground shelter. I went to get a pick to make their digging easier. They'll cover the hole with boards and use it as a special retreat. I guess it's hard to do this back at their homes. Perhaps the biggest benefit the older group is getting is a warm, close human interaction with each other. They stay close together and socialize in a tent after our meetings. I wonder how much they will take advantage of the beautiful Adirondack wilderness.

August 16—This afternoon the staff expressed their concern over "helping" the campers too much. They found that they made many decisions for the kids that the kids could be making. They felt sucked up into a trap of "helping" and providing too many answers and too much structure. It was decided that we would bring this concern up at the meeting tonight. We are confused sometimes about our role in the total community and how much we should lead compared to allowing leadership to emerge from the campers. The goal is to place more responsibility on the campers gradually and help them develop self-reliance and group cooperation. We want to share more of the leadership with the campers, but the weaning process is difficult. We want to maintain control over camper safety, health, menus, and food preparation. It's sometimes hard to know where to step in and where to step out.

Some campers are relaxing in the cabin with books and letters while others are improving the road, building a tree house, and making candles. Sue and Bob deliberately walked out on the tree-house group because they believed they were taking charge too much. They thought this would enable the campers to make more decisions. My only hope is that the safety aspect is maintained. I think I'll go check that out now . . . After putting that extra spike in the tree, I can breathe easier now.

August 17—We went to Mt. Jo in the morning with all but two campers. The climb was steep, but we did it in less than one hour. On top, we made lunches and ate them quietly. For part of the time after lunch, we had twenty golden minutes of silence. I'm glad we forced that twenty minutes on the group because some of them mentioned it as their "new and good" for the day. I wish I would have remembered the topographic map of the area, but they enjoyed the view anyway. We stopped by the nature center for help with some local nature, but most of the campers were anxious to hike. We had problems with Kevin's acute littering habit. Nothing seemed to work to stop him. There must be a better way than telling him in front of the rest of the group as well as privately. He's got to really care about the beauty of an unlittered environment.

The community meeting was led by Darby. I find that the campers share some of the same values as I do about living together and they raise issues that I would. I try to maintain a low profile at the meetings and generally my concerns are dealt with. Of course, I bring up topics that really bother me. The meetings are aimed at making our lives together more smooth and rewarding.

August 18—Writing this beside the stream is peaceful and relaxing. The rains today came down hard after lunch. After a week of blue sky and warm sunny days, it just had to rain. The stream is way up and churning beautiful black patterns in front of me. Every once in a while, a fish feeds on the surface. A hummingbird just buzzed in to taste the jewelweed nectar close by.

August 19—Inspired by Backwards Day, Stream wrote this poem, which may be read either forwards or sdrawkcab:

> Love of flowers
> symbolizes love of life;
> Breathing of fragrant winds
> brings new hope,
> recharging tired spirits,
> strength returns again.
> Low time contrasts with soaring,
> touching inner caverns,
> awakens knowing of strength within.
>
> Flowers of love
> life of love symbolizes;
> Winds fragrant of breathing
> hope new brings,
> spirits tired, recharging,
> again returns strength.
> Soaring with contrasts, time low
> caverns inner touching,
> within strength of knowing awakens.

August 20—Judy took my watch and Sue made my lunch. They are clearly telling me this is a day off. It is sorely needed. There isn't enough time this summer to really enjoy a pressure-free Adirondacks romp. Hiking, fishing, and reading would be an improvement.

Creativity night was good. Trish and Jenny are leaving tomorrow and we will be poorer for their going. I was presented with a validation sheet tonight which made me feel good. Love is growing in our community as time passes.

Bear Pond Reflections

Pond surface shimmering
carved with little V's by insect swimmers
dimpled by newts coming up for air
dragonfly runway that is never used for landings
reflections of a distant shoreline
morning mist magically drifting across
pond surface always alive
What is happening underneath?

People calmly conversing
sharing past events of life
gathered around the campfire
carving woodchips from forest branches
laughing or staring into nowhere
reflections of their past life at home
people always alive
What is happening underneath?

August 21—We bid Jenny a tearful farewell. We talked about crying when a few of the campers responded to her goodbye tears. There were warm hugs that came naturally out of love and caring. This must be a different kind of community because of the coming together and leaving of each other, all in the course of three weeks. Saying tearful goodbyes will occur over and over again in our lives. It feels good to provide support for this way of expressing sad emotions when someone special goes away.

I wanted to prevent the people in our community from taking blueberries home with them and Vera thought that it was OK to pick as many as possible. I agreed to discuss the issue at the community meeting that night. There was mixed reaction to my concerns and we decided to bring the question to a higher authority—the director of NHEC, our sponsoring organization. Since the director owned the land and the blueberries, it was his decision to make. We also asked him another question we had about letting people walk on the cabin roof. We respected his decisions on these issues and it became clearer that the power and authority rested in different hands with different issues.

August 22—John Simon spent the whole day with us and everyone loved having him sing and play his guitar with us. When he was ready to leave, I suggested that everyone express their thanks to him after the meeting in a nonverbal way. It was good to see many people hug him, especially the boys. It feels good to encourage touching as a way of expressing caring. The outside world is often afraid to encourage touching as a form of human expression. Living together like this provides special events that are hard to match in public schools. Why can't we find ways to spread what we have learned in this community to others in other settings? The dramas coming out of feelings of caring, sadness, anger, joy, and fear are real and important mediums for learning about our humanness.

August 23—We had a terrific totem-raising ceremony. The campers had a chance to change their names and think about changing a part of themselves too. We gained more insight into each person when we heard how each would like to change themselves.

This is my philosophy of camping: I believe that kids are persons with many of the same rights as adults. They deserve to be heard, to direct their lives in most areas, to speak out for what they like as well as against what they don't like, to structure their time and to share in responsibilities of everyday living. Camp purposes should focus upon human growth about self and others and nature awareness and knowledge. Campers ought to be placed in environments which encourage decision making and self-reliance whenever possible. Taking responsibility for themselves is a gradual process and should be increased with each day spent in camp. Cooperation among all members of the community should be stressed and structured. Competition in which there is a winner and loser should be underplayed. Activities

LESSER

can be structured so that all people win. Rewards for excellence in skills should be largely the pleasure and knowledge one gains from doing the activity. Choice within a structure should be encouraged. The camp should be run like a community—with all pulling together cooperatively. Everyone can contribute their talents to the task of living and growing together.

Child-adult dependency patterns can be gradually broken as the staff works with the campers. Attention should be paid to how each person is interacting with every other person. Putting this philosophy into practice is difficult and never fully polished. Understanding humanity and becoming more human is a lifelong venture.

August 24—This morning has given me time for myself and packing. I am feeling less tense about "doing things" even if I don't feel like it. The community can almost run itself now. I don't feel that its success rests totally with me anymore. What a relief!

We are a close-knit community of people who come together to search for better ways of living together. For three weeks, we try to have fun while learning about ourselves and others in a wilderness setting. We try to face joys as well as problems head-on and experience them fully. We try to create a small society which takes the very best from our larger society. We understand that we have the power to make a difference in our lives when we return to our homes. Since we live in the wilderness, each day brings new awareness and appreciation for nature. Because there is no electricity or running water, we work hard tending to the basics of living. We have used the earth's resources to make dye from plants, to find driftwood carved by lapping waters, to erect a giant totem, to make a tree house and underground shelter, and to eat from wild plants. We have built a sauna, shower, rock drains, and a nature trail. We have felt the wind on our faces, heard the rain tap our tents, and experienced the strains of rappelling over a rocky cliff or carrying a loaded backpack. The morning and evening chill have helped us appreciate our warm sleeping bag cocoons more. Wilderness adventure and encounters with the natural world happen every day.

We are continually involved in thinking about people-to-people interaction which helps us grow. We are aware of our different values and interests, but at the same time know that we have many things in common. We stress cooperation over competition, caring over contempt, and sharing over selfishness. We value trust in ourselves and in others. We focus upon what is new and good in our lives and on what we appreciate in others. Our goals are never easy, but we try to stretch ourselves every day. The one thing that we can all say we know for sure when it's time to return home is that we have a feeling for the rewards and problems of living together closely. We have attained a sense of community that so many others in the world hunger and strive for and never achieve.

A Letter to the Staff

September, 1975

Dear close friends,

Our Human Relations Youth Adventure camp has been over for almost a week as I write this. I wanted to communicate with you soon to appreciate you and to reflect upon our accomplishments before the memories blur.

Vera and I considered the camp a success and we want to do it again next year. With every successful project there are elements which can be improved. That thought is comforting because it tells me that I've learned something and am growing in a good direction. I will not dwell on how we can do better, because I know each of you has clearer personal guidelines for the future.

I would like to appreciate each one of you for being you and for giving part of your life to an experiment in community building. It was an experiment and will always be an experiment. Each time we do it we will know more and will change and improve some of our approaches. I appreciate each of you for being the trusting, loving, caring, happy, cooperative, understanding, real, honest, open, helpful, listening, and just plain nice persons you were. All of these adjectives describe you well. The words also came from the campers when they wrote down the best things about our community. We *were* an effective community and we had more joy and hope for the future than in most communities I know. I appreciate you because you cared enough about building an ideal community and you devoted as much personal space as you could to that end. I know how difficult it is to give the space to a single goal. I appreicate you because you shared the good things in your lives with others both young and old. You spent your lifetimes getting ready and preparing for these times together. I have often boasted, half jokingly, that we have the longest staff training session of any camp in the world. I have also claimed seriously that we have one of the best camp staffs anywhere. You shared activities with others because they were fun and beneficial to you in your life. You also responded to what the campers wanted to do if you saw that it was valuable and worthy of the precious time involved. I appreciate you because you took active roles in improving our community whenever you thought your idea would work. I appreciate you also for the silence and patience you exercised when you thought something someone else tried wouldn't work. Sometimes it's harder to do nothing and let things happen than to do something which inhibits a learning opportunity. I appreciate you because you lived what we were trying to teach to the campers. Our staff interaction was a microcosm of what we wanted to happen to the whole community of forty. We expressed our thoughts and feelings, we cared about each other, and we worked hard at implementing a common goal. You all gave permission to everyone else to live out the loving, understanding, and intelligent parts of us that sometimes are hidden beneath the armor of our back-home "make the change from being a hard, cold person to survive in my town to a warm, loving person which I really am." You made it easier for him and for all of us to be that kind of person.

What was it about each one of you that made a difference in our quest? It was certainly more than your guitar, kazoo, washboard, ax, or camping equipment. It was more than your wilderness skills, cooking ability, singing voice, dramatic flair, or collection of inspirational readings. It was all of these and more. It was all that made you the human beings you are. Thank you.

The list of appreciations would not be complete unless I appreciated myself. First, I appreciate the same things in me that I appreciated in you. I appreciate my wisdom in gathering all of you together and allowing you to be yourselves in all your magical manifestations. I appreciate how consciously I provided permission and encouragement for you to practice the best skills you knew for building a solid community. I appreciate my trust in everyone and the faith that we would succeed in taking the best from our outside-world community. I also knew that we would try very hard to eliminate the worst from our larger society such as verbal putdowns of ourselves and others, hatred, greed, violence, and all the other cancers that could grow from living together closely. I appreciate myself for having the courage to make this camp a part of my life and to shoulder responsibilities involved with a community of this size. All of the difficulties in making our community work were outweighed by the tremendous gratification I received. Thank you for being part of my personal excitement in living out a dream.

I know that we will keep in touch throughout this year. Good luck in trying to spread the sense of community to the world around you now.

See you on the trail,
Cliff

Impressions of a New HRYAC Camper
(By Cliff Knapp)   August, 1976

The first day of camp finds me a little nervous inside.

I wonder to myself, "What will happen next?", "How will I fit in?", "Who will become special to me?"

There is a friendly tone in the air and a sense of something different.

Music and song smooth the way for learning more about the persons behind the faces.

Gradually and magically, the caring sides of people emerge like caterpillars from crysalises.

"What is happening to me?" I ask, pinching myself to see if I am dreaming.

I feel better about myself in a way that's different.

Can this be real?

I begin to see how I fit into our community.

I marvel at my goodness and strengths.

We are becoming less like isolated individuals and more like members of a close group.

People really do care about me, and I care about them. This feeling is strange but nice.

You mean that I have a say in this community? I really have some power to make a difference here?

It's scary to face up to knowing what happens to me is mostly my responsibility—that I can control much of my own life here.

I feel like a fish trying out a new set of fins or a bird testing out new wings.

I wonder where this will take me as I navigate toward my future.

The staff must trust me to make the right decisions. Wow that *is* strange!

What if I just wanted to sit in my tent all the time and play cards? Would they let me?

Wait a minute, that would only hurt me! That is not what I came here for.

I want to know more about the wilderness and the people gathered around me.

I want to try some new things and go different places.

I want to be a bigger and better person when the times comes to leave.

I want to do this to me and for me.

What can I give and what can I take?

I want to keep the giving and taking in the right balance.

What can I create with my own hands and brain?

How can I make the world a better place here and after I leave?

How can I take more of this caring community and plant these seeds in the outside world?

Can I do it alone? Where can I get help? Are people really different out there?

Will I have to leave the sense of my own power in the Adirondacks?

No, I can find the caring sides of people everywhere.

I can take this personal power with me when I leave.

Yes, I have grown with the wilderness this summer and I will not stop now or ever.

HRYAC: What Is It?

(By Cliff Knapp)   August, 1977

Whenever people ask me to describe our camp, I have difficulty. The best way for them to understand what we are is to live with us for three weeks. Since this is impossible, I try to use words to paint pictures of HRYAC. When I do this, I wonder if the words really do it. How can words describe feelings and experiences if another person has never known them? People also ask me how I create our community. I tell them my secret formula: First, I invite the best people I know to join our staff. Then I give them lots of room to be themselves and to do what they enjoy and do best. Then I find a wilderness environment where we can live together. Then campers join us who want to share outdoor adventure and improve their skills with people. The last step is to give a great deal of mental and physical effort to make the community ideal work. All of you know that fun, learning, and caring just don't magically appear in our lives. We plan specific kinds of activities to reach our goals.

Here are some of the words I use to describe HYRAC to others: Our camp is now four years old. Each year I learn more about how to help our community reach some important goals. One goal is for people to become more trusting of others and be honest about their feelings. At the same time, I want to see people act in caring ways toward others and to be gentle and considerate. I want to see people recognize their strengths and to love themselves more. I want to see people become more in touch with their thoughts and feelings and be clearer about what is important in their lives. I want to see people learn more skills of communication and use them to solve the problems of living together. I want people to feel a sense of community oneness and to work toward common purposes. Also, I want people to celebrate their differences and to respect others who are different. I want people to take more charge of their lives to get what they need and want.

HRYAC is based on the assumption that people will make the world a better place if they know how. The power of touching is used a great deal to communicate caring. Music is another tool for reaching some of the community-building goals. The daily community meeting is an important part of solving the problems of living together. Everyone is given the opportunity to be heard and to influence many decisions. A great deal of freedom to decide how to spend each day is necessary for growth in self-responsibility. Self-confidence and direction in life result from opportunities for risk taking and self-stretching. Individual and group needs are both considered important.

These are some of the words I use to describe our camp. I know that they fall short because they don't have the same meaning to everyone. The true meaning of these words are within each one of us. We know what HRYAC is for us and no one can take our memories from us. We have lived together for three weeks. We have laughed, sung, hiked, swam, touched, talked, cried, rejoiced, sweated, and been hurt and angry together. We know what camp is. We can describe our camp to others by the special way we live and interact with people. I know that the world is a better place for our being here and for spreading our community goals to others. Enjoy the adventure of living in your own separate communities and use some of what you have learned here.

The HRYAC Experiment
(by Cliff Knapp)   August, 1978

Some people may wonder why I still call our camp an experiment after five years of operation. HRYAC will always be an experiment no matter how long it continues.

Experiments are valuable ways of finding out new things. What we learn from experiments stays with us longer than if someone just told us about something. Good experiments are conducted under suitable laboratory conditions. They follow intelligent guidelines and are based on accepted assumptions. Experiments attempt to answer important questions. An experiment well done requires skilled experimenters. Good experiments involve mixing known substances in safe ways to avoid explosions or other accidents.

We are trying to find better ways of building a close, supportive community of people of all ages. We are striving to create a place for everyone to be somebody special. We want to create an atmosphere where people will have a sense of personal power to get what they need to live a rewarding life. Our goals include giving people permission to touch other humans in caring ways. We want people to like themselves more and to fill time with worthwhile things to do. We want them to express thoughts and feelings easier in ways that consider others. We want them to be able to listen to others by "walking in their moccasins" for a while. Along with these human relations goals, we want people to love the natural environment and to work to improve the quality of life on earth. There are more goals of our camp. To allow people to meet some of their own personal goals is a goal in itself.

What have we learned after five years? Occasionally, I am asked, "Does this kind of camp work?" My answer is clear, "Yes." In saying "yes" I know that we all take away different things in different amounts. Every year we ask our community members to honestly tell us what they have gained in three weeks together. Even if some people don't fully believe they have changed, they say that they feel more loving, caring, trusting, important, and able to solve problems of living together. All of these changes don't last when they go home, but some do. In general, they feel more in control of their lives and confident of their abilities. Most people agree that they have grown to be better than they thought they were before.

What are the conditions and guidelines under which all this happens? In order to grow, people need safety to make mistakes. We strive to eliminate put-downs. They also need recognition of their successes. We validate each other with words describing the strengths we see. We also support each other with lots of physical touch. Our environment is shared as much as possible to allow freedom to make decisions and to experience self-power.

Our community rules are established to maintain our good reputation, to consider the needs of others, to maintain health and safety, and to care for personal property. We believe that expressing feelings of anger, joy, fear, and sadness are fine and normal. We encourage openness and attempt to deal with human conflicts directly. We have made other assumptions about people too. We believe that people are lovable and capable, that they are able to live together with people of different backgrounds. We assume that differences can be resolved satisfactorily without one winner and one loser emerging. With a skilled staff who cares about creating a human-growing camp, we can effectively conduct the HRYAC experiment. Our staff is the vital ingredient in our recipe. It is they who help to create the norms that make our camp different. However, without the cooperation and commitment of our total community, our experiment will fail. We all know that our task is not an easy one and that there is always more to do. This is true of other types of experiments as well, so we continue our search for growth. HRYAC has always been an experiment in community building and that is the way it will remain.

The Campers and Staff Have the Last Word

It is appropriate that we end this chapter by letting the camp participants speak for themselves and their own experience in the Human Relations Youth Adventure Camp. What follows are excerpts from the HRYAC HOTLINES camp newspaper spanning the years . . .

Raft Painting

"How about pink with elephant polka-dots?"

"Naw, I think a gigantic IALAC button in phosphorescent purple and green would be perfect."

"Could we each paint three-fifths of a board our own favorite color?"

And so, after careful deliberation and consultation among all concerned, it was decided that the best decision would be to compromise and paint the raft a beautiful shade of strato-cumulus grey. Mostly because it was the only shade of grey that we had.

Plus, it's Howie's raft. (Alan)

Utensils Meal

On Friday, August 4, at suppertime, everyone lined up to have tacos for supper, just as usual. Only one thing was different—we didn't use any forks, or spoons. Instead, we used spatulas, potato mashers, strainers, soup ladles, huge spoons, peelers, and other strange kitchen utensils. Everyone seemed to have a good time trying to eat tacos and jello with our strange silverware. (Reenee)

'50s Night

The main attraction of the night was the '50s dance. All the girls came in high pony tails, rolled up blue jeans, sweatshirts, and bobby socks. The guys came with white tee shirts, blue jeans, and, of course, slicked-back hair. The music was '50s tapes, and everybody really had a lot of fun. Thanks to Boo, Wendy, Peter, Maria, and Erika, the barn was in really good shape. Priscilla was there, of course, to chaperone, making sure there was no funny business.

Of course we can't forget our live entertainment. Manhattan John made a special guest appearance. The crowd of teenage girls went wild and tried to tear at his clothes, but he kept cool and calm. He sang wonderful songs, and everybody was dancing and singing. Unfortunately, Big Ernie wasn't here so he couldn't sing the camp's favorite '50s night song, "Acne Blues." Manhattan sang and everybody danced and had a great time. Fifties night wasn't the same without Big E, but it was still great. Everybody had a great time. It might have been the best '50s night in the history of HRYAC. I think it was. (Maria)

> As I look into nature's mirror
> after the rain I see the clouds,
> the birds, the trees,
> and someone's eyes looking back at me.
>
> Who is this strange but familiar looking person?
> Why is he in the mirror of nature?
>
> As I look into the mirror I see the
> feelings that lurk inside me.
>
> Why does he feel the feelings I
> do?
> Why does he think like I do?
>
> The answer lies not in the mirror
> but in his eyes. (Adidas)

On Friday night we had the first Saturnalia. Saturnalia is the Latin word for festivity or festival. It was more commonly known to the camp as the celebration of life.

To start the celebration we had previously picked people's names to make gifts for. We busily slaved over beautiful gifts for two days.

On the festival night the gifts were given and appreciated. Singing, laughing, and eating made it a real celebration. An evergreen tree in the cabin added a touch of festivity to the occasion. It was almost as good as Christmas. (A.A.)

Thank You

I came
    alone, scared—anticipating what?
I was touched, cared for
why? You hardly knew me
        but you cared
I decided to try
       I opened up a little
       I shared a little
I was unsure. Am I doing alright?
You said, you're doing great, just fine.
I smiled. I like this
      being supported, feeling special
a new feeling
    It crept up on me
        it was unexpected
but I finally realized it. These weeks we spent together
that feeling, a feeling of love I had never had before.

Thank you (Sandy B.)

Rappelling

(Editor's note: Although rappelling was named on the final evaluations as a thing that took the most courage, the scariest thing, and the hardest thing to do, Tom offers us another side of rappelling.—AB)

Rappelling with Sunshine, Boo, and Dean is very fun. You're entirely sure that they won't let you drop for very far. When you first go down you're very nervous. But the second time you go down, it's a snap. The beginner slope isn't anything compared to the intermediate slope, although they both have hard parts to them. When you get to the bottom, you feel so proud of yourself for doing the rappel down that slope. (Tom)

Earth Day

EARTH DAY was a spectacular experience. It was done in the
rain which was very different
and very successful.
You heard and felt the rain hit
your face as Elizabeth and Big
Ernie talked about the beauties
of nature and life. You had a
nice dream and clean feeling

BROWN

after the showers. Everything
was sparkling. A dance of giving
gifts to trees was beautifully
portrayed by Elizabeth, Ann, Mitzi,
Jenny, Bev, and Sandy M. It was
fantastically done with creative
movement.
THE WILDERNESS WONDERS
drama troupe pantomimed "HOPE
FOR THE FLOWERS" by Trina
Paulus. The troupe included Scott,
Chris, Mitzi, Wayne, Becky, and Eve.
Thanks, Elizabeth, for a neat idea.
(Eve Knapp)

Where are all the stars?
The stars have fallen to the ground
There's not a star around

The earth is sourcefull
It gives life to many things
Mud forms when it rains
The plants and flowers float away
The sun comes back again. (Mitzi)

My Spot

I have a spot
I call my own
It is a place where
I can be alone
I love my spot, I do
It's my spot
       my own. (Jocie)

You Mean so Much to Me

Of all the people that make up
the world—I love you the most.
Nowhere do your smiles dominate
the environment—like they do in
this community.
I look at you and I see—I feel love
You touch me with so much care
When you sing to me, my being
overflows with happiness.
And most of all you share your-
self with me—
All of you—you mean so much to
me.
I love you so. (Big Ernie)

He rises majestically over his people,
allowing wind to sway his arms
    to and fro,
He is King.
His back is bent from time,
gnawed from wind and rain.
His figure silhouetted against the
    starry sky shows his wisdom.
He is the mighty pine tree. (July)

My Back Rubs

When I feel the need to have a backrub, I just come up to someone and say, "Would you please give me a backrub?" They usually say, "Sure." Then I lay down on my stomach and relax. Then they give me a soothing backrub. Occasionally a couple of "Just a little bit up more's" or "A little to the left's" come out. When someone comes up to me and says they need a backrub I do the same. I sooth their muscles and scratch their mosquito bites. I try to give them a backrub they will *never* forget! (Kara Cutbill)

Climbing a Mountain, Mirror of Life

"How many flights of stairs in an apartment building does this
mountain equal?" "We figured we would walk 190 blocks if we were
in the city." "Are we at the top yet?" "I can't go any farther."
"Let's count steps to see how many we can go before we rest again . . . "

When you approach a high peak hike, Phelps Mt.—4161 ft., what appears
to be a hill to climb becomes a battle between mind and body. The
way you decide to solve this adventure, oftentimes, reflects the
ways you handle other life situations.

You Bring Your Self to the Mountain

    You make the decisions when to rest, and when
to go, and how to hold on.
    You make sure your footing is steady,
your hands embrace the bark of a tree's trunk
for support.
    You are on your own and yet together.
    Another's hand reaches out, contact,
and then letting go.
    Where do you need to stop for yourself?
    Is it the mountain's summit?
    WE ALL WENT HIGHER . . . (Bev Lazar)

Why Do We Have to Go?

It is so peaceful here, where the rivers flow,
so why do we have to go back?

BROWN

Being in touch with nature,
learning with the trees,
so why do we have to go?

Sweetness is in the air,
times are changing, we are growing,
so many problems, we can solve them here.

Look around at your friends,
people who love you so
So why oh why do we have to go?   (Erika)

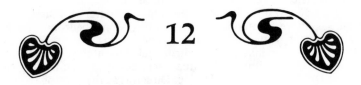

Resources: Where Do You Go from Here?

Our hope is that the preceding eleven chapters have tickled your curiosity and have inspired you to explore further ways of humanizing environmental education. This chapter describes different paths you might take from here, including organizational, book, and article resources.

Organizational Resources: Sagamore Institute

Founded in 1971, Sagamore Institute is a nonprofit, tax-exempt educational conference and resource center devoted to furthering theory, research, and practice in humanistic education and in the helping professions. Sagamore Institute's programs and services include: (1) sponsoring workshops at its home bases in Saratoga Springs and Raquette Lake, New York, and at numerous locations around the country; (2) sending educational and professional development materials (books, articles, tapes, films, posters, etc.) throughout the United States and abroad; (3) providing consultation services to school systems, camps, human service agencies, businesses, and community organizations throughout the world; (4) offering a professional development training series for the directors and staff of nonprofit agencies; (5) coordinating a national network of professional support groups; (6) focusing on new approaches to environmental education through its Adirondack Bound Program and the Human Relations Youth Adventure Camp; (7) funding innovative projects that are important to the future of education, the helping professions, and the environment (through the Sagamore Institute Project Fund); and (8) developing networks (bringing people and organizations together in cooperative and collaborative efforts).

As a national center for innovative thinking, research, and practice, Sagamore Institute focuses on such approaches as: values clarification; creative problem solving; enhancing self-esteem in schools and homes; humanizing environmental education; leadership training; grantswriting and effective public relations for nonprofit agencies; preventing burn-out; humanistic curriculum development; organization development; family team-building; life skills approach to drug abuse education/prevention; the implications and applications of humor; communication skills; career development; and more.

The national office of the Institute is at 110 Spring St., Saratoga Springs, NY 12866 (518-587-8770). The organization's conference center is the magnificent Sagamore Conference Center, a forty-three bedroom, twenty-six fireplace, former Vanderbilt family retreat, sitting on the shore of a totally private mile-long lake in the Adirondack Mountains. For more information about the Institute's resources, services, and membership program, contact Dr. Joel Goodman (Project Director) at the Saratoga Springs office.

Selected Book Resources
from the Field of Humanistic Education

**Briggs, Dorothy Corkille. *Your Child's Self-Esteem*. Garden City, NY: Dolphin Books, 1975.

This is a practical, helpful, and clearly-written book for parents and educators, grounded in a knowledge of self-esteem theory and research, and also filled with practical applications for numerous daily situations.

**Canfield, Jack and Wells, Harold. *One Hundred Ways to Enhance Self-Concept in the Classroom*. Englewood Cliffs: Prentice-Hall, 1976.

Numerous strategies are presented for teachers and parents to use to enhance self-concept. The strategies are drawn from many different approaches (e.g., values clarification, magic circle, effectiveness training, achievement motivation). This is a real goldmine of practical activities.

Combs, Arthur. et al. *Humanistic Education: Objectives and Assessment*. Washington, D.C.: Association for Supervision and Curriculum Development, 1978.

This booklet gives an update of some of the latest thinking of leaders in the field with regard to the goals and objectives of humanistic education. Research guidelines and findings are shared, along with a helpful checklist for humanistic schools.

**Goodman, Joel and Furman, Irv. *Magic and the Educated Rabbit: A Handbook for Teachers, Parents, and Helping Professionals*. Paoli, PA: Instructo/McGraw-Hill, 1981.

This is a collection of easy-to-do and powerful magic tricks. What is unique about this book is that the authors describe hundreds of ways of using the tricks to address important learning objectives (e.g., using magic as an aid to: learning subject matter, creating a positive learning environment, helping young people learn such life skills as observing, communicating, enhancing self-esteem, etc.).

**Goodman, Joel and Huggins, Ken. *Let the Buyer Be Aware: A Practical Handbook for Consumers, Teachers, and Parents in the 1980's*. La-Mesa, CA: The Wright Group, 1981.

This involving book includes hundreds of practical activities and ideas for: taking charge of your lifestyle; making sense of important consumer issues; developing life skills for the '80s; helping students to become more effective consumers and citizens; and applying the values clarification approach to consumer education. The authors also provide a powerful curriculum-development model which teachers and parents can use to generate millions of ideas for classroom lessons and family discussions.

**Goodman, Joel (editor). *Turning Points: New Developments, New Directions in Values Clarification, Volume I*. Saratoga Springs: Creative Resources Press, 1978.
    This book contains a stimulating and varied collection of twenty articles by leaders in the field who explore the very latest thinking on values clarification theory and practice. This volume explores the applications of values clarification to education, families, business, youth organizations, and trainers/consultants. It also contains sections on new practical strategies, questions and answers about values clarification, and annotated resource lists.

**Goodman, Joel (editor). *Turning Points: New Developments, New Directions in Values Clarification, Volume II*. Saratoga Springs: Creative Resources Press, 1979.
    There were so many good contributions to the first volume that a second volume was published. Like *Volume I*, this book has sections on innovations in theory and practice, new strategies, and resources in the field. It includes descriptions of how to apply the values clarification approach to a wide variety of fields and helping professions.

**Gordon, Thomas, with Burch, Noel. *Teacher Effectiveness Training*. New York: David McKay, 1974.
    Gordon applies the important communication skills of Parent Effectiveness Training to the classroom. The book explores the use of "I Messages," "Active Listening," and "No-Lose Problem Solving" (along with many examples from real classroom situations). This book will help educators to improve their own (and young people's) communication skills.

**Harmin, Merrill, Kirschenbaum, Howard, and Simon, Sidney. *Clarifying Values Through Subject Matter*. Minneapolis: Winston Press, 1973.
    The subtitle of this book, "Applications for the Classroom," describes the focus. There are many suggestions for how to use the values clarification approach in content areas. The activities are also useful in camps, especially the chapter describing fifteen values strategies in environmental education.

**Harmin, Merrill and Gregory, Tom. *Teaching Is . . .* Chicago: Science Research Associates, Inc., 1974.
    This "teacher education" guidebook contains essays, quotations, and poems from leaders in the educational field as well as significant literary figures. It also includes many experiences and activities to help the reader personalize the meaning of these writings and to clarify professional values issues. This is a good text for helping professionals to use in clarifying their own roles.

**Howe, Leland and Howe, Mary Martha. *Personalizing Education: Values Clarification and Beyond*. New York: Hart Publishing, 1975.
    This book contains over one hundred strategies, worksheets, and sample units designed to build four facets of a humanistic educational environment: (1) establishing trust and good human relationships; (2) clarifying students' goals and values; (3) building a personalized curriculum; and (4) organizing and managing the classroom.

**Howe, Leland. *Taking Charge of Your Life*. Niles, IL: Argus Communications, 1977.
    Here is an involving sequence of life-planning, value-clarifying activities. The reader does the activities right in the book, identifying strengths, goals, and barriers while exploring and planning future alternatives.

**Johnson, David and Johnson, Roger. *Learning Together and Alone*. Englewood Cliffs: Prentice-Hall, 1975.
    The Johnsons show how teachers (and other leaders) can use a combination of coopera-

tive, competitive, and individualized learning activities to maximize cognitive and affective educational goals. The authors' theory is firmly grounded in research, and is complemented by practical applications and techniques which flow directly from the theory.

**Kirschenbaum, Howard. *The Catalogue for Humanizing Education.* Saratoga Springs: National Humanistic Education Center, 1978.
This is a valuable new resource for educational consultants, teachers, administrators, parents, camp leaders, human service agency personnel, and students. It gives complete annotations of over 600 books, tapes, articles, student materials, and films. It is the most comprehensive resource guide of its kind. Instructions on how to obtain all of the listed resources are included.

**Kirschenbaum, Howard and Glaser, Barbara. *Developing Support Groups: A Manual for Facilitators and Participants.* La Jolla: University Associates, 1978.
After two years of field-testing, this manual provides a clear and useful structure for on-going, shared-leadership learning and support groups for professionals. This important model, which is gaining momentum around the country, can be applied in all kinds of settings. The manual offers practical suggestions on how to start and maintain ongoing support groups.

**Kirschenbaum, Howard, *On Becoming Carl Rogers.* New York: Delacorte Press, 1979.
The life and work of America's most influential living humanistic psychologist and educator is portrayed. This is a thorough personal biography from childhood to age 76, as well as a complete study of Rogers' professional development and lifelong contributions.

**Larson, Roland and Larson, Doris. *Values and Faith: Value Clarifying Exercises for Family and Church Groups.* Minneapolis: Winston Press, 1976.
This book presents eight basic valuing strategies and their applications to religious education in the church and the family. Strategies focus on such themes as "valuing my faith," "valuing my family," "valuing myself and my gifts," "valuing others," and "valuing the old and the new."

**Norem-Hebeisen, Ardyth. *Peer Program for Youth.* Minneapolis: Augsburg Publishing House, 1973.
This describes a structured group interaction plan designed to develop self-esteem, self-understanding, and communication skills. In the form of helping youth to create their own support groups, this approach can be useful in retreats, classes, camps, and ongoing groups.

**Norem-Hebeisen, Ardyth. *Exploring Your Self-Esteem.* Saratoga Springs: National Humanistic Education Center, 1976.
Here the author describes her multi-dimensional concept of self-esteem and provides numerous exercises to positively influence young people's self-esteem. This teacher's guide is a good complement to *Self Assessment Scales*, which is a self-scoring, self-esteem inventory for adolescents and adults.

**Parnes, Sidney, Noller, Ruth and Biondi, Angelo. *Guide to Creative Action.* New York: Charles Scribner's Sons, 1977.
This is the most complete resource on creativity and problem solving available. It is filled with readings, activities, and hundreds of books/films/programs/instruments and other resources available.

Education is a basic process—finding ways to be human.
                                                              BILL STONEBARGER

Purkey, William, *Self-Concept and School Achievement*. Englewood Cliffs: Prentice-Hall, 1970.
This classic gives the educators and parent an excellent grounding in the importance of self-concept to the educational enterprise. It explores theories of self-concept, documents powerful research findings, focuses on the direct relationship between self-concept and success, and suggests some practical implications for the teacher.

Raths, Louis, Harmin, Merrill, and Simon, Sidney. *Values and Teaching: Revised Edition*. Columbus: Charles E. Merrill, 1978.
This is an updated version of the basic book on the values clarification approach, with discussion of new theoretical issues and research and insights resulting from twelve more years of experience with values clarification. As with the original edition, it also includes a number of practical strategies that educators can employ to clarify values.

Read, Donald, Simon, Sidney, and Goodman, Joel. *Health Education: The Search for Values*. Englewood Cliffs: Prentice-Hall, 1977.
This volume is filled with scores of essays by most of the leading figures in the humanistic education field. About half the book consists of essays dealing with theoretical issues, the other half focuses on specific techniques for the classroom and other applications of humanistic education.

Read, Donald, Simon, Sidney, and Goodman, Joel. *Health Education: The Search for Values*. Englewood Cliffs: Prentice-Hall, 1977.
This book presents new developments in how the values clarification approach is defined, along with new applications to the field of health edcuation. The authors present dozens of practical activities focusing on such content areas as human sexuality, drug abuse, and nutrition, while simultaneously showing how these can be used to develop valuing skills. The book includes an innovative chapter on humanistic approaches to evaluation.

Rogers, Carl. *Freedom to Learn: A View of What Education Might Become*. Columbus: Charles E. Merrill, 1969.
This is one of the basic texts in humanistic education. Rogers presents his own concept of human growth and development and shows how educators can facilitate "significant learning" in this context. He provides a number of case studies which illustrate his principles of student-centered learning.

Roger, Carl A. *A Way of Being*. Boston: Houghton Mifflin Company, 1980.
Carl Rogers continues to think and write about important person-centered ideas he has formulated during his career of more than fifty years. In his latest book he writes about his experiences and experiments in humanizing education in the 1970s. The book uncovers many essential topics for humanizing environmental education. Of special importance are the chapters on communication, empathy, supporting research, community building, affective-experiential learning, and education for the future. This book should be important reading for leaders who implement humanizing programs of all kinds.

Simon, Sidney. *I Am Lovable and Capable*. Niles, IL: Argus Communications, 1973.
"*Ialac*," a story presented in an attractive pamphlet, shows what can happen to a person's self-esteem in a typical day. This colorful story is an excellent allegory on the classical put-down. Simon also provides suggestions on how to use the story as the basis for discussion and activities.

**Simon, Sidney, *Negative Criticism.* Niles, IL: Argus Communications, 1978.
This follows up on the *"Ialac"* story by exploring the effects of criticism on self-concept. The author also looks at what we can do to stop putting each other down, and how to appreciate ourselves and one another more. Again, Simon does this in a colorful, creative way.

**Simon, Sidney, Howe, Leland, and Kirschenbaum, Howard. *Values Clarification: A Handbook of Practical Strategies for Teachers and Students: Revised Edition.* New York: Hart Publishing, 1978.
This is still the most extensive activity book on values clarification with over 2,000 examples of seventy-nine strategies described. These strategies cover a wide variety of values-rich topics. This book is a goldmine.

**Standford, Gene and Standford, Barbara. *Learning Discussion Skills through Games.* New York: Scholastic Magazines, Inc., 1969.
This little classic has two major sections—the first providing a developmental sequence of discussion skill-building activities, the second describes fifteen remedial exercises for dealing with group problems. This book is very useful for groups of all kinds—classrooms, camps, families, etc.

**Stanford, Gene. *Developing Effective Classroom Groups.* New York: Hart Publishing, 1977.
This is a superb collection of practical activities and games to help students (all levels) build trust, group responsibility, cooperation, problem solving, group decision making, and other skills.

**Weinstein, Matt and Goodman, Joel. *Playfair: Everybody's Guide to Non-competitive Play.* San Luis Obispo, CA: Impact Publishers, 1980.
This is the most recent book in the field of humanistic recreation, and provides a good bridge between humanistic and environmental fields. The authors describe sixty new games that invite cooperation, inclusion, and self-esteem. The book also includes an excellent chapter on how to invent your own positive games, along with a stimulating chapter on commonly-asked questions about cooperation, competition, and play. There is also a chapter which provides the reader with an opportunity to clarify his/her own values about cooperation and competition. This is a very playful book—and a serious one.

Selected Book Resources
for Humanizing Environmental Education

Allen, Rodney F. et al. *Deciding How to Live on Spaceship Earth: The Ethics of Environmental Concern.* Evanston, IL: McDougal, Littell and Co., 1973.
This is an excellent book to help students explore issues in environment quality. A broad range of topics are covered through the use of background material and student activities. The authors advocate humanistic processes of inquiry in dealing with environmental problem solving.

"A child cannot reach self-actualization until his needs for security, belongingness, dignity, love, respect, and esteem are all satisfied."

(MASLOW)

**Charlotte-Mecklenburg Schools. *Valuing the Environment* (Two volumes— Grades K-6 and 7-12). Funded by Project SEED (State Experimentation in Educational Development), Division of Development, North Carolina Department of Public Instruction.
This is a collection of environmental lesson plans by a number of writers. The format for each lesson includes an introduction, objectives, activities, values clarification exercises, and resources. The topics of the lessons cover a wide range in both the social and physical/ biological sciences.

Cornell, Joseph Bharat. *Sharing Nature with Children.* Nevada City, CA: Ananda Publications, 1979.
The author has collected forty-two games that will open up nature to children and adults. The games are divided into the following categories: calm/reflective, active/observational, and energetic/playful. The book contains many new ideas for increasing both nature and people awareness.

Environmental Studies for Urban Youth Project (sponsored by the American Geological Institute). *Essence I* and *Essence II.* Reading, MA: Addison-Wesley Publishing Co., 1971 and 1975.
This is a collection of cards on which many open-ended assignments are written. *Essence I* contains seventy-eight cards dealing with outdoor investigations and ways to open up the classroom environment. *Essence II* consists of 171 awareness cards divided into ten mini-units and a make-your-own game. Both sets of cards provide many hours of stimulating and rewarding invitations to explore many environments. This is an excellent resource for inter-disciplinary environmental education involving human interaction.

DuShane, Judy and Hug, John. *A Future Look at Environmental Education* Occasional Paper #1 and *Forward to Fundamentals: The Complete Education* Occasional Paper #4. Columbus, Ohio: Ohio Department of Education, Office of Education. (1978 and 1979 respectfully)
These two brief monographs outline a philosophical base and an example of what the authors term Whole Earth Education. Four components of Whole Earth Education are outlined—personal growth, learning processes, learning climate, and the themes chosen for study. A useful list of resource materials is supplied in the appendix of Occasional Paper #4.

**Fluegelman, Andrew (editor). *The New Games Book.* New York: Dolphin Books:Doubleday and Co., Inc., 1976.
Using the slogan, "Play Hard, Play Fair, Nobody Hurt," the New Games Foundation has published a book of games in the following categories: games for two, games for a dozen, games for two dozen, and "the more the better." The book provides background on theory and practical hints for leadership. The games are good vehicles for helping people get to know each other while having fun outdoors.

Franck, Frederick. *The Zen of Seeing: Seeing/Drawing as Meditation.* New York: Vintage Books (a division of Random House), 1973.
The author describes how he hit upon an idea for increasing awareness and connectedness with nature. He explains the technique of "seeing/drawing" and how it is useful in achieving an intimate relationship with the environment. The book is full of drawings by this talented writer/artist.

**Glashagel, Jerry, Johnson, Mick, and Phipps, Bob. *Digging in . . . Tools for Value Education in Camping (Camp Director's Handbook* and *Camp Counselor's Handbook).* New York: National Board of YMCA, 1976.
This publication uses the values clarification approach to help camp counselors clarify their own values and begin to build a valuing environment for campers. These books contain many practical suggestions for implementing a values education program in camps. Strategies are provided for mealtimes, campfires, hikes and nature study, sports, etc.

McInnis, Noel and Albrecht, Don (editors). *What Makes Education Environmental?* Louisville: Courier-Journal and Louisville Times Co., 1975.
This is an important collection of over forty essays by some of the leading figures in the environmental education field. It provides an overview of key issues in environmental education. Topics include strategies, approaches, projects, teacher training, evaluation, and funding.

Orlick, Terry. *The Cooperative Sports and Games Book: Challenge Without Competition.* New York: Pantheon Books, 1978.
Orlick combines many useful chapters in providing a brief overview of the cooperative-games movement. He supplies much of the information needed for leaders to humanize contemporary games. The author divides a variety of cooperative games into age categories from preschool to adults. A rationale and philosophical foundation are clearly outlined as well as many practical suggestions for creating your own games, conducting cooperative play days, playing games from other cultures, remaking adult games, and finding more resources on this topic.

**Project Adventure Staff. *Teaching Through Adventure: A Practical Approach.* Hamilton, MA: Project Adventure, 1976.
Most of this book consists of descriptions of specific programs that have been implemented in public high schools and middle schools. It describes how exploration of the community and surrounding areas can be used to teach and learn subject matter. The book stresses adventure, cooperation, problem solving, and direct experience with ideas and human nature.

**Rohnke, Karl. *Cowstails and Cobras: A Guide to Ropes Courses, Initiative Games, and Other Adventure Activities.* Hamilton, MA: Project Adventure, 1977.
This book outlines an approach to physical activity which combines a joyful sense of adventure, a willingness to move beyond previously set limits, and the satisfaction of solving problems together. The book uses group and individual challenges and "initiatives." The activities have application far beyond physical education. They encourage group cooperation, trust formation, risk-taking, and communication.

Stapp, William B. and Cox, Dorothy A. *Environmental Education Activities Manual* (six books). Farmington Hills, MI: Thomson-Shore, Inc. (7300 W. Huron River Drive, Dexter, MI 48130), 1974.
This is a compilation of writings of teachers who applied an environmental education model to lesson planning. The series of six books includes: (1) Concerning Spaceship Earth; (2) Lower Elementary Activities; (3) Middle Elementary Activities; (4) Upper Elementary Activities; (5) Junior High Activities; and (6) Senior High Activities. The authors advocate a values clarification approach in the solving of environmental problems.

The American Forest Institute, Inc. *Project Learning Tree* (two volumes). Washington, D.C.: The American Forest Institute, Inc., 1977.
These two volumes, "Supplementary Activity Guide for Grades K-6" and "Supplementary Activity Guide for Grades 7-12," provide an interdisciplinary approach to environmental education. Trees are used as vehicles to begin the exploration of our natural resources and human inter-relationships to the total environment. Human communication and valuing are used as techniques to understand culture. The activities are varied and creative and have been field tested in schools to assure validity.

Torbert, Marianne. *Follow Me: A Handbook of Movement Activities for Children*. Englewood Cliffs, N.J.: Prentice-Hall, Inc., 1980.
Torbert has compiled a book of more than 100 movement activities designed to humanize play. Each activity is accompanied by information about the physical, social, emotional, and cognitive benefits that can be derived. Chapters include skill topics such as perceptual motor development, listening, release of tension, self control, and thinking processes. Leaders will find many suggestions for using these movement activities as well as the reasons for doing them.

**Van Matre, Steve. *Acclimatization: A Sensory and Conceptual Approach to Ecological Involvement* and *(**)Acclimatizing: A Personal and Reflective Approach to a Natural Relationship*. Martinsville, IN 46151: The American Camping Association, 1972 and 1974.
Both books provide a conceptual framework and practical suggestions for nature awareness and ecological education. Leadership techniques are described as well as many activities which blend nature with human nature. These books are classics in the field of nature awareness and revitalized nature programs.

Van Matre, Steve. *Sunship Earth: An Acclimatization Program for Outdoor Learning*. Martinsville, Indiana: American Camping Association, 1979.
In this book Van Matre and associates puts it all together with a complete five-day program ". . . for helping kids to understand how their world functions." The program includes activities which encompass both conceptual and affective learning. As in his previous two books, the author provides practical suggestions for leaders in implementing this human relations/ecology program about our planet.

**Wurman, Richard Saul (editor). *Yellow Pages of Learning Resources*. Cambridge, MA: The M.I.T. Press, 1972.
This is a catalogue of different settings in the community and a description of the kinds of things students can learn there. The butcher, city hall, electricians, gas stations, junk yards, and restaurants are a few of the places to explore. This book could open up many possiblities for exploring the rich learning opportunities in every community.

Yarrow, Ruth. *Exploring Environments: A Handbook of Environmental Exercises*. Staten Island, NY: High Rock Park Conservation Center.
Here is a collection of nature activities written by people who are practicing naturalists. There are four chapters: "Awakening Sensory Awareness;" "Basic Ecosystem Processes;" "Discovering Adaptations;" and "Environmental Consequences." The last chapter contains many valuing activities.

"Now I see the secret of making the best persons: it is to grow in the open air and to eat and sleep with the earth." (WALT WHITMAN)

Selected Articles on Environmental Attitudes and Values

Allen, Rodney F. "This World Is So Beautiful . . .: Feelings and Attitudes in Environmental Education." "But the Earth Abideth Forever: Values in Environmental Education." "Environmental Education as Telling Our Stories." National Council for Geographic Education (*Instructional Activities Series*), 1975.

Baker, Milton R. et al. "An Analysis of Environmental Values and Their Relation to General Values." *The Journal of Environmental Education.* Vol. 10, No. 1 (Fall 1978), pp. 35-40.

**Cullinane, William and Santosuosso, John. "Values Clarification and the Summer Camp Counselor." *Adolescence.* Vol. 11, No. 44 (Winter 1976). pp. 636-642.

Genge, Betty and Santosuosso, John. "Values Clarification for Ecology." *Science Teacher.* February 1974, 00. 37-39.

**Goodman, Joel and Knapp, Clifford. "Making a Difference: Values Clarification and Social Issues." *Turning Points: New Developments, New Directions in Values Clarification, Volume II* (edited by Joel Goodman). Saratoga Springs: Creative Resources Press, 1979.

Iozzi, Louis. "The Environmental Issues Test (EIT): A New Assessment Instrument for Environmental Education." Seventh Annual Conference, National Association for Environmental Education. Chicago, May 1978 (unpublished manuscript).

Harshman, Ronald. "Value Education Processes for an Environmental Education Program." *The Journal of Environmental Education.* Vol. 10, No. 2 (Winter 1978/79), pp. 30-34.

Knapp, Clifford E. "Environment: Children Explore Their Values." *Instructor.* Vol. 81, No. 7 (March 1972), pp. 116-118.

_____. "Attitudes and Values in Environmental Education." *The Journal of Environmental Education*, Vol. 3, No. 4 (Summer 1972), pp. 26-29.

_____. and DuShane, Judith. "Clarifying Values for a Better Environment." *Counseling and Values.* Vol. 18, No. 4 (Summer 1974), pp. 266-271.

_____. "Outdoor Environmental Values Clarification." *The Communicator: Journal of the New York Outdoor Education Association.* Vol. 7, No. 1 (Fall/Winter 1975), pp. 9-11.

_____. "Open Space Learning Activities." *Science and Children.* Vol. 51, No. 7 (April 1976), pp. 10-12.

_____. "Values that Make Better Camping." *Camping Magazine,* Vol. 51, No. 5 (April 1978), pp. 8-9.

_____. "Impact on Teaching Values." in *Fifty Years of Resident Outdoor Education: 1930-1980: Its Impact Upon American Education.* Martinsville, IN: American Camping Association, 1980, pp. 58-64.

_____. "Developing an Environmental Ethic: A Values Education Model" *Science Activities* Vol. 17, No. 2 (April/May 1980) pp. 39-42.

_____ and Woodhouse, Janice. "Camping and Value Changes" Research edited by William M. Hammerman. *Camping Magazine,* Vol. 52, No. 7 (June, 1980) pp. 26-27.

LaHart, David and Tillis, Richard. "Using Wildlife to Teach Environmental Values." *The Journal of Environmental Education,* Vol. 6, No. 1 (Fall 1974), pp. 43-48.

Lamb, William. "Classroom Environmental Values Clarification." *The Journal of Environmental Education*, Vol 6, No. 4 (Summer 1975), pp. 14-17.

Miles, John. "Humanism and Environmental Education." *The Journal of Environmental Education,* Vol. 7, No. 3 (Spring 1976), pp. 2-10.

_____. "The Study of Values in Environmental Education." *The Journal of Environmental Education*, Vol. 9, No. 2 (Winter 1977), pp. 5-17.

**Paulson, Wayne. "Environment: Where Do I Stand?" Minneapolis: Winston Press, 1974.

Shaver, James P. "Environmentalism and Values." *The Journal of Environmental Education*, Vol. 4, No. 1 (Fall 1972), pp. 49-53.

Tomera, Audrey. "A Compendium of Values Clarification Research in Environmental Education at Southern Illinois University-Carbondale: Kindergarten through Middle School." (Unpublished manuscript, Department of Curriculum, Instruction, and Media.)

Quinn, Ray. "Using Value Sheets to Modify Attitudes Toward Environmental Problems." *Journal of Research in Science Teaching.* Vol. 13, No. 1 (1976), pp. 65-69.

Yambert, Paul A. "Impact on Environmental Ethics." in *Fifty Years of Resident Outdoor Education: 1930-1980: Its Impact on American Education.* Martinsville, IN: American Camping Association, 1980, pp. 65-74.

Each book or article that has a double asterisk (**) in front of it is available through the mail-order bookstore of Sagamore Institute. For more information about these and other titles, contact the Institute at 110 Spring St., Box E, Saratoga Springs, NY 12866.

Photo Credits

The photos in this book were submitted by Paul J. Brown, Clifford Knapp, and Tom Lesser.

Cover

The cover was designed by Jan Woodhouse, Oregon, Illinois.

Background on Clifford E. Knapp

Clifford Knapp is the Director of the Lorado Taft Field Campus and Chairperson of the Outdoor Teacher Education faculty at Northern Illinois University. He is an Associate Professor in the Department of Curriculum and Instruction. The Field Campus, in Oregon, Illinois, is a 141-acre resident environmental education center.

Dr. Knapp holds a Bachelor of Arts degree in Junior High School Education from Paterson State College, a Master of Science degree in Educational Administration and Supervision, and a Doctor of Philosophy degree in Curriculum and Instruction from Southern Illinois University.

He has taught at all levels of education from elementary school to the graduate level. Dr. Knapp has taught science and outdoor education in public and private schools in New Jersey and New York. He has served as Assistant and Acting Coordinator of the Outdoor Education Center for Southern Illinois University. While there, he taught courses in Nature Interpretation, Conservation/Outdoor Education, Camping, Arts and Crafts, Science Methods, and General Elementary Methods.

Knapp has had extensive experience in summer camps as counselor and director in New Jersey, New York, and Illinois. He originated a unique camp dedicated to human relations and outdoor adventure. This Human Relations Youth Adventure Camp is sponsored by the Sagamore Institute. As environmental specialist for the Institute, he has also led adult workshops in human relations and environmental/outdoor education. He is a member of the editorial board for *Camping Magazine*.

In addition to teaching courses at Southern Illinois University, Knapp has taught at Montclair State College, Rutgers: The State University of New Jersey, Marywood College, Kean College of New Jersey, and Northern Illinois University. He has also taught in-service workshops for teachers in humanistic education, values education, stress management, and environmental education. He has also served as a speaker and consultant in these areas for many groups across the nation.

In addition to administering summer camps, Knapp has served as Director of Environmental Education for the Ridgewood, New Jersey, Public Schools. He also was a science specialist and science department coordinator at the junior high level.

Dr. Knapp has published extensively in the education field. He has written more than thirty articles which have appeared in various journals, including *Science and Children, Instructor, Camping Magazine, Environmental Education Report, Science Teacher, Science Activities,* and the *Journal of Environmental Education.*

His articles appear in the following books: *Fifty Years of Resident Outdoor Education: 1930-1980 (1980); Turning Points: New Developments, New Directions in Values Clarification: Volume II* (1978); *Environmental Education in the Elementary School* (1977); *What Makes Education Environmental?* (1975); *Teaching Subject Matter with a Focus on Values* (1973); *Readings in Values Clarification* (1973); and *Helping Children Learn Earth-Space Science* (1971).

In addition, he has authored or coauthored the following books: *Bulletin Boards for Environmental Studies* (1973); *Outdoor Activities for Environmental Studies* (1971); *Selected Sources of Information for Interpretive Naturalists* (1969); and *Exploring and Understanding Our Changing Earth* (1968). Knapp has published multi-media instructional materials with accompanying teacher's guides titled, "Open Lands and Wildlife" (1975), "Eco-Problem Posters" (1971), and "Ecology Poster Series" (1970).

He holds professional memberships in the American Camping Association, National Association for Environmental Education, National Wildlife Federation, New York State Outdoor Education Association, Environmental Education Association of Illinois.

He enjoys reading, writing, fishing, woodcarving, jogging, human relationship groups, and retreating to the wilderness. He has been successful during most of his career in the art of combining his work and play into a life of continuous growth.

Background on Joel Goodman

Joel Goodman is Project Director at the Sagamore Institute, a nonprofit educational training and resource organization based in Saratoga Springs, New York. Here, he directs the Consulting Program, coordinates the Professional Development Center, and directs The HUMOR Project. Dr. Goodman has served as Assistant Director of the National Humanistic Education Center, has taught graduate and undergraduate courses at a number of universities (e.g., University of Massachusetts, Russell Sage College, Bowling Green State University, Hampshire College, Marywood College, etc.), has worked with elementary and secondary school students for a number of years, and has served as a resource person to many nonprofit agencies.

Complementing these activities, Joel has been a consultant, speaker, and workshop leader for hundreds of schools, businesses, and human service agencies throughout the United States and abroad in such areas as the nature and nurture of humor; values clarification; training and staff development; enhancing self-esteem; creative problem-solving; humanistic curriculum development; motivation; leadership training; team-building in families; organization development; preventing burn-out; magic as an aid to teaching; cooperative approaches to play; and creating professional support groups.

He has authored or co-authored eight books, including: *Health Education: The Search for Values* (Prentice-Hall, 1977); *Turning Points: New Developments, New Directions in Values Clarification, Volume I* (Creative Resources Press, 1978) and Volume II (1979); *Creative Problem Solving Playbook* (NHEC, 1979); *Magic and the Educated Rabbit* (Instructo/McGraw-Hill, 1980); *Playfair: Everybody's Guide to Noncompetitive Play* (Impact Publishers, 1980); *The Power is in the People; A Consumer Education Handbook* (Pennant Press, 1980). Joel is presently completing a new book,

Making Sense of Humor; Laughing for Learning, Healing, and Growing.
In addition, he has written over a score of articles for such national
magazines as *Today's Education, Learning, Nation's Schools, Today's
Catholic Teacher,* and *Scholastic Teacher.*

Joel brings a great deal of warmth, expertise, and energy to his teaching,
group leadership, speaking, writing, and project development. He combines
a delightful sense of humor with a serious commitment to the people with
whom he works. Joel enjoys having friends over for potluck dinners and
game nights, playing basketball, giving magic shows to local elementary
school classes, photographing and videotaping, getting sent to the punitenti-
ary for playing with words, taking late-night walks, and combining dreaming with doing.